RADICAL CURRENTS

IN

CONTEMPORARY PHILOSOPHY

A *Monograph in*

MODERN CONCEPTS OF PHILOSOPHY

Series Editor

MARVIN FARBER

State University of New York at Buffalo
Buffalo, New York

Books currently appearing in this Series

Walter Cerf—*On Space and Time: Kant, Strawson, Heidegger*

David H. DeGrood, editor—*Radical Currents in Contemporary Philosophy*

Rollo Handy—*The Measurement of Values: Behavioral Science and Philosophical Approaches*

Donald Clark Hodges—*Socialist Humanism: The Outcome of Classical European Morality*

William Horosz—*The Promise and Peril of Human Purpose: The New Relevance of Purpose and Existence*

William Horosz and Tad Clements, editors—*Religion and Human Purpose*

Paul Kurtz, editor—*Language and Human Nature: A French-American Philosophers' Conference*

D. C. Mathur—*Naturalistic Philosophies of Experience: Studies in James, Dewey and Farber Against the Background of Husserl's Phenomenology*

Jitendra Nath Mohanty—*The Concept of Intentionality: A Critical Study*

John L. Pollock—*An Examination of Set Theory*

Lynn E. Rose—*Plato's Dialectic*

N. Rotenstreich—*Power and Its Mould: An Essay on Social and Political Philosophy*

Xenia Atanassievitch—*Metaphysical and Geometrical Doctrine of Bruno*

Roy Wood Sellars—*Principles of Emergent Realism: Philosophical Essays.* Edited by W. Preston Warren.

RADICAL CURRENTS
IN
CONTEMPORARY PHILOSOPHY

Edited by

DAVID H. DeGROOD

University of Bridgeport

DALE RIEPE

State University of New York at Buffalo

JOHN SOMERVILLE

California Western University

WARREN H. GREEN, INC.
St. Louis, Missouri, U.S.A.

Published by

WARREN H. GREEN, INC.
10 South Brentwood Blvd.
St. Louis, Missouri 63105, U.S.A.

Library of Congress Catalog Card No. 73-110806

Printed in the United States of America

4-A   (184)

To

Roy Wood Sellars

V. J. McGill

Marvin Farber

and

to those philosophers who continue

to make philosophy

vital

The Greek coup d'état (1967)

The new four are in;
    The old three are out.

They used to pull the strings—
    Clotho, Lachesis and Atropos.

Now others run the telegraph
    Signalling the sentences—

Guanine who beds with Cytosine;
    Adenine in league with Thymine.

ALAN MACKAY

FOREWORD

THE EDITORS have asked me to write a little foreword saying what I think philosophy "should strive to do." The contributors will say, in part at least, what philosophy is about; I am to say what it is for. I suppose I shall need to give some argument to the effect that what I think philosophy is for is what it really *is* for; otherwise my view is left to be merely personal. Possibly, in the end, that is what it is.

I regard philosophy as the area of largest generalizations and of discourse upon ultimates. All the sciences, achieved or aspiring, describe the behavior of various sorts of things, and therefore describe change. But each science describes change as its particular subject-matter reveals change. No one science or combination of sciences will yield, though of course it will support, a description of change in general. The largest generalizations about change belong to philosophy.

It is well known that, for the past two hundred years and more, the chief or at any rate the favorite problem of philosophy has been the problem of knowledge. And what is this problem? It is, to find the rule that will enable us infallibly to distinguish between true sentences and false ones. Any such rule will be an "ultimate."

Or suppose we take the various linguistic philosophies. Whether the effort is to establish a language that shall say everything clearly, or whether the effort is to clarify "ordinary" language by showing what it ordinarily means, there evidently is an assumption that some rule exists which will show us when a locution is clear and when it is not. This rule, too, will be an "ultimate."

The agreed tasks of philosophy have no doubt shrunk since the spacious days of Bradley, Bosanquet, Royce, when a work on logic (in two volumes, of course) was a disquisition upon the cosmos. The shrinkage, however, has been, so to say, horizontal and not vertical.

Contemporary fashion allows philosophy fewer problems, but these still have the largest generalizations and they touch upon ultimates. Philosophers, it seems, still know what they ought to be doing, and know, further, that what they ought to be doing is rather more than ease or safety suggests.

My notion is that the task, purpose, function of philosophy follows from the nature of our human species, exposed as it is to conditions of life upon this planet. We all have needs that require to be satisfied. Satisfaction is easier and surer when we cause events to behave as we want them to behave. This becomes possible when we know and understand how events really do behave. Hence the problem of knowledge and the search for a rule that distinguishes true sentences from false.

Because of circumstances within each personal life, needs are often in conflict: we can't always do all we need to do. When thus we have to choose one need rather than another for satisfaction, the question arises as to which is more important. The same question comes, socially, when we have to ask, *Whose* need is more important? Hence ethics and the search for a rule that governs choices by determining what importance is.

Some of the things we do are a sort of playful excursion from all this "serious business." There is a delight in showing our skills just as skills, and in enjoying the sight of them. Hence the arts, which allow skill to be seen and estimated—estimated most adequately, perhaps, when they are still in touch with "serious" material. Hence the notion that there is a standard of beauty, and that your old piano teacher is not Beethoven. In short, esthetics.

There can be, and, it may seem, must be, an account of the whole thing: the nature and history of men, of their general environment, of the rules applicable to their conduct, and of the gross or subtle interplay of all these. Once upon a time this would have been called Ontology. I have never much liked the word, but the thing signified —the vast, whelming tide of events and values—is still there, awaiting description. The chance to describe it all is philosophy's.

Now, it may be wondered whether the thing, or indeed any part of it, is better described from being looked at or from being acted in. Observers are, as such, not participants; and participants, though they can't very well help observing, will have trouble observing the whole. Thus the case seems to be that observers know things participants don't know, and participants know things observers don't know. Detachment is at odds with intimacy, theory with practice.

This sort of opposition, grounded in our nature as that is exposed to our conditions of life, must somehow be overcome. Theory, detached from practice or from some possible connection with practice, tends to be trivial—the fate, alas, of many a philosophy. On the other hand, practice, detached from theory, moves, nearly blind, in pragmatic shadows. It is then not much more than mere exercise of power, and may become a kind of tyranny.

It seems, therefore, that we must do two contrary things at once—no surprising task, indeed, since few of our problems are of any other sort. We must join the observer's eye with the participant's touch; otherwise we won't know all we need to know. If we succeed, we shall find ourselves changing the world by having accurately described it, and describing the world accurately by having changed it. If we fail, the world will merely have changed us, with little sign of our presence in the process. I cannot think that this much submission to outward power is any part of philosophy's intent.

If it is not this, the intent presumably is so to unite knowledge of fact with knowledge of value that our choices will be right and our deeds effective. Then perhaps (but only perhaps) we shall be safe and happy. And then the hopes of philosophy will have been fulfilled.

BARROWS DUNHAM

PREFACE

I T IS MORE than twenty years since the publication of a significant cooperative volume edited by Roy Wood Sellars, V. J. McGill, and Marvin Farber. The title of their volume, *Philosophy for the Future: The Quest of Modern Materialism* (1949), was a challenge for philosophers to consider carefully the naturalistic and materialistic alternative to Continental European Existentialism, Anglo-American "analytic" movements, and the traditional supernatural frameworks. In the hope of continuing within the tradition of the Sellars, McGill and Farber volume, I contacted numerous scholars, many of whom had contributed to the earlier volume, about the possibility of bringing out a companion text. The present work represents the active participation of these scholars. Naturally, the contributors take responsibility only for their own articles, since many different kinds and ranges of naturalistic and materialistic tendencies are represented here, as will be obvious to those familiar with the literature. Uniformity in a narrow sense was not sought, but rather I tried to exhibit the vitality and multiplicity of "scientific philosophy" today throughout the world.

It seems to me to be of paramount importance today that narrow specialization, trivialization of philosophical activity, and assorted anti-scientific irrationalisms have profoundly distorted the activity of philosophy and have unfortunately retarded the progressive role which philosophy must assert in helping to shape the events in today's fast-changing world. It seems to me to be a great tragedy that in much of the "civilized" world philosophers have ceased to exercise their traditional role of critically evaluating existing beliefs and institutions.

In our attempt to challenge anew established dogmas and institutions, we have tried to set a balance between the generation of *Philosophy for the Future* and the newer generation so eager to transform the present into the future. Moreover, a balance was also set between materials already printed (and worthy of being considered again) and materials to appear for the first time. Furthermore, it is a great honor for me that some of my former teachers and classmates have consented to join in this effort in portraying philosophical trends of many continents.

Works such as these, however, are not only the result of the labors of an "intelligentsia," they are also grounded in the strenuous labors of an academic "proletariat." Naturally, in all areas of human activity, reflection and labor complement one another. I wish to express my appreciation to the following secretaries and typists: Donna Aiple, Jacalyn Berger, Janet Chubak, Patricia Grose, Virginia Martin, Paula Martinelli, Susan Schiffman, and Natalie Silverglide. As usual, my lovely wife performed as typist and co-worker without hesitation and with her usual vigor. Also those holding rights to some of the papers contained in the cooperative volume anthology are offered our profoundest thanks.

My fellow editors, Dale Riepe and John Somerville, served graciously in making this volume worthwhile. I also wish to thank the following University officials for their encouragement: President Henry W. Littlefield, Chancellor James H. Halsey, Vice-President Robert A. Christie, and Head Librarian Lewis M. Ice. The hundreds of fellow students who have voiced their hopes that these essays would be printed are also extended my gratitude. Special thanks must go to Professor Howard L. Parsons, my colleague, who has always been ready to give constructive suggestions during this book's production. I should also enjoy thanking Dean Donald W. Fletcher for his generous assistance in having certain technical problems alleviated.

The responsibility for any errors of judgment which remain, naturally, is my own.

DAVID H. DEGROOD
Editor-In-Chief

CONTENTS

PART IV

LOGIC AND PHILOSOPHY OF VALUES

RADICAL CURRENTS
IN
CONTEMPORARY PHILOSOPHY

Part I

THE NATURE OF PHILOSOPHY

CRITIQUE OF IDEALISTIC NATURALISM: METHODOLOGICAL POLLUTION IN THE MAIN STREAM OF AMERICAN PHILOSOPHY

Dale Riepe

INTRODUCTORY REMARKS

IN THAT landed geographical region south of Canada and north of Mexico there have been four main philosophies. They all had three features in common: they were dedicated to individualism rather than to the common good, they all emphasized method, and they were all optimistic. Puritanism dominated American thought from 1600 to 1840. From 1840 to 1878 Transcendentalism was triumphant. With Charles S. Peirce's enunciation of the principle of pragmaticism, Pragmatism was ascendant until the end of the first World War. From that time until 1950 Naturalism prospered. Each of these philosophies concentrated on method: Puritanism on self-abnegation and hard work; Transcendentalism on inwardness and upwardness; Pragmatism on utility; and, finally, Naturalism on scientific method. Until the closing of the geographical frontiers, Naturalism shared the customary American optimism, which gradually dwindled after the second World War. The euphoria concerning method continued until recently when instead of assuming that the method would find its own goal, philosophers began to ask what the aim of the method was to be. To leave this question undecided was a grievous error as Aristotle claimed. He said "the master arts are to be preferred to all the subordinate ends; for it is for the sake of the former that the latter are pursued." One art "is most truly the master art. And politics appears to be of this nature; it is this that ordains which of the sciences should be studied in a state."[1] And it will ordain the method or methods to be used.

---

[1]Aristotle, *Nichomachean Ethics*, 1049, trans. W. D. Ross.

METHODOLOGICAL MONOMANIA

Even though none of the philosophies, from Puritanism to Naturalism worked out a systematic or integrated plan toward any particular goal, their emphasis upon movement, action, practice, and utility reached its culmination of sterility in Naturalism. The Naturalist believed that the common surd of his program was "the whole-hearted acceptance of scientific method as the only reliable way of reading truth about the world, nature, society and man."[2] It is significant that the method here does not have any such goal as changing the world, but the passive one of "reading." As we might expect, John Dewey's statement along this line was more cautious: "The naturalist is one who has respect for the conclusions of natural science."[3] The salvational method was to provide "reading" matter for Hook; for Dewey it provided an object of "respect." On this view many philosophers who would not have called themselves naturalists were so designated, for example Kant or C. S. Peirce. A tighter claim than "respect" for scientific method was that of Y. H. Krikorian who maintained that "For naturalism as a philosophy, the universal applicability of the experimental method is a basic belief."[4] There were and are naturalists who would deny that scientific method is the *only reliable* way of "reading" truth, including Dewey, Abraham Edel, G. P. Conger, and Thelma Lavine; and there are naturalists who would question the necessity of having as a basic belief universal applicability of the experimental method. As was pointed out by O. K. Bouwsma, the scientific enterprise accepts as *more basic* the laws of thought which are unverifiable scientifically. Furthermore, he emphasized that "scientific method has never been justified from a purely intellectual point of view."[5] This leaves us with Dewey's less demanding "respect for the conclusions of natural science." "Respect," of course, does not imply whole-hearted acceptance and this is to the good because we do not know when the conclusions of science are finally ready for unqualified and passionate devotion. Scientists tentatively accept scientific conclusions; sometimes they ignore or question them. If scientists are so cautious, how can philosophers be so intrepid? I believe that one reason for this is

---

[2]Sidney Hook, *Naturalism and the Human Spirit*, ed. Y. H. Krikorian (New York: Columbia University Press, 1944), p. 45.

[3]*Ibid.*, p. 2.

[4]*Ibid.*, p. 242.

[5]Bouwsma, *Philosophical Essays* (Lincoln: University of Nebraska, 1969), p. 79.

that the Naturalistic philosophers are not scientists, no more scientists that Henri Bergson, Albert Camus, or Martin Heidegger. Their detachment from the actual operation of the scientific enterprise [of the interlocking scientific trusts] makes them outsiders whose opinions on the worth of scientific conclusions, on the tentativeness, makeshift, probatory, speculative nature of experimentalism is not worth much. The Naturalistic philosopher should do philosophy rather than (1) serve as an unpaid [?] publicity agent for scientific method, and (2) uncritically accept scientific method without analyzing its use in terms of social goals, and (3) assume without scientific evidence that the scientific method is simply inviolable and that by employing it mankind will be led straight to the Holy Grail or Nirvāna.

But some of the Naturalists themselves are not really serious about the scientific method of the scientist. While pretending to praise it, Dewey attacked scientific method by replacing it with what he called "common sense inquiry." This "common sense inquiry" which has its counterpart in the "ordinary language" of linguistic philosophy has been described as "a cognitive counterrevolution."[6] This cognitive twilight of Dewey fortunately ended in sunset. In Dewey's method of inquiry, which purports to be consistent with scientific method, one is not allowed qualitative distinctions, cannot separate object from subject, cannot find the "situation" or "field" about which he makes so much. For if one cannot carve out an object, how does one recognize a field? He recognizes it by the quality and quantity of objects surrounding it or included in it. Otherwise a "field" is like Nagarjuna's non-ontological Void. Dewey believed that inquiry consisted in discovering "the relationships of facts and conceptions to one another [which] is dependent upon *elimination* of the qualitative as such and upon reduction to non-qualitative formulations."[7] This implies, as Paul Crosser has shown, "the elimination of any meaningful interpretation, in the sense of the relation of outer forms to a material content"[8] and the elimination of science as known by scientists. But this should surprise no one who knows the works of Dewey beginning with his article "The Metaphysical Assumptions of Materialism" (1882).[9] Here Dewey attacked what-

---

[6]Paul Crosser, *The Nihilism of John Dewey* (New York: Philosophical Library, 1955), Chap. i, ii *passim*.

[7]Dewey, *Logic, the Theory of Inquiry* (New York: Henry Holt & Company, Inc., 1938), p. 65.

[8]Crosser, *op. cit.*, p. 85.

[9]Dewey, *Journal of Speculative Philosophy*, XVI, pp. 208-213.

ever he thought materialism was because (1) "it assumes the possibility of ontological knowledge," and (2) "it assumes the reality of the causal nexus." In its place we have the immaterialism that Dewey professed for the remainder of his life. Yet, how can Dewey favor the reduction of cognitive concerns to the qualitative when he has neither *ontos* nor nexus?[10] What, is the quantitative, quantitative *of*? I can only hypothesize that they must be quantities of mental events in Dewey's central nervous system. Dewey also had trouble finding objects in aesthetics. What are his art objects? They are such mentalistic *qualities* as "job satisfaction," indeterminable sense reactions, the "colorful drama of change," "fingering of the stretched string," and "tribal customs."[11] Dewey's idealistic nihilism arrives at the same place found by the famous Buddhist nihilist Nagarjuna, yet he mistakenly believed that he was respectful of scientific method. Not all the Naturalists were as idealistic and mentalistic as Dewey, but some of them were not quite sure that there was an independent material world existing apart from any minds contemplating it.

AIMLESS ACTIVITY

It is in examining the role of Naturalism in American social thought that we discover another weakness closely allied to an infirmity of Pragmatism. Pragmatism was first seriously attacked by social critics during World War I. Randolph Bourne, trained at Columbia University under Dewey, thought that he had put his finger on the greatest weakness of Pragmatism. This weakness is shared by Naturalism. Bourne thought that the infirmity appeared during periods of crisis. "What is significant is that it is the technical side of the war that appeals to them [the Pragmatists], not the interpretative or political side."[12] "The American," Bourne says, "in living out this

---

[10]George P. Conger says that if Dewey was to be asked: " 'Is there a physical world?' the answer is a shaded 'Yes.' " "Pragmatism and the Physical World," *Philosophy for the Future*, ed. R. W. Sellars, V. J. McGill, Marvin Farber (New York: The Macmillan Company, 1949), p. 524. Conger, a student of Dewey, believes this, but Arthur Murphy stated that he could not get Dewey to admit to this in conversation.

[11]Dewey, *Art As Experience* (New York: Minton Blach & Co., 1934), pp. 4-6.

[12]*The History of a Literary Radical & Other Papers by Randolph Bourne*, New York: S. A. Russell, 1956), p. 252.

philosophy, has habitually confused results with product, and been
content with getting somewhere without asking too closely whether
it was the desirable place to get."[13] Furthermore, according to Bourne,
"In the application of their philosophy to politics, our pragmatists
are sliding over this crucial question of ends."[14] And in discussing
the realm of ends, he notes that "when the emphasis is on technical
organization [the scientific method of the Naturalists] rather than
organization of ideas [philosophizing] on strategy rather than desires,
one begins to suspect that no programme is presented because they
have none to present."[15] The Pragmatists were "pitifully unprepared
for the interpretation or the idealistic focusing of ends."[16] One might
add that they were even less prepared for a materialistic focusing of
ends. What was at fault, then, with this evolutionary philosophy was
not the unawareness of change and the rationalistic-idealistic traditions that seemed to prevent them, but heedless that the real end of
human thought was politics, a social order that was to be formed by
intelligence—not just any intelligence, but an intelligence in favor of
the great majority of the people not simply its theater-filling rulers.[17]
Intelligence uses the best tools available unless these are observed to
be too dangerous. Dewey used tools that had grown out of Utilitarianism, Free Religion, Transcendentalism, Leibnizianism and Right-wing
Hegelianism.[18] By fusing these, he thought perhaps we can build
a better society. Yet "social change is to be a matter of individual
choice and individual moral change . . . a slow day-by-day, almost
non-temporal process."[19] As Dewey says "thus can we be sure that
we face our problems in detail *one by one as they arise*, with all the
resources provided by collective intelligence operating in cooperative

---

[13]*The History of a Literary Radical & Other Papers by Randolph Bourne*, p. 253.

[14]*Ibid.*, p. 248.

[15]*Ibid.*, p. 249.

[16]*Ibid.*, p. 251.

[17]It is the view of John Kenneth Galbraith, America's best-known establishment
economist and confidante of former President J. F. Kennedy, that the rulers or
decision-makers of this country would fit handily in a modest sized-theater.

[18]"His implication of a 'social soul,' of a 'community of religious feeling' is indeed
not so far from Emerson and Hegel." Waldo Frank, *The Re-Discovery of America*
(New York: Charles Scribners Sons, 1929), p. 170.

[19]Harry K. Wells, *Pragmatism: Philosophy of Imperialism* (London: Lawrence &
Wishart, Ltd., 1954), p. 164.

action."[20] Piecemeal, partial, pluralistic,[21] non-visions through the developing present, seen individually and morally in a field of objectless, subjectless non-cognitive unrealizations is the a-scientific model presented to us by Dewey, the Vermont Zeno.

The constant flux and change, the evolutionary march which Dewey saw was the march of the productive system of capitalism armed with scientific method and control of the forces of production. There were other forces at work also, hangovers from feudalism such as the church, nobility, serfdom, and the apriori and authoritarian methods. From the standpoint of this tradition, both Pragmatism and Naturalism appeared as radical philosophies because they embodied the claims of "progressive" capitalism. At their best both combined mechanical materialism (Dewey's belief that the field must be reduced to quantity) with historical idealism. Even today Naturalism appears radical to religious fundamentalists unless they have been sniffing in the populist gluepot.

Pragmatism collapsed in the disillusionment created by the exposure of nationalism and imperialism during the first World War. Although Dewey rarely made derogatory references to imperialism he had such an unclear notion of what composed it that we must assume that he had never even read Lenin on the subject. But even so, Dewey's doctrine had by that time spread throughout the American educational system and its influences were seen everywhere, especially in Naturalism and to some extent in its European cousins: logical positivism, general semantics, and unity of science. Operationalism was perhaps an offshoot of Peirce's pragmaticism. Pragmatism and Naturalism, however, were not so much inclined towards open espousal of neutralism and objectivism (social neutrality)[22] as the imported philosophies of Austria, Germany, and Central Europe. The neo-positivists relegated politics to the non-empirical realm along with ethics and aesthetics. Political philosophy was conveniently

---

[20]Dewey, *Freedom and Culture* (New York: G. P. Putnam's Sons, 1939), p. 7, my italics.

[21]George P. Conger makes this comment: "By its doctrine of truth as satisfaction and the obvious plurality of satisfactions in an individual or a group, pragmatism has tended to pluralism; and pluralism whatever be its proper status as a philosophy, can evade many an issue by saying both Yes and No." "Pragmatism and the Physical World," *Philosophy for the Future, The Quest of Modern Materialism*, ed. R. W. Sellars, V. J. McGill, and Marvin Farber (New York: The Macmillan Company, 1949), p. 524.

[22]Social "neutralism" by its silence encourages the establishment.

buried under the "Theory of Valuation" by the end of the second World War. Nevertheless, what nearly all the empiricists had in common, whether Pragmatic, Naturalistic or Positivistic was the denial that objective reality may be rationally understood, the espousal of the relativity of truth, and a common hostility to materialism. They refuted materialism on the following grounds: (1) it is dogmatic; (2) it is unscientific; (3) it undermines individual freedom, and (4) it favors authoritarianism.[23]

An analysis of the social function of the "Theory of Valuation" requires a separate paper, but let us at least see what Dewey believed that its function was. He said: "A theory of valuation *as* theory can only set forth the conditions which a method of formation of desires and interests must observe in concrete situations."[24]

What is a method of formation of desires and interests? Psychological conditioning? Does the theory "set forth the conditions" of psychological conditioning? Do these conditions include a theory of politics? If not, what is the theory of valuation all about?

Let us then turn to the Valuationist, C. I. Lewis, who cunningly failed to state what his position was: Naturalist, neo-Kantian, or Pragmatist. He asks how can we determine the "social value of an objective existent?" First, we determine a linear series of values (higher and lower), he responds. Second, we count up the satisfactions such as beauty and instrumentality and then decide where in the linear scale the social value belongs. To quote Lewis himself: "The conjunction of two such value-potentialities in the object give value to it in accordance with the principle that the conjoint value of two satisfactions, A and B, is determined by the place of (A and B both) in our series of immediate values in general, as determined by direct preferring. If having the satisfactions A and B both, is preferable to experiencing satisfaction C, then an object having the

---

[23]Maurice Cornforth, *In Defense of Philosophy* (London: Lawrence & Wishart, 1950), p. 242. The so-called open society desired by K. R. Popper, Bertrand Russell and associates is the society open for the predatory activity of the world jet set enjoying the fruits of socially un-neutral scientific enterprise.

[24]Dewey, *Theory of Valuation,* International Encyclopedia of Unified Science II, 4 (Chicago: University of Chicago Press, 1948), p. 57. Dewey's italics are everywhere used as escape hatches. The turgidity of his mind is well brought out here when he emphasizes "theory *as* theory." How about theory as cigarette-holder or garbage can or snow plow? Or even cleverer; how about theory as non-theory? That will take several generations of conjuring! Think of the Ph.D. theses devoted to *that.*

potentiality for satisfactions *A* and *B* both is, on this point, preferable to one affording satisfaction *C* only, and is in like manner a more valuable object. To be sure, such direct preferring is required to be rational; but so far as is here concerned, *to be rational means only to value a satisfaction not presently realized as we should value it if and when experienced.*"[25] To be rational implies valuing a satisfaction that cannot be felt and hence not a satisfaction. To be irrational then would be to not value a satisfaction as we should value it if and when experienced. Why cannot an individual do both or neither? What has rationality to do with it? This is just another attempt to continue the atomistic tradition of theoryless empiricism. Behaviorism is no substitute for a social theory seeking a common good.

What on earth is Lewis trying to say? I think that we can tell what he is trying to talk about by examining what he says in the light of the Physiocrats. Of them Marx wrote: "Their method of exposition is, of course, necessarily governed by their general view of the nature of value, which to them is not a definite social mode of existence of human activity (labour) but consists of material things—land, nature, and the various modifications of these material things."[26] That is why Lewis writes of "social objects" which can be plopped like commodities onto a supermarket checkout counter and jammed into the grocery box or bag in between two other objects.

If we can get philosophers to cogitate on such apparent trivia there is an excellent chance that they will be too busy publishing glosses on what Lewis and the other valuationists have to say about how to value a social *object* ever to raise a social *question*. Again the piecemeal, individualistc, pseudo-scientific, dust-raising trash is gravely treated as if it had something to do with our social life. In its favor may I recommend that it be used as a model for establishment attempts to raise the probability that what they do will be done with recondite pseudo-scientific flair.

The semi-progressivist "reconstructionist" Dewey of the teens and twenties succumbed, like a lady sinking back into the chaise longue with a sigh, to the scientificizing jargon of "verifiability," "valuation," "transaction," and empiricality. From the standpoint of a theory of society or genuine social evaluation commensurate with the needs of

---

[25]Lewis, *An Analysis of Knowledge and Valuation* (La Salle: The Open Court Publishing Company, 1946), p. 550, my italics.

[26]Marx, *Theories of Surplus-Value*, Part I (Moscow: Foreign Languages Publishing House, n.d.), p. 46.

American life, this amounted to a moratorium on critical social thinking among the academic philosophers extending from Peirce's early essays (1878) and his intuitional proof of God (1896) to the semantic idealism of Charles Morris, the Naturalistic liberalism of Morris Cohen and the other New York Naturalists. It is obvious that the post-idealist thought imported from Britain, from G. E. Moore to Wittgenstein and Austin, confused rather than clarified social thought and indeed stressed intuitionism and other forms of idealism.

The Naturalists might have laid up a bit of treasure if they had cried out like promethean souls to be released from the trivialities of their profit-seeking society. If they had turned to Nature, like the eighteenth and nineteenth century romantics, we should have known that they were not writing books for the dead. Their lifeless philosophy looked neither to the past nor the future nor to Nature for inspiration which must account for the undeniable fact that many of the Naturalists actually looked shockingly like half-living corpses and intoned their banalities as if they were speaking through winding sheets. This description was particularly true of those Naturalists who had studied Protestant theology and given it up out of respect for scientific method. There might also have been economic, social, and professional reasons. Once they had passed on the message that God was dead, they themselves died while their ghosts intoned the canons of scientific method. With the Death of God Naturalism lost its ogre and *raison d'être*. With nothing in particular to fight, since the whole domain of social philosophy and values was closed to it by the Postulate of Cautious Empiricism, it shrank into self-defeating non-prophecies. Naturalism might yet have unmasked the dried out shibboleths of bourgeoisdom or at least called attention to them from the philosophical belfry of the superstructure. Instead it chose to do logic without ontology, evaluation without issues, philosophy of science without objects, and philosophy of history without future reference.

Just as the office of the Attorney General did not ferret out Pragmatists, it also left the Naturalists unscathed. Why should anyone examine a philosophy that slid over controversial social issues, obstructed a clear vision of the economic and political consequences of monopoly capitalism and imperialism, and warned against a radicalism that it associated either with violence or dead European questions? Some Naturalists thought that they were treading on dangerous ground when they forthrightly remarked that "it is not completely outside the realm of possibility that deity may not exist, at least not in the sense encouraged by the church as an institution"; or when they bluntly stated that "man, after all, we must admit, is a part of nature." To demonstrate their loyalty to the status quo three well-known Naturalists included an essay, in their widely-sold elementary philosophy textbook of readings, written by the "Rationalistic" Naturalist Morris R. Cohen. It was entitled "Why I am Not a Communist." It is significant that they did not include another essay entitled "Why I am Not a Capitalist Monster."[27]

Pragmatism had seen happiness as capitalism had. Happiness is succeeding, going forward, adjusting [to market conditions], advancing [to new markets]. All this could be epitomized as "education for life," because that is what life turned out to be for Americans. But happiness is not a goal in itself. There is no goal in itself. There is no *end*. This is to carry out Leibniz's principle of continuity beyond all sense.

Dewey did not pass Pragmatism on to the business community; rather he incorporated the philosophy of business into his own psyche and rewrote it in the style that it deserved. This style Lewis Mumford characterized as "concrete in its object [but] as fuzzy and formless as lint." People of sensibility preferred the style of Bergsonianism as long as they were going to get a message aiming at the same result. Although no one believes that all the statements of Pragmatism can be made completely congruent with the views of capitalism, yet one can affirm the basic rationality of the capitalist order if only it operates with "the method of intelligence" and "scientific method."[28]

The Naturalists, except insofar as they were also Pragmatists, like Dewey, were academically more remote, but they carried out the traditions of methodological transubstantiation by turning social issues into problems of epistemology while frequently lifting the Host of scientific method. Despite this, Naturalism was an improvement

---

[27]I deliberately make this seemingly disparate parallel because to say that one was a communist after 1918 in the United States was tantamount to saying that he was a monster. The comparable term earlier was "atheist." Under capitalism, however, atheism has become philosophically respectable. See Daniel J. Bronstein, Yervant H. Krikorian and Philip P. Wiener, *Basic Problems of Philosophy* (1947, 1955, 1964).

[28]"John Dewey is in no rigid and excluding opposition to the American flux. His matter and method reveal a profound acceptance; indeed the younger generation (myself included) have attacked him on the ground that he accepted too lovingly the chaos of our world to lead us out of it." Waldo Frank, *op. cit.*, p. 168.

on Pragmatism.[29] It had fewer hangovers from feudalism such as a sincere interest in the viability of religion, it was scientifically cleaner, had fewer moving parts, and was more knowledgeable. "It expressed," better than Pragmatism, "the essence of advanced American technological society."[30] Naturalism was also somewhat less crassly untheoretical, made some gesture in the direction of trying to unite fact and value and attempted to emphasize the natural content of spiritual values. It failed to unite fact and value because it did not try to unite practice and theory. And the reason that it could not unite practice and theory is that then it would have had to settle questions of social aims, ends. If Naturalism had decided what the social aims were, it would then have been required to go back to make sense of ontology, ethics, aesthetics, and politics. As Harold Stearns stated at the end of the First World War: "Since we literally dared not be critical about the *aims* of the war, since we literally dared not examine realistically the glowing idealistic vaporings of the President [Wilson], we could be critical only of the *method* of waging the war."[31] With no recognizable (or only too recognizable) political theory and with an historical view that did not allow extrapolation into the future (in this it was even less optimistic and more cautious than Pragmatism), it confined itself to making the past a guide to understanding the present. Philosophically, this is too late. Value theory must refer to the future to be socially significant.

FUTURELESSNESS

Not following the biological and organic models so commonly dear to the Naturalists, would the Naturalist historicist wish to say that by studying the past of the horse we may know more about its present, whereas knowing both its past and present we will not know anything at all about its future? Is this true of society too? Will the past society give us some knowledge of our present society, but together they will not give us any clue to future society?

The Naturalist Edward W. Strong claimed: "[I have] taken seriously the attendant claim made by many historians that knowledge about the past contributes to an understanding of the present

---

[29]Although few of the proponents were any improvement on William James.

[30]*Il Pensiero Americano Contemporaneo*, ed. Ferruccio Rossi-Landi (Milano: Edizioné di Communità, 1958), p. 275, trans. Paul Piccone.

[31]Stearns, *Liberalism in America* (New York: Boni and Liveright, Inc., 1919), p. 94.

in which we live."[32] Strong also approvingly quoted Seignobos' view that "history enables us to understand the present in so far as it explains the origins of the existing state of things."[33] But what about the future? Strong rejects Allan Nevin's view that historical work "enables communities to grasp their relationship with the past, and to chart on general lines their immediate future course."[34] The most that Strong, the scientifically entranced Naturalist, can say in favor of learning about the future from the present and past is "summary opinion and more or less shrewd guesswork."[35] But can guesswork ever be "shrewd"? Just as Dewey occasionally slips into admitting something like class struggle, here Strong fumbles out an admission that there can be something "shrewd" about our guesswork concerning the future. But if we can't really know anything about the future, then no plans or aims for the future make any sense. So why worry about ethical or political questions?

George Boas, another Naturalist historicist, considered it important and perhaps imperative that the history of philosophy be understood in terms of *Kerngedanken* which dominate a period of philosophical thought. In our time, he said, philosophy of science and aesthetics are uppermost in [his?] philosophical circles. But these are not *thoughts,* but simply categories under which thoughts may be subsumed. Boas talked about "cosmological" periods, "scientific" periods, and "urban" periods. On a different level he differentiated the "end of a period," because "boredom explains much of what happens to the history of an idea."[36] Not only "boredom" but "conceptual inertia" is also responsible for much that goes on in the history of philosophy.[37] Let us examine boredom and inertia, factors so important in understanding intellectual history.

When students are bored, it may be because the teacher is not giving a full account of the subject. When there is inertia it may be caused by the mass media or education treating germane and relevant topics in a yawning manner in the hope that they will be forgotten. The inertia about social issues of students trained in parochial schools and most public schools as well has long been no-

---

[32]*Naturalism and the Human Spirit*, p. 176.

[33]*Introduction to the Study of History, ibid.,* p. 177.

[34]*Naturalism and the Human Spirit*, p. 178.

[35]*Ibid.,* p. 179.

[36]*Naturalism and the Human Spirit*, p. 141.

[37]*Ibid.,* p. 139.

ticed and tenderly induced. One thing we do know, Boas maintained, was that in accounting for how problems arise in philosophy "the answer given by that form of neo-Hegelianism known as dialectical materialism is more *terre à terre*: [he talks about Marxism like a Protestant divine about sex in the nineteenth century] but it is so overburdened with metaphysical baggage that it is not worth much more than its source."[38] Here one can reduce both father and son to ashes like the ancient Brahmins of India slaying the materialists. What does Boas propose that we replace the metaphysical baggage with? Well, how about the devastatingly sharp hypotheses of "boredom" and "conceptual inertia"? But where do these two small flight bags come from if not from the pre-Montesquieu idealistic checkroom?

Boas next asks: "What do we know about the history of philosophy?" At least the following: (1) There is no single subject matter which may be called philosophy and of which the history may be written. [Dewey was unable to find objects in a field or objects of art.] Boas cannot find a philosophical subject matter. (2) "Few philosophers had a system of philosophy in a geometrical sense." [How many had a system in an algebraic sense?] "[U]pon examination every system turns out to be, from the point of view of the subject matter, a group of interests *dominated by historical accident*."[39] [Like Dewey, Boas believes that subject matter has a point of view, and it is a good thing because its organizers in this case scarcely seem to have one.] A philosophy of history or a history of philosophy stuffed with historical accidents is going to be an embarrassment when the host begins to carve. (3) "Philosophical ideas . . . cannot be separated from the total *intellectual* life of a period."[40] [How about the material life also?] The philosophical idealism of Boas comes out more clearly and with less rending and tearing than that of most other Naturalists.

Another Naturalist, J. H. Randall, Jr., according to Dewey, should be given the credit for unmasking the *real* struggle that went beyond the historical materialist analysis. It is the "struggle between the active force of scientific knowledge and technical power and the deflecting force of the lag and inertia of institutionalized habits and beliefs."[41] Historical materialists, it would seem, must get off their

---

[38]*Ibid.*, p. 148.
[39]*Ibid.*, p. 152, "determined by" my italics.
[40]*Ibid.*, p. 153, my italics.
[41]Dewey, "Experience, Knowledge and Value," *The Philosophy of John Dewey*, ed. P. A. Schilpp (Evanston: Northwestern University Press, 1939), p. 522.

high horse and get down on all fours. But *who* and *what* lagged; *who* created the inertia; and *whose* habits are responsible for them? Dewey himself pointed out earlier "that the new science [after Francis Bacon] was for a long time to be worked in the interest of old ends of human exploitation."[42] Why didn't he write the obvious next sentence which would have been: "Now, instead of *old* ends of human exploitation, there are *new* ends of human exploitation." There were also new methods, one of them being the control of scientific method and technology for the end of profit for a tiny minority. Previous exploitation was developed under feudalism; the new under capitalism. Naturalism and Pragmatism before it, did not really go the whole way into social issues. They only seemed to. They kept whetting the knife and threatening to cut with it.

Why cannot the Naturalists talk about the future? One cannot deal with the future until one knows the present. And to know the present requires some form of transcendence, critique, philosophical criteria that enables one to judge the present from an unenmeshed point of view. Despite the mystical, mythological, and apparently non-sensible features of the book of *Revelation* what its writer[s] had was (1) an admitted knowledge that the present was intolerable (ca. 60-70 A.D.), (2) that a future must be hypothecated to give men hope and a sense of dignity, and (3) that this future would come in a relatively short time.

Under socialism events unfold according to the plans of future-oriented men who know that the present must be structurally changed to bring greater decency to mankind. The apocalyptic view of Revelation is future-oriented. Events will unfold according to the plans of God. A "faith survives only through active propaganda, unrelenting struggle against the internal and external enemy, the proud profession of the revolutionary standpoint before the heathen judges, and martyrdom, confident in victory."[43]

But in which direction is Naturalism oriented? Back upon itself, back upon the present, in a self-crippling gesture. Under Naturalism events do not unfold in any particular direction although accident, inertia, boredom, and the inscrutable may be thought of as controls.

---

[42]Dewey, *Democracy and Education*, reissue (New York: The Macmillan Company, 1962), p. 283.

[43]F. Engels, "On the History of Early Christianity," *Marx & Engels: Basic Writings on Politics & Philosophy*, ed. Lewis S. Feuer (New York: Anchor Books, 1959), p. 192.

If the Naturalists do not know what laws brought about the present, they surely will not be able to say anything about the future.

Much Naturalism is not shamefaced materialism, but a form of idealism.[44] We have been so hypnotized by its harping on scientific method that we have scarcely noticed that its metaphysics, ethics, aesthetics, history has been intellectual, geometrical, symbolic, logical, transactional, ideational, and mentalistic despite cant about the biological, evolutionary, organic, and quantitative. Scientific method was the Trojan Horse in which the Naturalistic idealists entered the Walls of Constructive Philosophy.

A CASE STUDY

Abraham Edel, of all the Naturalists, has tried hardest to overcome the barrier of fact and value. In addition he has had good things to say about Marxism. Furthermore, he has devoted serious attention to one of the behavioral sciences and has attempted to use it to strengthen his philosophical judgment. And he frequently gives the impression that he would like to see some major changes in the social order. With such strong recommendations, how is it that he retains his Naturalistic position? His misfortunes are perhaps the following: First, he believed that Dewey can serve as a useful guide. For he said, "Dewey's instrumentalist analysis of evaluation falls within a materialist tradition, broadly conceived . . . in approaching ethical problems Dewey definitely recognizes their social basis."[45] I think it would be fair to retort that Plato and F. H. Bradley also recognize the social basis of ethics. What is important is *how* the social basis is analyzed. Society could [it really couldn't] be made up of undifferentiated centers of subjectless and objectless experiences and I believe that it is on this that Dewey's alleged materialism is based. Second, like the Naturalistic historians, Edel is extremely cautious about the future. He said, "The Marxists . . . hold monopoly to be an inevitable product of capitalism and see government itself as an instrument utilized by monopoly interests. The question whether there is an ultimate clash of the interests [shall we wait for an atomic holocaust?] of capital and labor rather than merely occasional

---

44According to G. P. Conger "Pragmatism is a rear-guard action, A Battle of the Bulge on behalf of idealism—a thrust of emphasis on human experience or mind, reinterpreted to bring out its dynamic and practical functions." *op. cit.*, p. 539.

45Edel, *The Theory and Practice of Philosophy* (New York: Harcourt Brace and Company, 1946), p. 431.

temporary conflicts can thus be answered only in terms of the total economic functioning of a society, and a prediction of its future trend in the light of world developments."[46] To this one can only reply: how *much* evidence would convince anyone so precisely wedded to immaculate scientific methodology? Third, Edel believes that idealists are other-worldly, but since we know what they are by their actions as well as by their professions we know that they are this-worldly. I take it as a postulate that only the dead, if they, are other-worldly. The idealists are a hardy breed, as Bertrand Russell well demonstrates. It would be a frosty morning that they did not reach the hog troughs at least even with the simple-minded materialists! As a good Rajput intellectual has stated to me with some bitterness: "Why are the Idealists first in line when the honors, positions, wealth, and praise are to be distributed?" This is an important point and to miss it is to fail to see the true role of idealists in their ruling class orientation. Fourth, Edel gets more remote from questions of *praxis* from 1946 onwards. By 1968 he has really replaced any thought of major change in the social order with "a receptivity to possibly new qualities, a recognition of emergents in human life [by radiation?], and insistence on clearing the path for creativity."[47] The title of his first important book was *The Theory and Practice of Philosophy* (1946), of his last *Anthropology and Ethics: The Quest for Moral Understanding* (1959, 1968). The first was written at the beginning of the Cold War and the second just before the resurgence of practice in philosophy. In 1946 he said that "Sweeping changes must come from the war and the post-war reconstruction." But he did not foresee any more than anyone else that the reconstruction would be the resurgence of imperialism. Again he wrote in 1949, "On its active side . . . the theory of the role of ideas is the theory of how policies can and best may be formulated and become effective; in short, it is the theory of leadership as well as that of reflection."[48] This mood changes by 1959 to the resignation that about all we can do is to encourage "sensitivity." During the middle of the Joseph McCarthy period he said, "On the whole, while one may not minimize the basic disagreements that may exist in fact between nations and classes in the modern world, there is no ground for

---

[46]*Ibid.*, p. 455.

[47]May Edel and Abraham Edel, *Anthropology and Ethics*, rev. ed. (Cleveland: The Press of Case Western Reserve University, 1968), p. 237.

[48]Abraham Edel, "The Theory of Ideas," *Philosophy for the Future*, p. 450.

despair in the task of elaborating a stable moral core-conception of democracy."[49] I think I agree with Edel that we need not despair about elaborating a core-conception so much as we need to know whose core-conception to believe and act upon. It certainly cannot be that of the Naturalists who have not even tried to set forth the social goals towards which all men should strive.

I am not insensitive to the charm, style, and good intentions of the Naturalists who generally make up a group of ingratiating teachers, lecturers, and writers. The psychological and dramatic talent of Boas, the subtle interweaving of analysis and anthropology of Edel, the terse clarity of E. W. Strong, the complicated personal dialectic of W. R. Dennes, the breathless and complicated generalizations of Randall, the wit and clarity of H. T. Costello, and the salty gusto of H. A. Larrabee, who wrote the epitaph, he thought, of American idealism. What he said may just as aptly be applied to Naturalism: "The essential hollowness of the Genteel Tradition and its smug remoteness . . . from the actualities of American living, were suddenly exposed."[50] The genteel Naturalistic tradition has proved to be at most cautious and conciliatory and, at the least, contentless and irrelevant to the social issues of the day. And this avoidance of social issues, politics, and ends reflected back on its flaccid approach to other philosophical concerns. Larrabee goes on to say: "Just as the Civil War killed transcendentalism, so the first World War and its disillusioning aftermath precipitated the downfall of the feeble Roycean idealism which had succeeded it."[51] He might have added that the first World War made it possible for Pragmatism to cut its own throat and that the aftermath of the second World War provided an opportunity for Naturalism to do so. With Naturalism's demise the optimism that had saluted natural science for one hundred years evaporated. The manufacture and use of the A-bomb, biological and chemical warfare, the scientific use of human beings and the four pollutions (air, water, earth, and sound) created widespread negative reactions. There appeared to be one thing equally important to natural science and scientific method—

---

[49]Abraham Edel, *Ethical Judgment: The Use of Science in Ethics* (London: The Free Press of Glencoe, Collier-Macmillan Limited, 1964), p. 327. One notices that the "Free" Press has been swallowed up by the Collier-Macmillan conglomerate.

[50]*Naturalism and the Human Spirit*, p. 350.

[51]*Ibid.*, p. 351.

and that was *who* was to use it and for *what*. And no matter how these questions are asked, the answers will involve recognition and understanding of the class struggle.

The Naturalists' idealistic tendencies, from the most non-anti-materialistic (Edel) to the least (Boas, Eliseo Vivas)[52] is found in this notice, a choice that puts it nearly always in practice on the side of the establishment. The ruling class, it will be noticed, has not hunted down either Pragmatists or Naturalists, while keeping a sharp nose in the wind for non-mechanical materialists, Marxists, and socialists who indicate a belief in the existence of a fairly sharply defined struggle, and who have chosen to emphasize worthy ends and goals for an America up to its ears in scientific method.

This examination of Naturalism with its overemphasis on methodological considerations[53] exemplifies a wider truth than the one immediately apparent—that failure to consider goals and ends must lead to dangerous blind alleys. A wider truth to emerge from the entangling confusion resulting from focusing on exclusive features in philosophy is that disregard for the claims of ontology, social ethics, (politics) and aesthetics can only lead to warped and partial philosophy. When the special sciences and the whole of mankind are in need of a synoptic view, it is damaging to strum on partiality and speciality. American philosophy must now devote itself to supplying solutions to such a need.

---

[52]I have been told that Vivas abrogated Naturalism to join a group of "other-worldly" philosophers.

[53]The present discussion of American Naturalism is thus not intended to apply to all types of thought designated "naturalistic," and especially not to types which could equally well be called "materialistic" in a wider sense. Yet I stand guilty with the other idealistic naturalists, having spent too many years trying to clean the American henhouse with a methodological spoon. But from the bowels of decency and reason I exhort other naturalists to re-examine their positions so that they waste no more time in the futile chant:

"Scientific methodology without End, Amen, Amen."

EX NIHILO NIHIL FIT:
PHILOSOPHY'S 'STARTING POINT'

David H. DeGrood

PERIODICALLY, philosophers have had the feeling that some-how the entire weight of the traditional categories, doctrines, and problems should either be completely abandoned, permanently or temporarily, or else thoroughly redefined and reclarified. Though the ancient Skeptics (Pyrrho, Arcesilaus, Carneades, Philo of Larissa) perhaps have the right to claim "first fruits" in this domain of placing all things in critical suspension, it was to René Descartes in the late Renaissance that a great opportunity existed to undercut the vast wasteland of theological superstition and presumption. The "light of natural reason" was to inherit the power to determine belief, replacing the symphony of emotional and intellectual chaos pervading the age of "Reformation." In an atmosphere where religion was worth burning one's neighbor over, to alter slightly Montaigne's famous phrase, it was seen to be advisable by Descartes—who had "doubted everything"—to remove himself to a safer land. His pro-cedure, methodical doubting, is familiar, involving putting aside beliefs of which any doubt could be entertained. Since it is true that "from nothing, nothing comes," there would have literally been no Cartesian philosophy, unless something *resisted* the doubt. What had been smuggled[1] into the doubting procedure to begin with, the "I doubt" (*dubito*), or its semantic implication, "I think" (*cogito*); was to be the pole-star among all the innumerable dubitables (in-cluding empirical facts).

---

[1]See the excellent observations on this by Arnold Berleant, "On the Circularity of the Cogito," pp. 431-433. *Philosophy and Phenomenological Research*, XXVI, #3, March, 1966.

Fast and furiously, Descartes passed by logical scandal to some thoroughly scholastic conclusions;* for example, that a variation of the Ontological Argument of Anselm could be validated—thus giving him a metaphysical and eminent Ego, namely God, to solve his solipsistic dilemma, to resolve his doubts about the certitude of mathematics, and to grant sensory experience a degree of veridicity. In Cartesianism there is a mixture of defiance towards scholastic teleology and dogmatism and of seeming sycophancy towards those who rejected the concrete systematic doubting of the Copernican-Galilean science, a discipline about to undermine the Mediaeval ideology. Descartes' metaphysical dualism placated to some extent the conservative churchmen by placing the soul beyond scientific controversy. We can say, at least *almost* beyond scientific controversy. Descartes could not resist having the outlines of a complete system. Philosophers too abhor a vacuum! Descartes, therefore, proceeded to speculate on the possible function of the pineal gland, a gland he thought might serve as an intermediary (notice that the linking mechanism is corporeal) between the two disparate realms of the extended (*res extensa*) and the thinking (*res cogitans*). Granting the reactionaries the sop of their own special, though enigmatic, realm of the soul, Descartes set out to construct a detailed mechanistic world view, extending from physics to physiology. What it was that proved so eminently fruitful to humanity as a result of Descartes' work was not his method of doubting but the "geometrical method," that is, the hypothetical deductive reasoning of the revolutionary science of his time.

Though Francis Bacon, Thomas Hobbes, John Locke, and David Hume also allowed doubting to overthrow much of Mediaeval ideology, they did not necessarily begin with the *cogito;* in fact, Hume tried to undercut even that.[2] What these British philosophers did was to make liberal use of Ockham's Razor. They were moving in the direction of restricting knowledge-claims not necessarily to apodictic truth but to verifiable belief.

Both Bacon and Descartes saw that fruitfulness in philosophizing

---

*This is often the case with radicals in philosophy who try to begin completely "anew." With Descartes much of his philosophical set of premises smacks of La Flèche. A recent "radical innovator," Martin Heidegger, for all his "originality," is also not that far removed from his Roman Catholic, scholastic training.

[2]See David Hume, A *Treatise of Human Nature*, Bk. 1, Part IV, "Of Personal Identity"; & Bk. III, Appendix.

depended on the founding of a new *method*. Bacon saw systematic experimentation, leading to control over nature, as the key to scientific knowledge. From Bacon stems that tradition of philosophy which, in principle, begins in the midst of things, *in medias res*. This tradition does not seek an indubitable, incorrigible, presuppositionless "starting point" for philosophy. Rather, it sees the function of philosophy not in *a priori* declarations but in solving the problems of men, that is, in mastering nature and strengthening rationality in the lives of men. Examples of this "mid-stream," Baconian approach can certainly be found in more recent philosophy. Just after World War II in 1946, John Dewey in his paper, "The Problems of Men and the Present State of Philosophy," commented pointedly on the continuing tradition in modern philosophy of attempting to find some incorruptible starting point for thought, of attempting to "solve" the so-called "problem of knowledge":

> ". . . Practical problems that are so deeply human as to be the moral issues of the present time have increased their range and their intensity. They cover practically every aspect of contemporary life. . . . But during the very period in which this has occurred, philosophy, for the most part, has relegated them to a place that is subordinate and accessory to an alleged problem of knowledge. At the same time actual knowing and the application of science in life by inventions and technological arts have been going on at such a rate that the alleged problem of its foundations and possibility of knowledge are of but remote professional concern. The net result of neglect with issues that are urgent and of preoccupation with issues that are remote from active human concern explains the popular discredit into which philosophy has progressively fallen. This disrepute is in turn a decided factor in determining its role in the world."[3]

Philosophy has been caught in the compartmentalization of modern advanced industrialism. There is a pervasive tendency to find strict dichotomies between theory and practice, between fact and value, philosophy and politics, administrator and educator, and so forth.

In its most advanced stage of substantive paralysis, philosophy loses its function as the synthesis of the results of the sciences; it delivers itself from ethics, politics, and history. The American and British "linguistic" schools look to philosophy as a therapy for

---

[3]John Dewey, *Problems of Men* (New York: Philosophical Library, 1946), p. 7.

the bewitchment of the mind by our language. One of the founders of this way of doing philosophy, Ludwig Wittgenstein, manages to convey the neat way in which the problems of philosophy are solved or dissolved: "The solution of the problem of life is seen in the vanishing of the problem."[4] Philosophies are generated from "cramp" and "bewitchment"; we overcome these by investigating the logic of "our language." But what might happen to the "lucky few" who might get a "complete cure" *from* philosophy? The answer is, as Ernest Gellner has pointed out,[5] to artificially induce a cramp to be cast out later. This way of interpreting the role of philosophy could not stand in more marked contrast than it does to Marx's words in his last proposition in his "Theses on Feuerbach": "The philosophers have *interpreted* the world in various ways; the point however is to *change* it."[6] Like Dewey, Marx continued the Baconian tradition, despite important differences in emphasis and interpretation.

The starting point of the Marxist theory of history does not look to the certainties of intuition or even the bedrock certainty of a Cartesian God; its commencement sets forth premises by which man's historical achievements can be understood, just as Darwin's theory of Natural Selection lays down premises by which the origin of species may be discovered. In their treatise, *The German Ideology,* Marx and Engels explain:

> . . . "We do not set out from what men say, imagine, conceive, nor from men as narrated, thought of, imagined, conceived, in order to arrive at men in the flesh. We set out from real, active men, and on the basis of their real life process we demonstrate the development of the ideological reflexes and echoes of this life process."

As against the misty Idealisms of the past, they say:

> "Life is not determined by consciousness, but consciousness by life. In the first method of approach the starting point is consciousness taken as the living individual; in the second it is

---

[4] Ludwig Wittgenstein, *Tractatus Logico-Philosophicus,* 6.521 (London: Routledge & Kegan Paul, 1961).

[5] See Ernest Gellner, *Words and Things: A Critical Account of Linguistic Philosophy and a Study in Ideology* (Boston: Beacon, 1960), pp. 185, 246-247. Gellner's work of criticizing this philosophical school has also now been ably supplemented by Maurice Cornforth's profound study, *Marxism and the Linguistic Philosophy* (London: Lawrence & Wishart, 1965).

[6] In Friedrich Engels, *Ludwig Feuerbach and the Outcome of Classical German Philosophy* (New York: International Publishers, 1941), p. 84.

the real, living individuals themselves, as they are in actual life, and consciousness is considered solely as *their* consciousness."[7]

Starting points such as the above may be unsatisfactory for those philosophers who demand that premises have the upper limit of mathematical probability; but to those who are more interested in examining and testing consequences than they are in searching endlessly for unexceptional axioms whose truth is *guaranteed in all possible worlds,* such initial assumptions unlock the enigmas of economics, politics, law, religion, and philosophy itself.

Moreover, if one of the criteria of a sound philosophy is that it be able not only to account *genetically* for itself, but also that it be self-corrective, then it is difficult to imagine any historical variety of Idealism, subjectivistic, objectivistic, or positivistic, being sound. If we take Ralph Barton Perry's compressed definition of naturalism, it is plain that scientific philosophy or materialism, whatever word one wishes to use, not only can genetically account for itself through the techniques developed by social science, but as greater knowledge of the cosmos is revealed by the positive sciences, revisions within the naturalistic framework are cordially welcomed. As Perry declares, "By naturalism is meant the philosophical generalization of science— the application of the theories of science to the problems of philosophy."[8]

Speaking of the criterion above of judging the various competing philosophies, that is, the criterion that a philosophy should be able to account for itself genetically through its principles; a slight reservation in the case of Dewey's work must be made. It is not that Dewey's principles could not serve to meet this criterion, rather it is that Dewey himself seemed to want to exempt himself from the obvious reflexive nature of his socio-historical judgments. The reader is urged to judge this for himself in the reading of the apparently coy manner, if not of the ignominious manner, in which his exchange with Bertrand Russell was carried on in 1939. Russell said quite wisely:

"Dr. Dewey [Dewey hated the title "Doctor"] has an outlook which, where it is distinctive,* is in harmony with the age of

---

[7]Contained in Lewis S. Feuer (ed.); Marx and Engels, *Basic Writings on Politics and Philosophy* (New York: Anchor, 1959), pp. 247-248.

[8]Ralph Barton Perry, *Present Philosophical Tendencies* (New York: Braziller, 1955), p. 45.

*Nota bene!

industrialism and collective enterprise. It is natural that his strongest appeal should be to Americans, and also that he should be almost equally appreciated by the progressive elements in countries like China and Mexico." . . .[9]

Russell added an honorific comparison of Dewey to Jeremy Bentham.

Dewey's response showed a blindness to the significance of Russell's point, and certainly Dewey would not have accepted a response similar to his own that others might have given him after being sociologically analyzed by Dewey.[10] Though it is important to see how Dewey's interpretation of his own philosophy is limited, it does not follow from this that his peculiar narrowness on this point vitiates his philosophical perspective. The target of scientific philosophers is, as it has been historically, the particular variety of idealism contemporarily in vogue.

Though the older forms of Idealism seem to have suffocated with the steady success of science, and science has steadfastly remained realistic in its view of the relation of consciousness,* newer forms of Idealism, just as potentially injurious to the growth of man's knowledge, have appeared. Existentialism sees science as either falsifying or trivial with regard to actual human experience.[11] Generic pronouncement, uncontrolled metaphysical speculation, and viewing the world through the most morbid of emotions serve as catalysis for an academic irrationalism unmatched in history (Kierkegaard, Heidegger, Marcel, Sartre, Jaspers, Unamuno, et al.). Similarly, Husserlian phenomenology, entirely fruitful as a complementary method to the objective methods of the positive sciences, conceived as *the* portal to a complete philosophy of experience attempts to found all theoretical disciplines upon the basis of Transcendental Idealism. Husserl reverts to a Cartesian framework in terms of philosophy's starting point, though it must be added that Husserl's rigorous reduc-

---

[9]Bertrand Russell, "Dewey's New Logic." Paul Arthur Schilpp, ed., *The Philosophy of John Dewey* (Evanston: Northwestern University Press, 1939), p. 137.

[10]Cf. Dewey's rejoinder, Schilpp ed., *op. cit.,* pp. 526-527.

[11]For an examination of the social roots of this *malaise,* see Auguste Cornu, "Bergsonianism and Existentialism," pp. 151-168. In Marvin Farber, ed., *Philosophic Thought in France and the United States* (Buffalo: University of Buffalo, 1950). (Albany: State University of New York Press, 1968.)

*Roy Wood Sellars' term "mentation" is a more appropriate one admittedly. It puts "consciousness" within the skin, and sees consciousness as an instrument of social life and culture.

tions, exacting care at description, and his categorial apparatus are vastly more complicated than those of Descartes' *Meditations*. Like Descartes, Husserl looks back to Augustine for "inner truth";[12] but unlike Descartes, Husserl never leaves the inside of the looking glass. Unlike Descartes' descent into the empirical world to perfect a mechanistic cosmology, Husserl remains a philosophical narcissist. The student of philosophy might ask if the phenomenological philosophy could possibly live up to the criterion of a sound philosophy sketched above when we are told by Husserl:

> . . . "In regard to transcendental-phenomenological Idealism, I have nothing whatsoever to take back, . . . now as ever I hold every form of current philosophical realism to be in principle absurd, as no less every idealism to which in its own arguments that realism stands contrasted. . . . Over against the thinking, rich in presuppositions, which has as its premises the world, science, and sundry understandings bearing on method, . . . a radical form of . . . autonomy . . . is here active, in which every form of datum given in advance, and all Being taken for granted, is set out as invalid." . . .[13]

If Husserl would not have taken for granted the *conceivability* of "essences," in other words, if he would have actually done without presuppositions, there would never have been a phenomenological philosophy. Again, from nothing, nothing can come. Unlike phenomenology and existentialism, scientific philosophy explores every avenue of possible knowing, subjecting claims to "insight" into the nature of various levels of reality to test by critical experience. Naturalism or materialism is open textured, and it does not try to protect itself from scientific revolutions or from the implications of scientific knowledge concerning man's place in the cosmos, even when it becomes necessary to offset man's exaggerated self-importance in the scheme of things, a self-importance inherited from pre-scientific eras.

---

[12]Cf. Edmund Husserl, *Cartesian Meditations,* trans. Dorion Cairns (The Hague: Martinus Nijhoff, 1960), pp. 156-157.

[13]Edmund Husserl, "Author's Preface to the English Edition," *Ideas: General Introduction to Pure Phenomenology,* tr. W. R. Boyce Gibson (London: George Allen & Unwin, 1958), p. 19. For Husserl's detailed and quite assumptive polemic against naturalistic philosophy, see his "Philosophy as Rigorous Science." Contained in Husserl, *Phenomenology and the Crisis of Philosophy,* ed. & tr. by Quentin Lauer (New York: Harper, 1965), especially pp. 71-122.

For the naturalist, logic continues to be, as Russell has phrased it, the "essence of philosophy." Logic is the general tool of inquiry, in Aristotle's sense. That does not mean that the modern naturalist exclusively conceives of logic as formal deductive logic (as Russell does). Quite the contrary, the philosophical investigator sees even logic as corrected and modified by the needs of experimental inquiry. Inquiries may require a formal, postulational approach, or they may require generalizations from experimental data (inductive inquiry), or they may make necessary a dialectical approach (historical patterns, tense social situations, and certain aspects of thinking itself). Ordinarily and for the most part, logic will be the *critical control of inquiry* by various orders of concepts (deductive, inductive, and dialectical forms); and only rarely will the experimental situation thrust upon us the necessity of conceiving of different orders of logical concepts. The important thing to bear in mind, however, is that the logical concepts and categories are not in a "realm" of their own and *sui generis;* they reflect the structure of the world and the degree of imaginative ingenuity (in the case of fictive concepts) present in man at a given point in history.[14] Conceiving logic in its broadest sense as *methodology,*[15] is also the task of the philosopher to *clarify* the basic concepts required for intelligent action and scientific understanding.

In opposition to the uncontrolled philosophical speculations dominant in their youth, which were often anti-scientific and idealistic, philosophers such as Bertrand Russell and G. E. Moore in effect overreacted by starting a tradition where careful analytic thought and severely restricted claims became ends in themselves, rather than controlled starting points of investigation. This type of myopia tended throughout this century of "analysis" (especially in Anglo-America) to separate the philosopher from the *terminus* of analysis, that is, to keep him from applying concepts to the various levels of

---

[14]Cf. V. J. McGill and W. T. Parry, "The Unity of Opposites: A Dialectical Principle," pp. 418-444, especially pp. 439-442. *Science and Society*, vol. XII, #4, Fall, 1948.

[15]Cf. Dewey's usage and arguments for the identity of logic and methodology in his *Logic: The Theory of Inquiry* (New York: Holt, Rinehart & Winston, 1960), ch. I, 'The Problem of Logical Subject-Matter," pp. 1-22.

concrete experience and its problems.* The "analytic" philosopher has a predilection to avoid committing himself (qua philosopher should we say?) on political, economic, and religious issues, to "clarify" these issues, while abstaining from the fray. Nevertheless, clarification of basic concepts is a necessary condition of philosophizing; it is one of the aspects of "beginning" a philosophical inquiry without which nihil fit.

In combating the unverified, and often unverifiable, beliefs of the Middle Ages and ancient superstition, the empiricist tradition of Locke, Hume, and others made the theory of knowledge the prime starting point of philosophy. While philosophers such as Locke and Hume were enormously impressed by the Newtonian system of physics, and despite the fact that they attempted to set up a kind of "Newtonian system of psychology,"[16] their analysis of "experience" and "knowledge" ultimately failed to avoid skeptical conclusions of a far-reaching kind.** Hume could not only ultimately doubt the existential sufficiency of the external world, but he even failed to discover descriptively the ego which was reaching such skeptical conclusions. "Epistemological idealism," seemed to be the only consistent result of this atomistic type of analysis, the type of analysis also reflecting the rising social individualism of the age.

The "empiricist" begins with "uninterpreted" sensa as alone veridical, and he finds that everything else must be validated, if at all possible, by an extrapolative leap from those incorrigible sensa. He never really gets beyond these sensa, except by postulating "logical constructions"; hence he must ultimately undercut the work

---

[16]For an illuminating analysis of that development, see John Herman Randall, Jr., The Making of the Modern Mind, rev. ed. (Cambridge: Houghton Mifflin, 1954), pp. 261-271, 308-318.

*Russell, it can be said, did not restrict himself to analysis solely, nor could he endorse such artificial restrictions as the logical positivists and the "analytic movement" placed upon itself. Russell has continually applied clarity of thought, even when oversimplified and incorrect, to political ends, and he has made periodic excursions into "metaphysics."

**The use to which Lockean doctrines were put in France by Diderot, Helvétius, and d'Holbach launched a revolutionary tradition. That is because a general materialist theory of reality operated along with the epistemological system. With Hume, epistemologogy is allowed to undermine ontology; hence epistemology was allowed to weaken rather than strengthen the unity of theory and practice.

of other empiricists, working scientists.[17] The philosophical or epistemological empiricist fails to work with a fruitful general theory of
reality which will reflexively illuminate his own sense-data, which
will bring him out of his solipsistic "world." Whatever restrictions
may be imposed by the "epistemological empiricist" on himself, the
observer will always be able to notice how the scientific world view
of the day supplies much of the *content* of his epistemological speculation. Since the hypotheses of science will be present anyway, they
should be set down *explicitly* for intersubjective criticism. In other
words, a "metaphysic" should be allowed a cooperative role in developing a fruitful epistemology. The metaphysic or the epistemology
may be found to need modification or rejection in the course of
inquiry.* There is no reason that the investigator cannot critically
modify or reject initial "raw" or unclarified data. What the philosopher
should remember is that scientific results are really not often "undermined" by him, nor can the ideas of the positive sciences be
"suspended" from his philosophical system. As Hans Reichenbach
noted in this connection, "philosophical systems, at best, have reflected
the stage of scientific knowledge of their day. . . ."[18] This seems
an inescapable fact, a fact not to be bemoaned incidentally, but one
which requires tentativeness in philosophizing.[19]

Aside from the material fallacy which epistemologizing philosophers make who believe that they can generate a system free of
scientific content, there is another fallacy to consider. That fallacy
is that science has now advanced so much that philosophers must now
surrender wholly their constructive role in the history of thought.
This frame of mind is correctly identified with positivists such as

---

[17]This point is wisely brought out by Lenin in his *Materialism and Empirio-
Criticism: Critical Comments on a Reactionary Philosophy*, ch. 2, sec. 4, pp. 185-
194, especially p. 190. *Selected Works,* vol. XI (New York: International Publishers, 1943).

[18]Hans Reichenbach, *The Rise of Scientific Philosophy* (Berkeley: University of
California Press, 1957), p. 117.

[19]For a striking example of how quickly scientific-philosophical syntheses can be
dated, see my *Haeckel's Theory of the Unity of Nature* (Boston: Christopher,
1965).

*For those to whom the term "metaphysics" is anathema, they may substitute the
phrase "general theory of reality" or "results of the positive sciences taken as a
systematic whole." Even the positivist, Herbert Feigl, allows some types of
"meaningful" metaphysics. See his "Logical Empiricism," pp. 11-13. In *Readings
in Philosophical Analysis* (New York: Appleton-Century-Crofts, 1949).

Reichenbach. In the second part of the statement cited immediately above, he states about philosophical systems, ". . . they have not contributed to the development of science."[20] What does this imply for the philosopher currently? It implies a wholly *passive role* in analyzing scientific concepts and results. Constructive work towards new knowledge is seen as useless. This type of attitude, if taken seriously, would, in effect, emasculate philosophy. It is quite felicitous that Democritus, Aristotle, Bacon, Comte, Hegel, Marx, James, and Dewey did not adopt this passive attitude. Perhaps this passive attitude itself fits in better with a society in which individuals have little or no role in shaping their destinies, little or no power in directing their energies and technology.

Needless to say the exclusive reliance on metaphysical analysis may result in never bringing philosophy down to earth. Concepts such as "paratranscendence" (Oskar Becker), "nothingness" (Kierke-gaard and Heidegger), and "God" are notorious examples of meta-physics "unhampered" by critical standards of investigation, that is, uncontrolled by logic and epistemology. Such pathological appendages to various traditions in philosophy are linked to the inability of men at this point in history to satisfy their real needs.

For specialized studies, philosophers may take whatever starting points they like; their results will be critically weighed in terms of the developing sciences and the standards of logic. If a systematic, complete view is put forward, it must not only live up to the standards indicated above, but it must also be able to account for itself. If this manner of judging philosophies is rejected, we are entitled to remind the rejector that there is no presuppositionless way of philosophizing; "from nothing, nothing comes."

Given the present state of historical development, a new period of constructive philosophical work is sorely needed. If the philoso-pher's task is now to help to change the world, he must be able to interpret it correctly.

---

[20]Reichenbach, *ibid.*

AN HISTORICAL CRITIQUE OF EMPIRICISM*

James E. Hansen

MODERN Empiricism holds sway over virtually every scientific and pseudo-scientific discipline available to the interested student. The self-styled Empiricists have managed to convince most of us that their "methodological" approach to solving difficult problems is still the most viable that has been offered to Western man. Sidney Hook, for example, tells us that the knowledge gained by means of the "scientific method" is the *only* reliable knowledge, and, indeed, he who denies this is "palpably insincere."[1] Ernest Nagel, on the other hand, asks us to submit our findings to the experimental procedures of the sciences[2]—that is, we are to do so if we wish to be acclaimed "reasonable." The Positivists tell us that we must "verify" our claims if we desire them to be "meaningful" (although just what verify means at this date is not too clear). The psychologists working in the universities ask us to submit our findings to the laboratory or computer. Sociologists collect "data." And ethical philosophers insist that ethical claims be supported "scientifically." The science referred to in these appeals is the science of the so-called Empiricists. Although there are as many brands of Empiricism as there are claimants, certain generic traits exist by which all may be tied together. It is

---

[1]Sidney Hook, "Scientific Knowledge and Philosophical 'Knowledge,'" *Partisan Review*, Vol. 24, #2 (Spring, 1957), p. 223. This article was reprinted in Hook's *The Quest for Being* (New York: Dell, 1963), pp. 209-228.

[2]See Ernest Nagel's Presidential Address, "Naturalism Reconsidered," *Proceedings of the American Philosophical Association*, 1954-1955.

*An earlier form of this article appeared in *Catalyst,* Summer, 1967.

these traits and their presuppositions and consequences that are analyzed in what follows.*

One of the cornerstones of this view is that "facts" are "collected" by means of the "inductive method," and thereafter, and only thereafter, are legitimate theories and norms proposed. It is claimed that we are dealing with a world which is "objectively given." What the Empiricist claim amounts to is that we *really* have the methodological outline of all problems, and all we have to do is to subject whatever data we find to calculation. We have the Method, all we need is the data. Nothing is inviolate: everything can be analyzed "scientifically." Contemporary behavioral psychology, or neo-behavioral psychology, or neo-neo-behavioral psychology is well-known for this approach: give us the problem, and, with time (and money) we will supply the answer, for we possess the model Science. The fact that the present method is *one* among many historically implemented methods is blithely ignored. This emphasis upon the historical factors generating a theory of science is precisely what is abandoned to the junk-heap of "non-scientific" speculation.** Almost everyone is guilty of this form of *hybris,* except the dialecticians.[3] The dialectician investigates scientific theories and theories of science within the framework of their historical genesis and meaning. He does not accept as *a priori* or as "natural" that which is merely historical.***

---

[3]For example, see B. M. Kedrov, "Philosophy of Science," *Soviet Studies in Philosophy,* Vol. VI, #1 (Summer, 1967), pp. 16-27.

*We should point out that the remarks which follow are directed to a broad range of philosophical views of science. It is very likely that no one philosopher holds all the positions discussed in this paper (with the possible exception of Sidney Hook). What we have done is to deal with those views which must be defended if the contemporary, comprehensive theory of science is to remain intact.

**This is precisely how Ernest Nagel treats the attempts to utilize *Verstehen* in philosophical-scientific studies. See Ernest Nagel, "On the Method of Verstehen as the Sole Method of Philosophy," *The Journal of Philosophy,* Vol. I, #5, February, 1953, pp. 154-157. He rejects *Verstehen* on the grounds that it is not "scientific."

***For an example of how Marx deals with this, see *Capital,* Vol. III (Moscow: Foreign Languages Publishing House, 1962), Part IV, "Transformation of Surplus-Profit into Ground-Rent," pp. 600-793. Here Marx shows how certain central presuppositions of the classical economists were not "natural," but rather they were "historical" in character—and, thus, by no means "necessary" to doing Political Economy.

The Empiricist view of science closes the doors to any qualitative advance of either knowledge or activity, insofar as it maintains its methodological view (really a reified metaphysical view) as the one and only true view. Indeed, some Empiricists claim that there do not exist qualitative differences in either history or nature, and proceed to demonstrate their claim "methodologically," thereby closing the circle.[4] We shall analyze this view from the dialectical perspective, from the historical and non-reified perspective. To say that our approach is dialectical is to say that it is necessarily historical, although the converse is not true. One could be historical in one's view of science and yet be quite undialectical (for example, R. G. Collingwood). If the following analysis resembles some views of nondialecticians, this is more than acceptable. The dialectician attempts to avoid being exclusive, least of all on "methodological" grounds.

Dialecticians from Marx to Lukács have vigorously argued for the necessity of keeping all inquiry open-ended. They have continually pointed out the dogmatic character of any claim that purports to have grasped the one true set of conclusions to the one true set of problems, by means of the True Methodology. To oppose this extremely static, ahistorical conception of some kind of "universal" truth (apriorism), they have usually held something like the following: "one is always conscious of the necessary limitations of all acquired knowledge, of the fact that it is conditioned by the circumstances in which it was acquired." (Engels, *Ludwig Feuerbach and the End of Classical German Philosophy*, p. 67; Moscow ed.) Dialecticians, then, claim that knowledge is given meaning *historically*, and is not to be subjected to some alleged trans-historical, "methodologically pure" set of criteria deemed universally valid. Thus, one invariably comes across the insistent emphasis upon qualitative differences that are manifested in the different types of knowledge gained through varied and qualitatively different experiences. The knowledge of celestial mechanics possessed by a Greek of 500 B.C., for example, was qualitatively different from the knowledge that we presently possess,[5] a knowledge which itself will most likely be left behind as "magic" in the process of scientific advancement.

---

[4]This is very evident in the Empiricist treatment of history. For example see Carl Hempel, "The Function of General Laws in History," *The Journal of Philosophy*, Vol. 39, 1942, pp. 35-48.

[5]See Benjamin Farrington, *Greek Science: Its Meaning for Us*, Vol. I, *Thales to Aristotle* (Harmondsworth, England: Penguin Books, 1944).

There are those who disagree with such a view of science: these are the Empiricist scientists and philosophers of science. They argue that it is not historical influences that account for the growth and changing nature of science, but rather we should look to the "methodology" that deals with "brute facts" if we are to explain the growth of science. We are told that it is the formal character of science that accounts for its success. We are to look to *the* scientific method in all inquiry, both past and present. In this framework, we are told to observe "good scientific procedures." We are urged to accept the present norms of inquiry if we are to gain "knowledge." Indeed, one of these, Sidney Hook, argues that "those categories [of current science] are taken as fundamental which permit reduction to common factors;"[6] i.e., the present categories. This is the view of science as "normal science" of which Thomas Kuhn writes:

> "Normal science means research firmly based upon one or more past scientific achievements that some particular scientific community acknowledges for a time as supplying the foundation for its further practice."[7]

This type of science is prevalent in most lab work; the scientist "collects" facts in accordance with some pre-established paradigm. Kuhn opposes this type of science to "revolutionary science," wherein qualitatively new sciences are developed, sciences which cannot be made to fit within the old paradigm. The Empiricist argues that most if not all science is what Kuhn calls "normal science." This approach eventually leads to the claim that there are "limits to man's capacity to create concepts"[8] and that we have now arrived at *the* paradigm of scientific inquiry, a paradigmatic approach with which all other approaches must be "continuous" or "consistent." Qualitative differences are ruled out, and methodological criteria become the arbitration board which rules over all "knowledge."

Dialecticians, on the other hand, refrain from arguing that there should be a continuity of all forms, or contents, of historically concatenated knowledge. One would be surprised to find dialecticians first setting up criteria, frozen within limits, and then claiming that

---

[6]Sidney Hook, "Categorical Analysis and Pragmatic Realism," *Journal of Philosophy*, Vol. 24, #7 (March, 1927), p. 183.

[7]Thomas S. Kuhn, *The Structure of Scientific Revolutions* (Chicago: University of Chicago Press, 1964), p. 10.

[8]Niels Bohr, *Atomic Theory and the Description of Nature* (Cambridge: Cambridge University Press, 1961), p. 96.

all "knowledge" must submit to that set of criteria (alleged to be good for all time) if it is to be termed "real" or "scientific" knowledge. What they do claim is that we ought to seek a theoretical pluralism (in this historical period) which would allow for various interpretations of the existent domains of inquiry. These domains of inquiry are felt to be subject to the most widespread revisions when it comes to changing methodologies used to deal with them. The pluralism thus called for would prohibit any kind of Hookian reduction. This theoretical pluralism is one which is grounded in the knowledge that all inquiry, past or present, is the result of the generation of *theories*, "scientific" or otherwise. However, lest it be thought that the dialectician is one who throws limits to the wind, it must be remembered that any dialectician who argues for the pluralistic view does set up parameters of method, bound by certain conditions. (The Empiricists emphasize the *abstract limits* of inquiry, whereas the dialectician emphasizes the historicity of inquiry, thereby emphasizing the changeability of inquiry.) Although not restricted by any particular scientific use of "objective" references, the dialectician is bound by certain natural or ontological conditions, most of which may change —the possibility is not ruled out on methodological grounds. For example, the dialectician would not define an object in a way that would permit the attenuation of characteristics not permitted by that object, e.g., a person cannot be defined as capable of becoming physically identical with another person.[9] Nevertheless, the dialectician attempts to avoid the Empiricist trap of setting up particular criteria as *the* criteria. According to Paul K. Feyerabend:

> Not only is the description of every single fact dependent on *some* theory (which may, of course, be very different from the theory to be tested), but there also exist facts that cannot be unearthed except with the help of alternatives to the theory to be tested and that become unavailable as soon as such alternatives are excluded. This suggests that the methodological unity to which we must refer when discussing questions of test and empirical content is constituted by a *whole set of partially overlapping, factually adequate, but mutually inconsistent theories;* in short, it suggests a theoretical pluralism as the basis of every test procedure. ("Problems of Empiricism," in *Beyond the Edge of Certainty,* ed. Robert G. Colodny. Prentice-Hall, 1965; p. 175.)

---

[9]This example is from Herbert Marcuse's *One-Dimensional Man* (Boston: Beacon Press, 1964), p. 218.

This is a definitive refutation of Empiricism, from classical forms to the present. Here we should like to state our fundamental disagreement with Feyerabend. We do not, as Feyerabend does, argue for the necessity at *all* times of theoretical pluralism. We note, however, that in the present stage of the development of science and society—its "crisis" stage—a plurality of approaches is required if we are to arrive at an historical stage where a common humanity in a rational society could agree on a unified method to overcome *common* problems.

We shall explicate this claim by the use of examples. One case of this expunging of certain facts by the use of a theory is the example given by the "discovery" of oxygen. Because Priestley would not yield the phlogiston theory, he was unable to recognize the importance of the "discovery" of what he termed "dephlogisticated air." Lavoisier did reject the phlogiston theory (not an easy accomplishment in the face of his "scientific" colleagues), and was thus able to contribute to our growing knowledge of the chemical make-up of our world. Another example of the occlusion of "facts" by theories is the case of Maxwell's work in the electromagnetic behavior of bodies in motion. His discussion made no reference to a drag produced by ether, the ether theory being considered factual at that time, and his investigations caused no little difficulty for the ether theorists. For a long time the "scientists" attempted to work ether-drag into his theory, but, as is well known, were unable to do so. Now, the conclusion was: either accept ether theory as "factual" and reject Maxwell's work, or accept Maxwell's findings and reject ether theory. Eventually the earlier ether theory was dropped, and a new period of knowledge gathering was precipitated. If ether theory, and its accompanying machinery, had been held too steadfastly, Einstein would have found little road upon which to travel in order to develop his invaluable contributions to the growth of science.[10] Here, we must look to one of the eminent Empiricists to see how he would have handled the above issues, whether or not he would have accepted the new findings as scientific. Ernest Nagel tells us that science is cumulative, one branch being reducible to other branches dealing with the same domain. All we do is add "facts" to the "given" store of knowledge if we want to "expand" our knowledge.

---

[10]For a number of examples of this phenomenon, see Bernard Barber, "Resistance by Scientists to Scientific Discovery," *Science*, Vol. LXXXIV, #3479 (September, 1961), pp. 596-602.

He writes: "The objective of the reduction is to show that the laws or general principles of the secondary science are *simply logical consequences of the assumptions of the primary sciences.*"[11] A secondary science, for our purposes, might be the non-phlogiston oriented work of Lavoisier, whereas the corresponding primary science would be the work of Priestley. Is Lavoisier's work, we should ask, in point of the fact the "logical consequence" of the *assumptions* of Priestley's work? Could Maxwell have developed his electromagnetic wave theory if he had consistently included references to ether? The questions are rhetorical. What happened is that the results of the new work were grounded on *new* assumptions, new theories, which came about as a result of the inability of the older theory to explain certain critical developments. All this was not the result of the same set of assumptions logically extrapolated.

We mentioned earlier that the dialectician argues for a theoretical "pluralism." He argues that dialectics oversees scientific inquiry, in the sense that it insists upon the open-endedness of inquiry.[12] It is not, however, that he would argue that the scientific methods in use are to be replaced by dialectical methodology. It is simply that the dialectician would insist upon the fact that all inquiry is in process in history, and therefore it is nonsense to argue for any one Scientific Method as the ultimate court of judgment.* The Empiricists argue for just such a method, as for example when Hook argues that "all knowledge that men have is scientific knowledge,"[13] and then proceeds to set up as the necessary conditions of "science" those conditions which are merely historically important at this time, i.e., those that are accepted as the norm. Nagel is well-known for arguing for

---

[11]Ernest Nagel, "The Meaning of Reduction in the Natural Sciences," *Philosophy of Science*, ed. A. Danto and S. Morgenbesser (New York: Meridian, 1960), p. 301 (emphasis supplied).

[12]For an example of this, and a treatment of dialectics similar to ours, see Miladin Zivotic, "The Dialectics of Nature and the Authenticity of Dialectics," *Praxis*, Vol. III, #2, 1967, pp. 253-263.

[13]Hook, "Scientific Knowledge and Philosophical 'Knowledge' ", p. 219.

*Since science is a specialized pattern of inquiry, and dialectics an attempt at a total comprehension of and for *praxis*, how can it be maintained that dialectics is "scientific"? Engels seems to have thought that dialectics is "scientific," although he did not consistently maintain this approach.

such a procedure,[14] as is Reichenbach.[15] To oppose this view, the dialecticians argue that at any given period of the historical development of the sciences, any one method is a part of what constitutes the historically relevant possibilities of scientific inquiry. The dialectician warns us not to confuse actuality with potentiality; he warns us not to reduce all potentiality to actuality. As Feyerabend again tells us,

> "Dialectical philosophers have always emphasized the need not to think in a 'mechanical' way, that is, in a framework whose concepts are precisely defined *and kept stable in any argument,* and they have pointed out that arguments precipitating progress usually terminate in concepts that are very different indeed from the concepts in which the question was originally formulated. They have also paid due attention to the fact that the development of our knowledge presupposes the existence of at least two alternative systems of thought, of a thesis and an antithesis."[16]

In this way, the dialectician attempts to avoid stagnation, scientific or otherwise. We shall, for a moment, now analyze the metaphysics underlying the Empiricist methodology—namely, that there exist "brute facts" upon which our "mind" or "consciousness" or "behavior" clamps an "interpretation," and out of which a theory springs as if from Zeus' head.

The "objects of nature" with which science deals are without a doubt external to man's consciousness of them, but the *particular* characterization by which man knows them—and it is only because man knows them that they loom important—is a function of man in an historically determinate situation. It is a commonplace that there exists a natural world; no one except a wild-eyed constitutive idealist would deny this. But it is thought that the meaning of that world either remains constant or is immanent in the "facts." This is so because it is claimed that we "see" things as they really are. Like the phenomenologist, who "constitutes" meanings while not denying the

---

[14]See Ernest Nagel, *The Structure of Science: Problems in the Logic of Scientific Explanation* (New York: Harcourt, Brace and World, 1961).

[15]See Hans Reichenbach, *Experience and Prediction* (Chicago: University of Chicago Press, 1961).

[16]Feyerabend, *op. cit.*, note 142, p. 252.

existence of a referendum external to consciousness,[17] the dialectician argues that it is man in the world who is to be considered to be of primary importance in meaning determination; the dialectician wants to avoid the fetishism (reification) of facts and objects which man has created to serve his interests. He wants to avoid the transference of epistemological meaning into the world of ontological necessity. To effect such a transformation is to be subject to the most alienated type of fetishistic reification an "objectivistic" society (such as bourgeois society) can dictate. The situation of *praxis* renders the meaning-laden objects of scientific inquiry meaningful in man's world.* *Man* determines what he will investigate, why and how he will investigate it; without man there would be no science, for science arises in a specific historical period as a means to facilitate human responses to material conditions. The objects or "brute facts" of Empiricist "science" do not dictate to man either the methods or conclusions of his *praxis*. It is the difference between sensing a "field of existence"** and perceiving a "fact." We human beings predicate the "meaning" of the world, although it certainly is not argued that we in any way "create" the range of possible subject matter of inquiry. The relation of man and nature is a dialectical one. Man is "given" the possibilities of and in nature, and his activities are both determined by, and determined of, the field of existence through which he lives. He is not simply a passive object. The question is not whether he can direct and control nature, but how to do so rationally.

Even the so-called "Laws of Thought" are not *a priori* conditions

---

[17]See Marvin Farber, *The Foundation of Phenomenology* (Albany: State University of New York Press, 1967; Paine-Whitman, 1962), esp. chapters VII, XI, and XII. Also see Alfred Schütz, *Collected Papers* (The Hague; Martinus Nijhoff, 1962-1966). Farber's volume is an excellent explanation of the "meaning-constitution" process of phenomenology whereas Schütz' volumes are superb for their insights into the actual process itself, as a practicing phenomenologist engages in both the constitution of meanings and analyzes their role in the process of acquiring knowledge.

*Marx writes: "The question whether objective [*gegenständliche*] truth can be attributed to human thinking is not a question of theory but is a practical question. In practice man must prove the truth, that is, the reality and power, the this-sidedness [*Diesseitigkeit*] of his thinking . . . "*Theses on Feuerbach* II.

**This phrase is used by Marvin Farber, and we find it to be of great value in philosophic and social discussions. See Farber, *The Aims of Phenomenology* (New York: Harper Torchbooks, 1966), p. 34.

of knowledge. The Law of Non-Contradiction, for example, does not apply in certain areas of analysis, specifically when dealing with boundary conditions.[18] Indeed, we agree with Harris when he declares:

> "I think it is possible to show that the scientific evidence at our disposal is directly contrary to empiricist presuppositions and that it favours an entirely different conception of the world supporting a radically different philosophy and demanding a conception of logic wholly other than that which, fostered by Empiricism and elaborated by symbolic techniques, has gained such widespread prestige at the present day."[19]

What, then, constitute the criteria? Man, in his historically determinate natural and intersubjective relations must himself decide what shall and shall not be taken to be the "data" of experiments, let alone the necessity of choosing what experiments to undertake. As Engels says: "Taken historically the thing would have a certain meaning: we can only know under the conditions of our epoch and *as far as these conditions allow*."[20] From this it becomes obvious that any argument claiming the immanence of "natural fact" has objectified its *own* historical (or class) judgments to the stage of the "true" methodology. That is, an historically given methodology which deals with certain "facts" is claimed to be the one and only "pure" methodology. Certain methodologies, or theories, rule out the investigation of certain contradicting "facts." We can therefore say that any one methodology is *eo ipso* not exhaustive or descriptive, for this is what is meant by the *ceteris paribus* clause which is invoked in experimentation.[21]

---

[18]See V. J. McGill and W. T. Parry, "The Unity of Opposites: A Dialectical Principle," *Science and Society*, Vol. 12, #4 (Fall, 1948), pp. 418-444, for an excellent statement of this problem.

[19]Errol E. Harris, *The Foundation of Metaphysics in Science* (New York: Humanities Press, 1965), pp. 27-28.

[20]Frederick Engels, *Dialectics of Nature* (Moscow: Progress Publishers, 1964), p. 245.

[21]Carl Hempel has stated, however, that "in the formulation of physical hypotheses, the *ceteris paribus* clause is never used" ["Typological Methods in the Social Sciences,"] in Maurice Natanson, ed., *Philosophy of the Social Sciences* (New York: Random House, 1963), p. 225. This is a reprint of his article which originally appeared in *Science, Language, and Human Rights* (American Philosophical Association, Eastern Division, Philadelphia: University of Pennsylvania Press, 1952), Vol. I, pp. 65-86. We must confess that we have no idea what Hempel could possibly mean by such a statement.

Inquiry is value-laden, not only because it is one of many possible inquiries into the field of existence, but also because it is grounded in specific historically generated needs.[22] However spectacular the resulting abstractions may be, abstracted in order to expedite the satisfaction of those needs, the theory remains as a theory tied to history, and thus retains its present or previous value-orientation. As Kuhn says:

> "In a mature science . . . external factors like those cited above [social, political, economic] are principally significant in determining the timing of breakdown, and the area in which, because it is given particular attention, the breakdown first occurs."[23]

Hence hydrostatics retains its originary value-orientation, to use Husserl's phrase, as does sociology (confer Edmund Husserl, *Die Krisis der europäischen Wissenschaften und die transzendentale Phänomenologie*, Nijhoff, 1954). The clamoring for the "objective facts of nature" as divorced from theoretical presuppositions or value-interests is itself resultant from an historical *theoria*, one which, needless to say, requires historical analysis.[24]

Also, because the historical conditions of the facts of science are not of the same type-analysis as the facts of science are themselves, we are led to use history as the judge of science, and not the reverse.[25] By this we mean that history generates science and not science history. If we are to come to a full awareness of science and its facts, we must recognize that we are the inheritors of a tradition of inquiry, such a tradition, coupled with our goals, being constitutive of our methodology. We cannot simply ignore the historicity of the matter, and proceed to retrace historical growth in terms of the present methodology; by doing so, we fail to pay the appropriate attention to the very essence of science: its historicity. Much of contemporary linguistic philosophy fails in precisely this regard. It cannot deal with certain phenomena in linguistic terms because such phenomena did not at one time or another exist. Trans-

---

22See J. D. Bernal, *Science in History* (New York: Cameron Associates, 1954).

23Kuhn, *op. cit.*, p. 69.

24See Marcuse, *op. cit.*, *passim*.

25See E. H. Carr, *What Is History?* (New York: Vintage, 1967), for a treatment of this approach to history. We differ in certain respects from Carr, but find his views generally helpful.

lation also faces this dilemma, one which is not easily stuffed into a categorical analysis.[26]

The facts of science, because they are historical in their very essence, must be re-analyzed in each qualitatively different historical period.* When it is recalled that all facts are theory-laden, partially concatenated entities that are what they are only within the whole of a system employed as a background for study,[27] then it can no longer be maintained, in excellent Empiricist fashion, that the "empirical evidence in the nature of the case has to be piecemeal."[28] Piecemeal knowledge, or the result of a lot of running around by fact-collectors, is itself grounded upon an historically generated theory. Again, we must mention contemporary psychology as the paradigm of such fact-fetishism. We have indicated that conceptual structures (theories) *replace* other conceptual structures, and it is *not* the case that facts are simply added to other facts. It must be observed that the historical influences upon what can even be *undertaken* as science are constitutive of many facts. This is the whole point that the Marxist dialectic conveys. History determines facts, not facts history. In brief, then, this is what we mean: since all science utilizes *ceteris paribus* experimentation, and since the particular experiment conducted depends upon the value-orientation of the experimenter (historically determined), what was once "objective" may no longer be taken as such (e.g., witches, phlogiston, or ether). All this, of course, holds only if a new historical period has been attained. There is no *ceteris paribus* scientific model yet developed either by the "hard" sciences or the social sciences which can claim to absorb *all* variables.

If it were the case that there are "objective data" waiting to be investigated, and also that it was possible to arrive at a unified

---

[26]For a statement of this problem as it relates to Homeric Greek, see Bruno Snell, *The Discovery of the Mind: The Greek Origins of European Thought* (New York: Harper, 1960), especially Chapter I, "Homer's View of Man," pp. 1-22.

[27]See Norwood Russell Hanson, *Patterns of Discovery* (Cambridge: Cambridge University Press, 1965), esp. Chapters I and II, "Observation," and "Facts." Hanson is quite helpful here, although we in no way support many of his views, e.g., that there exists a "logic of discovery."

[28]Sidney Hook, "Dialectic and Nature," in *Reason, Social Myths and Democracy* (New York: Harper, 1966), p. 194.

*Carr in his *What Is History?* writes that we come to know history better as we proceed to the future, and science is as much a part of history as revolution.

method divorced from historical *praxis,* how would the great controversies in science be explained? For example, suppose, in earlier times, we were interested in finding out what scientists took the atomic theory to be. We take for our case an atom of helium, and ask a renowned physicist and a distinguished chemist whether or not this particular atom is a molecule, *in fact.* The chemist would reply that it is a molecule, because it behaves like one with respect to the kinetic theory of gases; whereas the physicist would reply that it is not a molecule, because it displays no molecular spectrum. Presumably, they speak of the "same" datum, although their replies are qualitatively different, and cannot be resolved on factual grounds.[29] This is so because their experience in problem-solving requires different answers to the same question, for the simple reason that they employ different *theories* (or theoretical frameworks) for different goals. Another example of a "factual" dispute would be the already mentioned case of oxygen. Is the newly "discovered" substance dephlogisticated air, or is it oxygen? Can we easily say that either of these examples serve to give us "brute facts" uninterpreted by theories? Or, to cite a more contemporary case, we can look to quantum theory. Where Heisenberg finds, "beneath" the sub-microscopic particles, some kind of "stuff" (reminiscent of Greek Pre-Socratic metaphysics), others, e.g., Bohr, find no such "stuff" and wish to press on with the investigation. Similar disputes in quantum theory may be found in arguments over Bohr's "complementarity principle." Again, we might ask whether a protozoan is a one-cell animal, or a non-celled coagulum. The answer to all these questions depends upon the theory one employs in one's analysis.[30]

Or, in the social sciences, how is it to be explained that Martindale and Bell treat Marx in such a superficial manner? For Sidney Hook, in contradistinction with many other of his statements,* the explanation for this is to be sought in historical terms, and not in

---

[29]This example is taken from Kuhn, *The Structure of Scientific Revolutions.*

[30]See Hanson, *op. cit.*

*Hook continually urges the acceptance of "class-less" sciences. In a paper entitled "Naturalism and First Principles," in his *The Quest for Being,* he claims that the proponents of the "class" view of science confuse the "objective data" of a theory and the uses to which that "data" is put. Also, in "The Mythology of Class Science," in his *Reason, Social Myths and Democracy,* Hook argues the same view. Most of the time, Hook is concerned to demonstrate the "pure" objectivity of science (in fine Empiricist fashion).

"factual" terms: "The cavalier dismissal of [Marx's] doctrines by most American sociologists is natural in view of their class origins, their persistent use of secondary sources, and their *conception* that social science is glorified fact-grubbing." (Sidney Hook, "Marxism—Dogma or Method?," *The Nation*, Vol. 136, #3532, March 15, 1933, p. 285—emphasis supplied.) The shabby treatment of Marx is not accomplished on "factual" grounds, according to Hook, but rather is accomplished within a framework that can only be understood in terms of historical relevancy and class orientation. Is the Marxist theory of the class struggle rejected because it is factually incorrect, or is it rejected because it does not fit within another theory (e.g., equilibrium models of social processes)? Must facts be consistent with theories in order to be accepted into the arena of "knowledge" or "science" (social or otherwise)? It would seem so. We must emphasize that this approach is the result of the Empiricist argument that urges us to accept "hard data" that is reified by a methodology, and thereby calls on other systems of argumentation to fulfill its criteria.

The difficulty with Empiricist historical research is that it ignores processes of *praxis* in favor of foregone conclusions generated by contemporary theories. The Empiricist method, therefore, cannot prevent the metamorphosis of *actual* history. The pernicious effect of the creation of mythical events can be seen very clearly in the rendering of social history. American history is replete with such a rendering; all the result of a *theory* that has Americans cast as superhuman Individualists. The Myth of the "Frontier Spirit" replaces the seemingly interminable slaughter of the American Indian; the existence of slavery is shunted off to a dusty corner in the name of "objectivity" (we must, after all, be objective about our analyses, i.e., cold-blooded and inhuman). In the present day, we are told that America is *saving* the Vietnamese from Communism—that most un-American and illiberal of institutions—whereas the fact that we are burning and destroying and poisoning the land in the process, is shunted off to "the hardships of war"; that we are maiming and killing the Vietnamese people is similarly apologized for. In short, another myth covers up one of the most barbarous acts man has committed.

Dialecticians, on the other hand, plead for a non-fictitious rendering of history. In Engels' words:

"The form of development of natural science, in so far as it thinks, is the *hypothesis*. A new fact is observed° which makes impossible the previous method of explaining the facts belonging to the same group. From this moment onwards new methods of explanation are required—at first based only on a limited number of facts and observations. Further observational material weeds out these hypotheses, doing away with some and correcting others, until finally the law is established in a pure form. If one should wait until the material for a new law was *in a pure form,* it would mean suspending the process of thought in investigation until then and, if only for this reason, the law would never have come into being."[31]

In the realm of natural science, the perihelion of Mercury required the abandonment of Newtonian Celestial Mechanics in favor of the Einsteinian formulation.

Lest it be thought that the dialectical viewpoint parallels the idealist view which would allow for all sorts of harebrained theories to account for man's experienced world, it should be pointed out that the dialectician requires historico-empirical evidence for any theory put forth, including his own properly scientific theories.°° What he does not do is rule out alternative theories (on *methodological grounds*) before they have had a chance to prove their mettle. There are a few exceptions to this rule, such as the rejection of Bohr's "atoms have freewill," but for the most part the dialectical scientists have proven to be a great deal less dogmatic in their methodological claims than have the Empiricists.°°° What must be remembered is the dialectician's insistence upon the historical or subjective (understood as inter-subjective) nature of all inquiry. Man is the agent of theorizing and "fact-collecting," and without

---

[31]Engels, *Dialectics of Nature*, p. 244.

°Instead of the expression "a new fact is observed," one might substitute Kuhn's terminology, a "crisis" of explanation is confronted, in which "discovered" phenomena cannot be explained in terms of the given theory.

°°Here it must be emphasized that dialectics is not specifically "scientific." Although this is so it by no means follows that dialecticians cannot be practicing scientists, a notion which the work of either J. D. Bernal or J. B. S. Haldane easily renders senseless.

°°°We should avoid operationally defining dialectical philosophy by reference to any particular nation, e.g., the Soviet Union.

man's intent there would be no "scientific facts" at all, let alone theories. In Engels' words:

> "Natural science, like philosophy, has hitherto entirely neglected the influence of men's activity on their thought; both know only nature on the one hand and thought on the other. But it is precisely the *alteration of nature by men*, not solely nature as such, which is the most essential and immediate basis of human thought, and it is in the measure that man has learned to change nature that his intelligence has increased."[32]

This is the goal of thought-in-history; we must avoid the trap of Empiricism at all costs. Man is not the mere receptor of stimuli, which he accumulates within the "basic unity" of the "scientific method" (Hook). Rather, the opposite is the case. Since a "statement will be regarded as observational because of the *causal context* in which it is uttered, and *not* because of of what it means,"[33] and since "meanings are the results of conventions,"[34] one of the primary tasks of the philosopher of science, or the scientist himself, is to investigate the origins and goals of certain theories, rather than presume their "objective validity." Certain sociologists (e.g., C. Wright Mills) pay lip service to this task, but do no more than scratch the surface of history.

However, this intersubjective and historical emphasis by the dialectician by no means rules out what has been termed "objectivity." The concept and theory of "objectivity" becomes sensible by reference to history. According to Enzo Paci:*

> "Objectivity is . . . a result of the operations of the various subjects, a result of *intersubjective* operations. . . . What is objectively valid is therefore constituted by subjects in history. . . . History is humanity 'collectivized,' as Husserl would say, and historical intersubjectivity constitutes objectivity *universally* valid for all subjects; objectivity is *constituted* by subjectivity understood as intersubjectivity, and it is here clear that the society of subjects cannot be an abstraction, but a society of integral and concrete individuals. . . . An abstraction would not constitute

---

[32]*Ibid.*, p. 234.

[33]Feyerabend, *op. cit.*, p. 198.

[34]*Ibid.*, p. 204.

*This remark is reminiscent of Lenin's notion of "relative absolutes."

anything. The humanly objective is constituted by the historically subjective. . . . This constitutes what is objective for *man*. . . . Science is *subjectivity that objectifies itself*."[35]

The "abstractions" of subjects which Paci refers to are precisely the abstractions with which "objective" sociology, economics, and psychology deal. This "objectivism," as Paci elsewhere argues, is nothing but the Empiricist alienation of science, alienated from man's role in its formulation. Man is not an object. It is now obvious that the "objective" is the reified intersubjective. By remembering that the relation of theory to fact is one of historically generated symmetry, generated from a material base for a purpose, the dialecticians point to the very essence of cognition: the interpenetrating relation of man and the objective natural world, *in history*. As Marcuse so precisely states: "The two layers or aspects of objectivity [physical and historical] are interrelated in such a way that they cannot be insulated from each other; the historical aspect can never be eliminated so radically that only the 'absolute' physical layer remains."[36]

What becomes of primary concern to the dialectician is the *telos* of scientific inquiry. Since it is absurd to claim a "value-free" science, insofar as any inquiry cannot with success be abstracted from its historical roots, it becomes necessary to choose the path science is to take. This must be done, for as Marcuse explains, "no matter how one defines truth and objectivity, they remain related to the human agents of theory and practice, and to their ability to comprehend and change the world."[37] It is because the Empiricist retains, although in a rather sophisticated and obscure form, the obsolete conception of an "objective nature" somehow distinct from and dictatory to man, that he cannot choose what becomes historically relevant for man. Historical significance thus becomes for the Empiricist a *non sequitor* in the pursuit of scientific knowledge. What this approach does to the practicing scientist is obvious. On the one side, he is a "scientist" interested in "truth"; while, on the other side, he is a "man" interested in ethics, social policies, and economic sys-

---

[35]Enzo Paci, *Funzione delle Scienze e Significato dell 'Uomo* (Milan: Il Saggiatore, 1963), p. 325. This selection was translated by the author in conjunction with Paul Piccone and Mary Iannacome. A complete translation of the volume is forthcoming.

[36]Marcuse, *op. cit.*, p. 218.

[37]*Ibid.*, p. 166.

tems: he is *alienated*. It is as if the sciences progress outside historical *praxis*, divorced from the historical and intersubjective needs of man. As opposed to this *sui generis* conception of science, dialectical philosophy seeks to go beyond what is historically given in order to better man's condition. Marcuse terms this "negative thinking,"[38] the purpose of which is to transcend the "Logic of Domination" predominating in contemporary society. He writes:

> "The power of negative thinking is the driving power of dialectical thought, used as a tool for analyzing the world of facts in terms of its internal inadequacy . . . while the scientific method leads from the immediate experience of *things* to their mathematical-logical structure, philosophical thought [i.e., dialectical thought] leads from the immediate experience of *existence* to its historical structure: the principle of freedom."[39]

What become important are not the "facts" of some abstract science, but the *possibilities* of man's factual world.*

The Empiricist forges ahead collecting and worshipping facts, leaving behind that for which the "facts" are gathered in the first place, the support of a *conception* or *value*.** In this regard, the social sciences utterly fail to provide us with meaningful options, the so-called "policy sciences," e.g., Game Theory, serving no interest but the intensification of the status quo.

Thus dialectical philosophy binds science to the social and historical character of existence, i.e., its very essence. Rather than accepting the fetishistic enslavement of man by the sciences he has created out of particular historical needs, an enslavement which threatens imminent holocaust, the dialectician offers a way out. Dialectics is to *serve* man by providing his *praxis* with the conceptual tool by means of which he may push aside the prevailing dogmatisms, so as to allow man the opportunity of determining the path of *his* future.

---

[38]Herbert Marcuse, *Reason and Revolution* (Boston: Beacon, 1960).

[39]*Ibid.*, p. viii ff.

*Maurice Merleau-Ponty has written: "One can be sure of facts only after giving up the attempt to change them." "Man, the Hero," in *Sense and Nonsense* (Northwestern University Press, 1964), p. 184.

**I would like to acknowledge Professor John Anton for this particular formulation of our thesis. [The thesis originates in F. Woodbridge, *Nature and Mind* (New York: Columbia, 1937) pp. 147-48—eds.]

Part II

COSMOLOGY, ONTOLOGY, AND EPISTEMOLOGY

EPILOGUE ON BERKELEY*

Roy Wood Sellars

M Y DICTIONARY defines an epilogue as a concluding part to a literary work; and it can be here so taken. What I shall be concerned to do is to comment very briefly on the course philosophy took in the period after Berkeley. I shall even comment on the present scene. I was early convinced that the *rise of human cognition* in the matrix of perceiving was a very basic philosophical problem. There was quite a flurry of energy devoted to the question in the first three decades of this century. Philosophers have differed as to what was accomplished. There is the negative attitude exemplified by John Dewey. Professor Schneider quotes Dewey as saying, "We did not solve the problem. We got over it." But, if I remember events correctly, Dewey came late into the field of epistemology after the New Realists and the Critical Realists had had their debate. He criticized both and kept to his logic of inquiry. I have argued elsewhere that both Dewey and Woodbridge were puzzled by the status of sensations, which seemed to be located in the brain. If these are the first objects of knowledge, how could one get to the outside world? Their gambit was to reject such entities and start with the outside world.

It seemed to me that this was a sort of begging the question. What was the status of consciousness? Dewey was always very vague on this topic. In fact, he moved to a modified kind of behaviorism.

I, on the other hand, persisted in thinking about it. It seemed to me that a new approach was needed. This would stress the use made of sensory factors in a frame of directed reference. These fac-

*Reprinted by permission from Sellars' book, *Lending a Hand to Hylas: A Restructuring of Berkeley's Famous Three Dialogues* (Ann Arbor: Edwards, 1968), pp. 92-102.

tors would operate in the directed act as informative. In animal life, they would have a guidance role, as even Berkeley noted. But, at the human level, there would be added the use of them as informative of the stimulating object which would also be the object cognized. From this situation would emerge the formulation of empirical facts about the object cognized. The base of these facts would be in the informational appearings found in the sensory data. This means that sensations would now function as disclosures, or manifestations, of the object. They should no longer be regarded as terminal entities, as they were for Berkeley and Hume. Instead, they function in a larger context. Concepts and language would now enter to aid in this cognizing effort.

Now I do think that human cognition is a wonderful achievement. But, surely, it had humble beginnings. As I see it, it developed in the matrix of guided response. Here we come to animal life and note the function of the sense-organs. The working unit is sensori-motor. Man has emerged with delayed responses and the use of his sensations for the deciphering of his environment. They clearly lend themselves to this employment. Mental ability is, of course, added. It is in this fashion that human cognition has emerged. The very word, *fact*, is a sign of this arrival.

Let me indicate some changes in analysis indicated by this approach. It was customary to speak of the *content* of perception as against the object of perception. In the older view the content could only be sensations and images. Now, as I see it, this content is changed into the operative use of this material into appearings of the object. Added to this transformation is the development of concepts *about* the object being perceived. The content ceases to be a *tertium quid* intervening between the knower and the object and becomes the instrument of knowing.

I am now going back to Berkeley, Hume, Reid, Kant and others to show why and how they "missed the boat." In all their ability, they did not understand the "from-and-to" mechanism of perceiving.

Berkeley, we saw, reflected the then current view of matter as inert, something pushed around like a billiard ball. Berkeley also accepted the view of sensations as terminal effects. I was told recently, during a visit to Trinity College, Dublin, the locus of Berkeley's early work, by Professor Furlong that Berkeley was as much influenced by Malebranche as by Locke. And I think one can see this in his theory of how ideas are inserted into the human mind.

The result of this view of matter as inert was that he could see no role for it in sense-perception. Spirit was introduced as causally active with volition as its paradigm. It is quite otherwise with us with our stress on energy. A weakness of Locke upon which he jumped was Locke's *substratum* view of the support and inherence of properties. I think we move from facts about things to our categorical notions of them. The object I look at may be cognized as red, round and so far away. There is no necessary finality about this cognition. It is a point of empirical departure. And we may decide that redness is correlated with light reflected from the object to our eyes. Properly interpreted, these cognitions do not conflict.

In our own day, science has developed *sensors* to gather information beyond the reach of our own sense-organs. The recent excursions to Venus illustrate this. The sensors are instruments which gather information and radio them to the earth. There the messages are decoded. And the decoding enables us to use the information about temperature on Venus. Now, as I see it, evolution developed our sense-organs for guidance and, ultimately, for cognition. Science assumes the fact of cognition. It has been one of the tasks of philosophy to try to understand it. I took the task seriously. I was recently told at Oxford that Professor Austin was inclined, after he had undercut phenomenalism linguistically, to leave the rest to science. I certainly wish to cooperate with science which has recently been doing such remarkable work on nervous receptors. But I still think that philosophy can supplement this work by undercutting some traditions in epistemology.

I pass now to Hume. He may be said to have continued the outlook of Berkeley and Locke in making sense-impressions and images terminal rather than, as I hold, informational. I shall argue that even Kant did not make this transition. His things-in-themselves did not manifest themselves in the sense-manifold.

Many hold that there was a touch of agnosticism in Hume. The mind and the material world may have "ultimate, original qualities" but these are beyond human knowledge. If so, his view may have resembled that of Gassendi, the father of modern atomism. What Hume did was to bring out into sharp relief the implications of his sensationalism. He belonged to the period of the Edinburgh Enlightenment and had no religious axe to grind. He even examined religious cosmic beliefs quite objectively. He was puzzled by the self for he could find no sensory basis for it. And with the Self went Berkeley's

Spirit and volition as causal. Causality became a case of routine expectation.

The critical realist cannot accept this reduction of the categories. To him, they need analysis but they are, essentially, well-based cognitions of the constitution of the world. Like space and time, they need refinement and clarification.

G. E. Moore was puzzled by Hume but he, himself, was unable to relate his sense-data to things. It is this that I have done in a functional way. Russell hardly made the effort. He swung to logical construction. I had conversations with him and he seemed to stress percepts rather than perceiving. My referential approach was quite alien to him. It has led me to wonder about the competence of logicians in epistemology. I shall mention no names.

I turn now to Reid. I have a certain sympathy with his rejection of ideas as primary objects. But I do not see that he reanalyzed perceiving in my fashion. He rightly stressed language and common sense but fell back on intuition too readily. He was convinced, however, that mental operations involve three factors: the mind which performs the operation, the object of the operation, which he seems to have thought was intuited or apprehended without any *tertium quid* intervening, and the operation itself. My reanalysis of the content of perception into sensory material and their cognizing use in the context of objective reference is, so far as I can see, not present. He appealed to language in a way analogous to the present "ordinary language" movement but, as I see it, he did not realize how ingenious nature had been. I, myself, moved between the introspective tradition and Watsonian behaviorism. Neither seemed to me to have an adequate epistemology. The introspective tradition stressed, like Russell, percepts rather than perceiving. How could one move from introspection to commerce with the world? Idealism beckoned. And Watsonian behaviorism just observed the behavior of rats and other mammals but had no curiosity as to the nature of observing itself. Why should it? Did not all the sciences make observations? How could one break down the barriers between introspection and behaviorism? My reply is that a good epistemology will help. But, even without that, I find that I agree with *Gestalt* psychology that traditional introspection did not do justice to sensory organization and the influence of the environment. Thus it tended to be reductive. As a philosopher, I would stress perceptual experience and its categories but I am, of course, interested in development.

John Stuart Mill struck out at Reid and Hamilton. But he, him-self, as I look at it, could not get to the external world. Matter was reduced to the possibility of sensations. There are a lot of blind alleys in philosophy. I suppose that proves its difficulties. It may well be that the attainment of an adequate epistemology may simplify many things. Many technical analyses may then fall into line. Reid's successors got into disputes. As James Ward pointed out in his *Naturalism and Agnosticism,* one dispute was over the question whether we see the sun itself or an appearing of the sun. I contend that we see the sun, itself in a referential way, in using its appearing cognitively. This, of course, is just a good start. But the right start is tremendously important. I think of the energy and ability that has gone into logical positivism, into existentialism, even into pragmatism. Many points are well taken, and yet are the foundations sound?

I leave Reid, and pass along. In France, Condillac identified knowledge with complexes of sensations. He was very ingenious and tried to show how we come to have the idea of an external world. Hume had worked on the same problem. We saw that Berkeley was aware of it. How do we two come to believe that we see the same thing? Since I start from a framework in which perceiving is externally oriented, I do not regard the problem as very difficult. It is solved, in part, behaviorally and, in part by communication. James gave the case of blowing out a candle. When I blow it out, your light also goes. But all this is made easier by the referential view of perceiving. Berkeley made it more difficult since he held the various kinds of sensations the primary objects of perceiving. I do not think we need Aristotle's common sense. The point is that the context of perceiving is referential and sensations are used in this context and subordinated to it. Pointing goes naturally with perceiv-ing. So do demonstratives. Since G. E. Moore made sense-data terminal, it is not surprising that he had heavy going with his proof of an external world.

When we pass to the United States we find John Dewey an inter-esting transitional thinker. Kant and Hegel had long come on the scene; and the result had been what is usually called Anglo-American idealism. Kant was alive to the science of his day, which was es-sentially Newtonian. He was, however, not a physical realist. While recognizing a sense-manifold, he did not appreciate its disclosing function. Rather he amalgamated it with *a priori* forms, such as space, time, causality, substance, and arrived at a phenomenal construction of the world. In this outlook he was motivated, I believe, both by his inadequate view of perceiving and his assumption that the physical world involves self-contradiction. This he thought he had shown in his *Transcendental Dialectic*. Modern logic and mathematics have undermined his arguments. But they played an important part in the ensuing rise of romantic idealism. Fichte took his departure from the Self while Hegel developed a logico-historical dialectic which paid small attention to the material world. One must remember that chemistry was just beginning to get a framework and that biology was still in the future. Technically speaking, the Hegelians rejected Kant's things-in-themselves as meaningless, as outside thought. These had been Kant's gesture to realism. One was now left to such terms as experience and thought. Not unsurprisingly, epistemology was downgraded. One heard, at most, of the subject-object relation.

There were protests outside official philosophy, as by Diderot and the scientists who began to flirt with the idea of a revival of materialism. But this was disregarded by official philosophy. Feuerbach, however, protested and influenced the rise of dialectical materialism, as expounded by Marx and Engels. It is only of late that Feuerbach has been carefully studied. And that is largely due to the rise of Marxism. I return to John Dewey and the United States.

Dewey had been introduced to Reid and Hamilton by Torrey of the University of Vermont. The stress was now on ontological dualism and intuition as a bridge. This seemed the sole alternative to the sensationalistic empiricism of Hume. After this, Dewey was brought to Kant and Hegel by G. S. Morris. Later he was affected by Darwin and William James and developed a logic of inquiry in which the stress was on the reflective solution of problems. William James, on the whole kept, with modifications, to the empirical tradition of Mill with, however, more stress on purpose and teleology.

Dewey moved to his experimentalism, instrumentalism and behaviorism in a quite logical way. As I have indicated, the idealistic tradition downgraded epistemology except as a reflection of its outlook. It is not surprising that the initiative here was taken by a group of younger men, the new realists and the critical realists. Dewey came into the situation from the outside, so to speak, and pointed out weaknesses in both. As regards critical realism, he devoted his attention to the "essence" doctrine of Santayana and Drake. So far as I know, he never carefully studied my analysis of perceiving. Hence I can appreciate his remark to Professor Schneider and also discount it. Schneider, himself, it would seem never understood my effort to get a new kind of direct, referential realism in which sensations are given an informational role. This, of course, undercuts both presentationalism and representationalism. Schneider decided that nothing new was offered. The next generation of American philosophers turned largely to Europe. There are some signs of a renewed interest in critical realism.

If I were asked why I turned to epistemology, my answer would be that I was interested in science and that I could not see how idealism connected up with it. Perceiving offered a linkage.

Like the Yellow River, philosophy frequently changes its channel. This is sometimes in the way of modification of emphasis, sometimes by means of a new approach. It is all very complicated with side-currents arising. In my own lifetime . . . I have had to take cognizance of pragmatism, Bergsonianism, new forms of realism, the idea of emergence, analytic philosophy, logical positivism, Wittgenstein, Whitehead, existentialism, ordinary language and Marxism. It follows that one has to have balance and a strong sense of priorities.

In this *Epilogue,* I am charting my course as I look back at it. Thus far, I have emphasized epistemology. But I want to add ontology. After all, Berkeley was an immaterialist and was fighting deism and materialism. One strand of his argument was to the effect that *to be is inseparable* from being perceived. I have argued against that. The other strand stressed ineptitudes in Locke's formulae. What is this unknowable substratum which supports primary qualities? And can an inert matter explain ideas and volitions?

This belief in the inertness of matter is, of course, dated. The stress now is on dynamism and energy. The sun's energy, or power to do work, keeps life going. And Einstein's famous formula is generally accepted, that is, that energy equals mass times C squared, C being the velocity of light.

But let us consider for a moment what and how we know about material things and their constituents. I have argued that we never intuit, or literally inspect, material things. That is an illusion nourished in us by presentational, or naive, realism. Instead, we can locate things and learn about them by using the data of observation. This operation gives us facts about them. What happens in science is a technical probing of things, particles and processes to get knowledge about them. Largely, it is an affair of asking questions and getting relevant answers. But these answers turn out to be mensurational reports about structure and behavior. It is in this fashion that we learn about atoms, molecules, electrons, positrons, etc. Huge machines are made for smashing atoms. These constitute the equivalent of a microscope. But, in all this, we learn only facts about the particles involved. We can never bypass information and arrive at some sort of inspective intuition of either molar things or particles. Matter is *that which* behaves in this sort of way and has this kind of structure. When chemists synthesize complex molecules, they work out relational patterns for the constituent atoms and get the same behavioral properties as the original substance had. I remember that Professor Sidney Hook once challenged me to tell him what matter was. It seemed to him a conceptual construct in what he called experience. Whitehead seems to have had similar ideas. That our tested thought about matter is conceptual I do not deny. But I hold these are concepts *about*, responsible to, garnered information.

The history of atomism is a long one, at first largely speculative, by noting states of affairs like the wearing away of stones and the drying of clothes. But Boyle developed his corpuscular hypothesis with considerable evidence. And this evidence increased after Dalton's work in chemistry. In these days of radioactivity and the atomic bomb few doubt the existence of atoms. Ernst Mach was one of the last to be skeptical but that was, I think, largely because of his epistemology, which was built of sensory elements.

I may here mention the point that when Lenin was trying to defend materialism against its critics he sought to show that science begins with material things and passes thence to reflected sensations. But his opponents to this day told him that cognitively we begin with sensations. Berkeley was still a hard nut to crack. But the reader will remember that I regard the material thing as the direct object of perceiving and the sensations aroused in the percipient are sources of information and so used. That is, the sensations are not terminal but functional. The significant use of the term, dialectical, is another question.

Locke's *substratum* idiom, which Berkeley rightly attacked, is no longer a natural idiom. It is the material thing we know in terms of achieved knowledge about it. As I have argued, we get no nearer to the object *cognitively* than facts about it, though we may handle it and tear it apart. But, in terms of facts and tested theories, we know a great deal *about* matter and energy.

Berkeley's was a mind of first quality and that is why I have concerned myself with him. I attacked Cartesian dualism from another angle. In my first book, *Critical Realism*, I argued that consciousness is extended in the way events and functions are. I was pleased that Woodbridge Riley noted this gambit in his history of American philosophy. So far as I know, no one else did. This, of course, led to my double-knowledge approach to the identity of mind and brain. I argue that one participates in brain activity. I am not an epiphenomenalist.

As against Berkeley, I have the benefit of scientific developments; one of the greatest of these is occurring in molecular biology. This fits in with my theory of emergence and levels in nature. It would seem that DNA and RNA work by means of codes. This is a new kind of causality to be added to feedbacks and homeostasis. I earlier saw the importance of organization in nature. I find my thinking is in line with *Gestalt* in that I think nature organizes itself while man makes machines. This is what Köhler calls a dynamic view. He stresses sensory organization as following stimulation. As nearly as I can make out, recent work on retinal receptors, such as that of the Nobel prize winners, Dr. George Wald, and Dr. Hartline, move in that direction. Upon this base, learning advances. Epistemology, as I see it, starts in its examination from the level of perceptual claims and these concern outer things. It is this tree that I am looking at and judging about. I pointed out the preparation for this. Cognition emerges within a context. Wittgenstein stressed facts but I do not think he looked on them in this way. He seemed to me to give them more an ontological status. But I am not an expert on his perspectives.

Now all this sums up to emergent, or evolutionary, materialism. This is non-reductive in perspective. In a way, it culminates—so far as we know—in man. And the job of philosophy is to cooperate with the sciences in understanding the situation. I can quite appreciate the immaterialism and theism of Berkeley. For him, as a bishop, it was a natural stance. And he added a Platonic note in his later writings, much as did Whitehead in our own day. But I can get no nearer to Platonism than words and concepts and their cognitional application. Here we are at the level of the working of the new brain and its linguistic centers. Professor Wilfrid Sellars connects thinking with verbal expression, "The learning to use symbols in accordance with rules is a pervasive feature of concept formation." As I see it the resultant capacity operates even when we are not talking. Language is a social achievement whose origins are lost. But its logic and psychology are now being closely studied. A new kind of empiricism is resulting. I take this to be a continuation of critical realism. It is a compliment to a framework to seek to develop it. I believe this is being done.

I shall now move to the close of this *Epilogue* by means of some remarks on the past and the present.

When, in 1916, I published my first book, *Critical Realism,* I sent a copy to the famous British idealist, F. H. Bradley. He was kind enough to read it and to write me his reaction. It was to the effect that he could see that realism had much to be said for it but that he, personally, could not conceive how we could get beyond *appearances.* His effort, accordingly, was to indicate how appearances could be organized logically in terms of increasing coherence. I take it that Professor Blanshard is pursuing that objective. In a way, it goes back to Berkeley. Kant and Hegel had, of course, been added. It has been my endeavor to show how appearings are referentially used in cognition. I take a less skeptical view of categories than does Bradley. I regard them as cognitive achievements which can be developed.

Some years ago there appeared a book in England called *The Revolution in Philosophy.* It largely devoted itself to showing the importance of the advances in logic to relationalism. Little attention was paid to epistemology. Because the book did not broach the question of the nature of perceiving which, obviously, played such an important part in Bradley's thinking, I could not regard it as very revolutionary. It seemed to me to be marking time. I wanted to get down to fundamentals.

I have already paid my respects to phenomenalism and logical positivism. The burden of my reproach was their neglect of epistemology. These writers were ingenious and learned within their assumptions and added to philosophy's technical equipment. Nevertheless, they wrote off the whole idea of transcendence as meaningless. I, on the other hand, had correlated transcendence with (1) reference and (2) the use of sensory information to give facts about objects. It is, of course, a worldly kind of transcendence which does not lead to a supernal realm. But it is transcendence, nevertheless. It gives a base for ontology and, if you will, metaphysics.

I have paid my respects to pragmatism in the persons of Dewey and Sidney Hook. With the former with respect to realism. With the latter with respect to the status of matter. There is much practicality in American pragmatism, perhaps too much. It seems to me to go, at times, three quarters of the way to clarification of problems and to leave it there. Had I more space I should like to illustrate what I mean by this. But my remarks on both Dewey and Hook are samples.

I want, in conclusion, to say a few words about Existentialism. My technical complaint is that it has no clear epistemology or ontology. I have no objection to a stress on *Angst*. I feel it myself sometimes. Nor do I want to treat persons like things. The human situation is very important. Call it, if you will, philosophical anthropology. It is a reflection on human life.

But my objections go deeper. So far as I can make out, the existentialists build on Kant and Husserl. They are suspicious of empiricism, naturalism and evolutionism. There is a marked subjectivistic element in their outlook. Take Husserl, for instance, one of the unwitting, founding fathers. By the use of his technique of "reduction," he arrives at the field of personal consciousness. External objects are reduced to a sensory pole in this field. Thence he moves to a Cartesian form of idealism. The realistic analysis I have sketched is completely alien to him.

Sartre has this background. The controversy between idealism and realism is to be disregarded. Material things become an affair of appearances, much as they are for the logical positivist. Hence he rejects realistic materialism. He regards himself as left with "being-in-itself," which is inert and passive, and "being-for-itself," which is active. There is no attempt to explain this contrast. In fact, there is a marked solipsistic note in Sartre. But Sartre is an able writer and stresses freedom and commitment.

Turning to Jaspers, we find him trying to get to transcendence and God by squeezing between Kant's subject-object relation. Somehow the world points beyond itself to an Absolute. This is an object of faith and not of knowledge. Jaspers is a brave and able man but, seemingly, out of contact with analytic forms of philosophy. There has been inbreeding here.

I cannot find much different in Heidegger and Marcel. The former makes much of ontology but seeks to reach it by a semi-poetic intuition. He rejects the correspondence theory of truth and hopes to unveil what is by verbal efforts going back to early Greek philosophy. Heidegger strikes one as a strong man in travail with he hardly knows what. Turning to Marcel, we find him putting stress on the difference between problems and mysteries. He challenges the sciences and the scientific view of the world. On just what grounds it is not clear.

Finally, we come to the theological existentialist, so popular in the United States, Paul Tillich. His background is, like that of Jaspers, of a Kantian type with introduction of transcendence to a God beyond any anthropomorphic God, to Being itself. I cannot, myself, find a basis for this projection. I have taken up this question in a companion book which I call *American Philosophy from Within*. What stands out is the separation of philosophical traditions. There is hardly genuine communication and mutual understanding. But I think this will pass. My own kind of materialism does justice to levels, the emergence of knowing, valuing and morality.

Thus ends my epilogue on Berkeley's famous *Dialogue*. As I look back on these sixty years, it seems to me clear that American philosophy as it came of age, deviated from the European in a certain explanatory openness. Of course Europe hardly took notice of it. And, as I see it, special circumstances, in my own case, favored a breakthrough on critical points.

MANDALA THINKING

Alan Mackay

IT IS DIFFICULT to explain why the geometry of symmetrical patterns should have such a perennial fascination, but it is certainly so.

In our own European culture-area the Pythagoreans were among the first to be seduced by the discovery of a set of pure relationships into the belief that, by pure numbers and without experiments, one could explain the structure of the universe. This trend culminated in Eddington's statement (Tarner Lecture, 1938): "I believe that there are 136 x 2^{256} protons in the universe and the same number of electrons"—although neutrons had been discovered in 1932! In modern terms, the Pythagoreans had discovered an infinite group (the integers). From many particular cases of $1x + 2x = 3x$ they had isolated $1 + 2 = 3$, existing entirely independently of x, this being the simplest kind of abstract relationship. Many peoples would subscribe to the statement "God made the integers; man made the rest" (Kronecker). For example, the Chinese, from the earliest ideas of the five elements, the eight abstract diagrams, the four books, etc., to the present-day slogans of the "three anti-s" have had a continual numerical cast of this kind in their thinking. We, too, still talk about the Trinity, though less than formerly, but we still attach the same sanctity as the Pythagoreans to the numerical ratios between the frequencies of musical notes. However, the mysteries of the Pythagoreans were largely geometrical and derived from Babylonia from whence they received Pythagoras' Theorem (and, perhaps, ideas of the transmigration of souls). This Babylonian tradition was also transmitted in the opposite direction to South India and even as far as New Guinea, and from time to time generated such number-intoxicated individuals as Ramanujan (1887-1920).

The Platonists inherited much of this numerical and geometric magic, the pure relationships of the integers and of geometry existing free of matter as ideas (which we would call the elements of group theory—universal relationships with particular representations). Plato's Academy had the slogan "Let none ignorant of geometry enter here" or so the legend goes. This was unusual for philosophers, but geometry was pure relationship and the Platonists were the most idealist of philosophers. It was also, perhaps, the beginning of the divorce of natural philosophy from "pure" philosophy.

The mystery of the Platonists was the five regular solids (the tetrahedron, the cube, the octahedron, the dodecahedron and the icosahedron), the only regular polyhedra. Again, we could call them geometrical representations of abstract symmetry groups, and we might remind ourselves that the "Eight-fold way" of Gell-Mann and Ne'eman, which is the current scheme of the fundamental particles, is just such an idea, and that the name is consciously chosen for its Buddhist associations. In the "Timaeus," Plato attempted to explain the structure of matter in terms of these regular solids, themselves made out of only two kinds of triangular sub-units. Plato would not have been surprised to see that the traditional set of architects' drawing instruments comprises, besides compasses for making circles, just the two triangles which he regarded as fundamental. Plato's system of fundamental particles was not as good as that of his predecessor, Democritus, but it was by no means contemptible. The trouble was that experiments which might have checked or modified the theory did not follow. It was the world which was imperfect, not the theory.

Later (about 350 B.C.), the abstract geometrical system reached its apex in one of the masterpieces of all time, the "Elements" of Euclid. Euclid of Alexandria began with his five axioms and proceeded step by step through 13 books to the construction of the icosahedron and the dodecahedron and the demonstration that there were no further perfect solids. Proclus, the neo-Platonist, claimed that Euclid's work was an essay for adepts on the regular solids. The "Elements" has remained a model of idealist thought and a textbook ever since, taking second place only to the Bible (the representative of entirely another mode of thought) . . . "Alone at nights I read my Bible more and Euclid less"—Robert Buchanan (1841-1901). Other Greeks did experiments to find out mathematical and physical laws but even Archimedes himself was a little ashamed at this earthy way of acquiring knowledge. The idea that the pure regularities of geometry lie at the basis of thought and of the structure of the universe is deep in our cultural tradition.

In what ways can we get to know things? If we exclude divine intervention as ill-attested, there are three main ways: experience of things at firsthand; knowledge transmitted from others by speech, books, etc., and genetic knowledge which is built in. What exactly we know genetically is difficult to determine, but we must assume, for example, that a spider knows because it has been furnished with the right genetic instruction on how to spin a web. Surely then, man, more complicated in every respect, must know many things genetically? C. G. Jung (if we interpret his pronouncements in the least mystical way) thought so. On the basis of observations, which are wide open to criticism, Jung concluded that there was a built-in tendency (genetically rather than culturally determined) for people to think in certain geometrical categories. He took as one of these archetypes (or images in which people tend to cast their dreams and thoughts), the Mandala—a pattern of concentric squares and circles associated with the iconography of Mahayana Buddhism. In Buddhist thought the Mandala represents, both a kind of ideological map of the universe (with Mount Meru—perhaps the Himalayas—in the center), and a map of the human personality. Jung suggested, for example, that architects built cities of concentric squares and circles because they have Mandala archetypes stored in their unconscious minds and not because of the physical properties of building materials or their social needs.

In Buddhism, no attempts were made in this particular tradition of thought to compare this geometrical world with reality, and consequently it did not make progress as regards the development of science and the achievement of control over the external world. The practitioners of "Mandala thinking" retreated and sought only control over the internal world of their own consciousness (and their own physiology). Mandalas were for contemplation—and very satisfying and soothing objects for contemplation they are, too.

In the Middle Ages, Johannes Kepler (1571-1630) looked at the five regular solids and the way (following Plato and Ptolemy) that they could be nested in spheres and made into a kind of three-dimensional mandala, his "Mysterium Cosmographicum." The language used for describing the crystal spheres of the planetary system has a remarkably oriental flavour. However, after being ensnared for many years by this idea, Kepler was finally great enough to take the enormous step of throwing away the Mandala model and enunciating his revolutionary three laws of planetary motion. This was really the beginning of modern science when the facts were taken as the final arbiter, and the squashed ellipse replaced the perfect sphere, which had been the self-evidently natural solution. Strangely, however, although Kepler was wrong about the macrocosm, the regular solids have turned up again in the structure of the microcosm. The solutions of the wave equations describing the state of the electrons in orbit around the nucleus of an atom involve angular terms, called "spherical harmonics" in the Ptolemaic style, which are really just the same regular solids as once played the music of the spheres.

William Davidson (1593-1669), the first British professor of chemistry, also represents a man just at the turning point. His book on chemistry contains both mandala-type drawings and realistic pictures of crystals. He thought that there must be a bridge between the Platonic solids and the structure of crystals but he could not step across it. Crystallography, the science and mathematics of the three-dimensional arrangements of atoms in crystals, waited for its beginning for Bravais and Häuy (1811-63 and 1743-1822). It did not really flower, however, until 1911 when the discovery of X-ray diffraction enabled experimental confirmation or disproof to be provided for the speculations by such as Barlow on the internal structure of crystals. The mathematics of repeating patterns did not wait for the physical realization but developed beforehand. Indeed it continues to do so still.

In recent times the biologist, D'Arcy Wentworth Thompson (1860-1948), had an outlook which was Pythagorean—"he saw numbers in all things. But unlike Pythagoras he was neither a religious prophet nor a mystic. Thompson was a naturalist, a classical scholar and a mathematician." In his great book, *Growth and Form* (1915), he said: "Cell and tissue, shell and bone, leaf and flower, are so many portions of matter, and it is in obedience to the laws of physics that their particles have been moved, molded and conformed. They are no exception to the rule that God always geometrises."

It is unlikely that the Islamic preoccupation with geometrical repeating patterns was entirely due to the prohibitions of the Koran (or rather the Ulama). At the time when Islam arose the Christian iconoclasts were also against figural art and indeed the whole Middle Eastern atmosphere was against natural representation. There must have been some positive features. Allah was, like the Christian God, also a geometer and the words of His Prophet were numerically arranged. Islamic decoration was concerned with infinitely extended two-dimensional repeating patterns and tessellations. Occasionally polyhedra occurred. These patterns also embody the abstract symmetry groups, particularly the 17 plane groups first explicitly described by Fedorov (1891). A mathematician would say that the patterns are representations of the groups. Islamic culture was, of course, well aware of Euclid and indeed transmitted his works to us.

Even today such major scientists as Linus Pauling and J. D. Bernal find their inspiration in the five Platonic solids. Pauling, in a very recent paper in *Nature* (p. 174, 9th Oct., 1965) on the structure of stable nuclei, even uses Pythagorean language and refers to "magic numbers." Both have suggested that the icosahedron is, as Plato believed, the key to the liquid element. It has certainly been shown by Bernal's school of crystallography to be the key to the architecture of the viruses, delighting the engineer, Buckminster Fuller, who had been building icosahedral domes for sound engineering reasons.

Whether Pauling and Bernal's geometrical theories of liquid and nuclear structure will become established depends on the results of the experiments suggested by the theories. If a theory does not fit the facts, then it will have to go, however sweet it may appear.

The geometry of the regular polygons and polyhedra still beguiles. Is nature really like that underneath, or is there some genetic mechanism which makes thinking in such terms so congenial? Is the web-spinning genetically or culturally conditioned? Certainly, geometrical doodling and speculation are part of our culture. Do we try to organize nature into such patterns, or just reflect the regularities which we find there?

I believe that we do not have built into us such specific ideas on how space should be subdivided as the spider, but that we have a more powerful and more generalized tendency to try to organize and control our environment. Such tendencies would have, in terms of evolution, considerable survival value. Enough of our geometrical speculations have been successful to give us confidence that such doodling is a healthy activity provided that now and again we find some use for parts of it—even if it is only an artistic application.

It is a sound heuristic technique to have, not only a stock of facts waiting to be fitted into patterns, but also a stock of patterns waiting for facts which will fit into them.

AN EMPIRICAL CONCEPTION OF FREEDOM

Edward D'Angelo

ALTHOUGH a great deal has been written about the problem of freedom, very little has been done to develop an empirical conception of freedom. Since "free" and "freedom" are valuation terms, it is often unclear what empirical referrent we are concerned with when we claim that man is free. A difficulty that arises with the problem of freedom is the formulation of an adequate set of criteria for classifying all types of human behavior and the development of a set of procedures to test empirically whether a man is free or not free.

Let us examine some of the criteria that have been used to determine whether an individual's actions are free.

John Wilson suggests that we distinguish between what he calls inside and outside causes as a means of determining whether a man is free.[1] An individual is free if his behavior is due to internal causes. He is not free if his actions are the result of external causes.

One of the problems with the inside-outside distinction is that some causes which appear to be internal are actually external. An individual may believe that his behavior is due to an internal cause and be unaware that the cause is really external. The individual who behaves in a given way because of a posthypnotic suggestion believes that the cause is within him. He is unaware of the fact that an external source is the cause of his behavior.

Another problem with the inside-outside distinction is that actions are not caused exclusively by inside or outside causes. In every situation there are some causal factors which are external to the individual. Phillipa Foot contends that the belief that some actions are caused solely by internal factors is the result of the ambiguity

---

[1] J. Wilson, "Freedom and Compulsion," *Mind*, LXVII (January, 1958), p. 62.

of the phrase "caused by my desires or character."[2] This phrase does not necessarily mean that my desires are the only factors operating. The fact that my desires are causal factors in a given situation does not preclude the fact that other causal factors external to me are also present.

Voluntary-involuntary is another criterion that has been used to determine whether or not an individual is free. A voluntary act is often defined as an act which is the result of a choice. When choices are ineffective in determining behavior, the act is considered involuntary.[3]

To define "free" and "voluntary" in terms of choice presents certain difficulties. Many of the things we do are not the result of a choice, and yet these behaviors are still considered to be free. In most cases the act of walking does not involve a conscious series of choices; yet it still would be considered a free act. There are also many habitual and impulsive acts that do not involve a choice. These nondeliberated acts are usually considered to be free, but they would not qualify as voluntary acts. If choice is a defining quality of a free and voluntary act, then some compelled acts would also be free. Choices can be either compelled or uncompelled. The man who decides to obey the orders of an armed bandit has chosen to do so rather than get shot. This is an example of a voluntary act that is compelled. Since some voluntary acts are compelled, we cannot consider them to be free.

The concepts of compelled and uncompelled also have been used to classify acts as free or not free. How do we determine whether a human act is compelled or uncompelled? If a man is chained to a rock and he cannot escape to fulfill a particular desire, he is compelled. He cannot act otherwise, even if he chooses differently. However, the act of the man who chained him to the rock was uncompelled. He chose to chain him and he was not compelled by anyone to do so. He could have acted otherwise, if he had so desired.

The difficulty with this position is that choices and desires can be just as compulsive as external causes. The behavior of an individual who has a compulsive desire to steal is just as constrained as the individual who is forced to act contrary to his desires. There exist not only external compulsions, but also internal compulsions.

---

[2]P. Foot, "Free Will as Involving Determinism," *Philosophical Review*, LXVI (October, 1957), p. 44.

[3]J. Laird, *On Human Freedom* (London: Allen & Unwin, 1947), p. 34.

A distinction needs to be made between acts which are internally constrained and acts which are internally nonconstrained.

To illustrate the difference between these acts, A. J. Ayer refers to the thief and the kleptomaniac.[4] According to Ayer a kleptomaniac does not deliberate, or if he does, he would steal anyhow. Deliberation does not causally influence the behavior of the kleptomaniac, but it does affect the behavior of the thief. The behavior of the kleptomaniac is compulsive because he would steal regardless of the consequences of the situation. The thief's behavior is not compulsive because he will refrain from stealing at times.

It is interesting to note the lack of empirical evidence to support Ayer's description of a kleptomaniac. Donald Cressey, the criminologist, claims that most kleptomaniacs do not have an irresistible urge to steal. In some courts "the policeman at the elbow test" has been used to determine whether an individual had an irresistible impulse. Most kleptomaniacs would not pass this test. The desires of a kleptomaniac can be controlled to an extent if he knows that he is being watched by a clerk or a policeman. Cressey maintains that thieves and kleptomaniacs are motivated in many similar ways. They make their plans in advance, select secluded areas, and they are aware that they will be arrested if they are apprehended.[5] This evidence indicates that the distinction between the kleptomaniac and the thief cannot be used to distinguish internally constrained acts from those which are internally nonconstrained.

Another difficulty with the compelled-uncompelled distinction is that we cannot fit some types of behavior into these two categories. Some kleptomaniacs do not have a compulsive urge to steal, and yet it is not exactly accurate to maintain that their acts are uncompelled and free. From an empirical point of view, can we accurately classify all types of behavior within the two categories of free and not free?

In the development of a science a two-category system is sometimes used to classify all substances. For example, in order to understand the nature of particular substances, we can use "soft" and "hard" to classify all minerals. The problem with a two-category

---

[4]A. J. Ayer, "Freedom and Necessity," in his *Philosophical Essays* (London: Macmillan, 1954), p. 277.

[5]D. R. Cressey, "The Differential Association Theory and Compulsive Crimes," *Journal of Criminal Law, Criminology, and Police Science*, XLV (May-June, 1954), p. 35.

system of this type is that it is often difficult to fit all minerals into these categories. Some substances may not be exactly soft or hard. The varying degrees of softness and hardness of minerals make the two-category system inadequate.

One way out of this difficulty would be to introduce intermediate terms, such as soft-hard and hard-soft. Although this may enable us to classify these minerals more accurately, it still presents the problem of classifying future substances which do not fit into these categories and understanding the relationships between them. Additional categories can always be created, but one wonders whether a more efficient system can be devised to resolve this problem.

Another approach would be to use comparative concepts to classify all substances. A may be the softest known mineral and Z may be the hardest. The comparative concepts "softer than" and "harder than" can be used to classify all substances between A and Z. When new substances are discovered they can be classified between A and Z, or they may be considered softer than A or harder than Z. The comparative concept approach enables us to express the difference between substances in terms of degrees as well as to define operationally these concepts in reference to a particular empirical test.

It is my contention that a comparative concept approach can be used in relation to the problem of freedom. The two-category systems of rational-irrational, voluntary-involuntary, internal-external and compelled-uncompelled present innumerable difficulties. We cannot always fit all types of behavior into these categories. The history of the free will problem has been to invent new categories (conditioned-constrained) to meet these difficulties. This approach will probably always fail given a diversity of conditions and behaviors.

Felix E. Oppenheim uses the comparative concept "more freedom than" as a means of describing the differences of behavior in various social and political situations. He develops a system of degrees of freedom to describe these differences.[6] I believe that a similar approach can be used in relation to the traditional problem of freedom.

The comparative concepts "more free than" and "less free than" can be used to classify all types of behavior. Freedom would be defined in terms of specific behavioral relationships. As a relational concept, it would be defined in a contextual situation. In this sense

---

[6]F. E. Oppenheim, *Dimensions of Freedom* (New York: St. Martin's, 1961), p. 181.

it would be meaningless to ask whether an individual's act is free or not. It would also necessitate that we no longer use "free" and "not free" and substitute certain comparative concepts to denote the empirical differences in human behavior.

Let us examine certain possible uses of the comparative concepts "more free than" and "less free than." Mr. Smith claims that he is more free than he was in the past in doing X. "More free than" in this case refers to the behavioral changes from the past to the present. In the past he could not return any merchandise which he had purchased and found to be unsatisfactory. Today, in approximately fifty per cent of the cases, he can return unsatisfactory purchases. There is a behavioral difference between the past and the present concerning this particular act. He is freer than he was in the past in returning unsatisfactory purchases. Mr. Smith claims, however, that he is less free than Mr. Jones in returning unsatisfactory purchases. Mr. Smith can do it fifty per cent of the time, whereas Mr. Jones can do it ninety per cent of the time. In general, Mr. Smith is less free than Mr. Jones, relative to returning certain unsatisfactory purchases.

Within contextual situations, however, the results may be different. What if we know that a certain shopkeeper is infuriated when someone returns a particular purchase? Under these circumstances Mr. Jones may not be able to return the merchandise, whereas Mr. Smith might do so without any difficulty. In this case Mr. Smith is freer than Mr. Jones. In specific situations, either one may be freer than the other, depending on his ability to return the merchandise. Of course, in situations where both men can return the merchandise, the comparative concepts "more free than" and "less free than" have no meaning.

"More free than" refers to growth in relation to a particular act and also to the ability to modify one's behavior relative to different acts. What if the shopkeeper is not only infuriated, but will also kill anyone who returns any merchandise? Mr. Smith and Mr. Jones discover this fact just as they are about to return some merchandise. Mr. Smith changes his behavior but Mr. Jones does not. Mr. Jones says that it is a matter of principle and that he is going to return the merchandise regardless of the consequences. Mr. Smith is freer than Mr. Jones in this situation because he is able to modify his behavior in more diverse ways to correspond with certain changes that have taken place in the environment.

Freedom in this sense is equivalent to varied and flexible growth. There is a significant difference between an individual who will behave in a single way and an individual who will behave in various ways. The individual can behave in various ways because he has been influenced by the introduction of additional preferences, knowledge of the consequences of the act, changing conditions in the environment, an awareness of the various alternatives, and other factors. Since these factors can offset prior causal conditions, this individual is capable of changing his behavior. He can make different kinds of adaptations and satisfy a greater variety of needs than the individual whose behavior cannot be influenced by these causal conditions.

The use of the comparative concepts "more free than" and "less free than" involves not only the principle of growth, but also a standard of a desirable goal. Not all growth is desirable. This is what we mean when we say that an individual has grown worse. We need to include a value judgment of a better state of affairs when judging an individual's behavior to be more or less free than others.

Within the framework of the traditional problem of freedom it has been difficult to fit certain types of behavior into the two-category system of free and not free. The behavior of the kleptomaniac is not considered free and uncompelled, and yet empirically we have found that not all kleptomaniacs act compulsively. The comparative concepts "more free than" and "less free than" will enable us to evaluate the different behaviors of all kleptomaniacs. A system of degrees of freedom needs to be established in order to express the differences between these behaviors in relation to a particular act in a given situation.

An empirical conception of freedom is a relational concept involving changes of behavior from one state to another. It includes the principle of growth and the recognition of a desirable goal as the basis of empirically testing whether certain behaviors are more or less free than others in a contextual situation.

APPENDIX

What are the social and political implications in using a comparative concept of freedom? An empirical concept of freedom that employs the concepts "more free than" and "less free than" enables us to note the actual differences between specific acts, rules, and behaviors of certain institutions in different countries or in opposing political and social systems. The judgment of labelling one system as free and another as not free obscures the similarities and differences between the institutions within these systems.

In using the comparative concept of freedom we notice that there is more freedom in the Soviet Union than in the United States concerning representation of minority groups in the legislative body of the government. The Soviet of Nationalities, a body of the Supreme Soviet, is composed of deputies who are elected by all minority groups in the various republics of the Soviet Union. All minority groups have no assurance that their interests will be represented by elected officials in the legislative body in the United States. On the other hand, there is more freedom for a writer and artist in the United States to express various forms of art than in the Soviet Union. If we compare France with the United States and the Soviet Union, we may find more freedom for the writer in France to describe certain sexual acts in his writings than in these other countries. People living in Japan who desire an abortion for economic reasons have more freedom than people living in other countries where abortion is illegal for such reasons.

A detailed analysis, using the comparative concept of freedom, is needed of the institutions of similar and opposing political, economic, and social systems of different countries. This approach will enable us to destroy some of the myths about the function of particular institutions within different political systems. A comparative concept of freedom has tremendous possibilities as an educational instrument in understanding and changing human behavior and the institutions of society.

HEIDEGGER ON THE ESSENCE OF TRUTH*

Marvin Farber

TO MANY readers of philosophical literature, Martin Heidegger appears to have made great contributions to philosophy. But to those who have taken the trouble to read his writings with logical standards in mind, he has very little to offer, and he rates primarily as a pretentious verbal philosopher. He has taken care to create severe linguistic barriers between himself and his readers, which serve to make plausible the claim to untold profundity and novelty. It will be instructive—and quite disillusioning to some—to examine a piece of Heidegger's more audacious writing carefully. Nothing could be better for this purpose than his essay on "The Essence of Truth."**

The reader has the right to expect something definite from any discussion of the concept of truth. He is not likely to be deceived, or impressed, by anything else. Once he has departed from the murky intricacies of the language dealing with "being" and "existence," Heidegger becomes quite a different kind of figure. The change is, roughly, from tragedy (a linguistic tragedy, at least) to comedy— or the commonplace. Heidegger asks a good question to begin with (321): "What do we ordinarily understand by 'truth'?" The word truth means, in his words, "that which makes something true into a truth." This is hardly subtle, and not at all new. Much better is Heidegger's subsequent recognition of truth as correspondence, whether of a thing with an idea, or of a statement with a thing. He does not justify his assertion, however, that propositional truth (*adaequatio intellectus ad rem*) is only possible on the basis

---

*Reprinted by permission from *Philosophy and Phenomenological Research*. Vol. XVIII, #4, June, 1958, pp. 523-532.

**Cf. M. Heidegger, *Existence and Being*, Henry Regnery Company, Chicago, 1949, pp. 319-351.

of objective truth (*adaequatio rei ad intellectum*). It is interesting to note that "the reduction of propositional truth to objective truth" is called a "theological explanation" (325). The theological notion of creation of the world of things, and of minds as well, hardly requires a "reduction." Such a designation is more appropriate for scientific philosophers.

A promising element in the discussion is the consideration of the view that truth is "the likeness or agreement of a statement to or with a given thing" (326 ff.). The author properly attempts to analyze the meaning of "agreement." By agreement can be meant "identity of appearance" between two coins, for example. Or, the statement "This coin is round" "agrees" with the thing. At this point, Heidegger's acuteness runs away with him, for he finds it necessary to observe that the coin is metal, and the statement is in no sense material; the coin is round, and the statement is not spatial. He is quite right in pointing out that with the coin you can buy something, but that the statement about it can never be legal tender. And yet, the statement "agrees with and is true of the coin." If the agreement is supposed to be an "approximation," then how can such a completely unlike thing like a statement "approximate" to the coin? The author reasons that it would have to *become* the coin, which would remove the basis for agreement. It follows that "approximation" cannot mean a material likeness between two unlike things. The kind of relationship obtaining between statement and thing is then declared to determine the nature of the approximation. Although this theme has been treated at length in an abundant literature, Heidegger approaches it as though it were waiting for his clarification for the first time. Thus he writes, "So long as this 'relationship' remains indeterminate and its nature unfathomed," all argument about such approximation leads nowhere (327). Obviously, he is the person who has been called to fathom this hitherto unfathomed "relationship."

The matter must not be allowed to appear simple in any respect, for then there would be little to "fathom." The statement "represents" the coin, and states "how it is," "what it is like," in some respect or other. Much more could have been said on this point, but detailed analysis is not the author's objective. "Representation" is taken by him to mean "letting something take up a position opposite to us, as an object" (328); and the thing that is "opposed" must, in the author's words, "come across the open towards us" while "standing fast" as a thing.

But does one always "*let* something take up a position as an object" when he makes statements? Is this not to ascribe too much autonomy and freedom to man as a knower? The activity of the knower must be duly recognized, but it is also important to bear in mind that the knower is causally conditioned, and that many events in the world force themselves upon him, no matter how unwilling he may be. It is a traditional philosophical disease to exaggerate the status of the mind in reality, thereby ignoring or falsifying the evolutionary perspective.

In the course of his discussion, Heidegger believes he has disposed of "the traditional practice of attributing truth exclusively to the statement as its sole and essential place" (329). He argues that "truth does not possess its original seat in the proposition." It may be observed that scholars have long known that there is a cognitive side and the side of reality (or of the objects) in talking of truth. The ambiguous expression "original seat" suggests order of time, but also logical or metaphysical priority. The statement is assumptive in any case, because "truth" is spoken of as somehow real in its own right. There is a set of truths; there is a concept of truth; but is there "truth" in the sense that the true is the whole? That would be a familiar idea, but it differs strikingly from the author's text because of its clarity and relative simplicity.

Quaint indeed is Heidegger's question (330): "Whence does the representative statement receive its command to 'right itself' by the object and thus to be in accord with rightness?" Quaint, but revealing. A command, indeed! He is unable to resist a linguistic *coup*, when he asks, "Why does this accord (*Stimmen*) at the same time determine (*bestimmen*) the nature of truth?" Had he written in English, that sentence might never have been born. His next step leads him quickly to a major objective. He asks how there can be "an approximation to a pre-established criterion, or a directive enjoining such an accord." Having just invented the "directive," he is free to use it as a means to an end. His answer is that "this postulate (*Vorgeben*) has already freed itself and become open to a manifestation operating in this openness—a manifestation which is binding on all representation whatsoever." This is as fast as it is fanciful. He does not show why it is "binding on all representation." What ulterior purpose may the author have in mind when he speaks of "this 'freeing' for the sake of submitting to a binding criterion"? It is declared to be only possible as "freedom to reveal something already overt" and being free in this way is said to point to the "hitherto uncomprehended nature" of freedom. If rightness is to be possible, the line of argument goes, there must be freedom. In short, "the essence of truth is freedom." (330). The author concedes that his version of the essence of truth (rightness of statement) as freedom must appear strange. Instead of attempting to give a precise answer to the question "What is truth?" he equates it to an even more misleading and difficult generality. There is an element of justification in introducing freedom, but it is not the central, or even an important part of the question of the nature of truth.

Heidegger weighs the consequences that might be drawn from "turning truth into freedom." Is that to undermine truth by delivering it up to the caprice of man, "to the whim of this wavering reed"? (331). Truth is now "brought down to the subjective level of the human subject." But all sorts of untruth are ascribed to man. That does not deter the author for a moment, for "this human origin of untruth merely confirms by contrast the essential nature of truth 'as such' which holds sway 'over' man" (332). This truth "as such" is portrayed as imperishable and eternal, and as something that cannot be founded on the transitoriness and fragility of mankind.

This is again a misleading formulation of the truth problem. The author uses merely pictorial language in saying that truth "as such" holds sway "over" man. There is no truth "as such"—that is merely an abstraction. There are truths, as best illustrated by verified scientific statements, or mathematical propositions, which are said to be objectively "true" or "valid," as the case may be. "Imperishable" and "eternal" are emotionally loaded words. Perhaps one should express them with bated breath, if not with the whites of his eyes. If "objectively true" (or valid) relates to a set of facts (or propositions), it may well be, as Bradley expressed it, that "Once true, always true." Every scientific proposition is subject to possible modification, all the way to possible repudiation. But *if* it is once true with respect to a given set of facts, or a given historical situation, then it is always true with respect to the same set of facts or historical situation. This is not to found truth on "the transitoriness and fragility of mankind," as Heidegger puts it. Man is to be sure transitory, and he is subject to error. The truths (not "truth") which are established, often with great travail, are "from below," and they do not hold sway "over" man.

Heidegger's next step is clearly indicated. If the essence of truth is freedom, as he declares, and if "essence" is "the basis of the inner possibility of whatever is accepted in the first place and generally admitted as 'known'" (331); then the question must be answered as to how the essence of truth can have "a stable basis in human freedom." It is an obstinate prejudice, in his opinion, to contend that "freedom is a property of man." If truth as such is above man, then the reader would expect that freedom must also be construed accordingly. Conveniently, there is experience of "a hidden ground in man's nature and being, so that we are transported in advance into the original living realm of truth." It now appears that freedom is only the basis of the inner possibility of rightness "because it receives its own essence from that thing of earlier origin: the uniquely essential truth." The term "earlier" is not explained, nor is it pointed out how one thing can "receive its essence" from another thing. If that could be explained, essences might well be rendered more fruitful. Neither is the meaning of "uniquely essential truth" explained. The proliferation of words cannot always be accounted for.

Whatever "freedom" may mean to the average reader—one thinks of freedom defined in terms of the satisfaction of his needs, or with respect to the fulfillment of a plan of action—it has a different meaning in the present context. Here it means "freedom for the revelation of something already overt" (333). Having defined the essence of truth as freedom, the author now asks for the essence of freedom. It would be precarious to attempt to apply his formulation, because the reader would be tempted to think of existing historical conditions (for example, slavery), and to interpret the author as suggesting that acquiescence is freedom. But this line of thought, which is at least as old as the Stoic tradition, appears to be on a more abstract, metaphysical level of analysis. His formulation reads: "The freedom to reveal something overt lets whatever 'is' at the moment *be* what it is. Freedom reveals itself as the 'letting-be' of what-is" (333). This is not held to imply indifference or neglect, but is intended to mean that one "has something to do with it," or to participate in something overt. The "ordinary idea of truth," as referring to the correctness of a proposition, is now revised and is traced back to "that still uncomprehended quality," the revelation of what-is (334). What-is reveals itself "as *what* and *how* it is, and the approximation which represents it in the statement may take it for a criterion. Unfortunately for the reader who insists on understanding what he reads, there are no examples of the revelation of "what-is." All the examples that would occur to one would have reference to limited situations in a selective manner.

The common-sense understanding of freedom is demeaned and

passed off lightly by the author. Thus he states that "freedom is not license in what we do or do not do" (334). It is evident from his text that he is aware of the distinction between positive and negative freedom and of the view that freedom is "a mere readiness to do something . . . necessary." Disclaiming these versions of freedom, Heidegger maintains that freedom is "a participation in the revealment of what-is-as-such." As distinguished from the vague, if not vacuous, freedom resorted to by the author, there is the concept of freedom construed in terms of taking one's place in the causal order, where "freedom" may be taken to mean relative self-determination. This conception of freedom would not be paraded as the essence of truth, however. It seems that a specially manufactured "freedom" is required as a prop for the present abstract concept of "truth."

Heidegger writes at times like a prophet. "In this *Da-sein*," he states, "there is preserved for mankind that long unfathomed and essential basis on which man is able to ex-sist" (335). Naturally, he is the man to "fathom" this "long unfathomed" thing. It is also interesting to note that there is an "essential basis" on which man is able to "ex-sist." To suggest food as a part of that "basis" would be an intrusion from the realm of facts. Is it something which the special sciences—natural and social—have missed? Or is it something they could never touch, if only because it is "unfathomable" by scientific means, and accessible only through Heidegger's linguistic usage. Perhaps he is right, after all: an artificially induced linguistic problem can only be met by linguistic devices.

With characteristic linguistic thoroughness and determination, the term "existence" is beaten into the desired shape. It does not signify an "occurrence" or thing, or the "presence" of an "existent." Neither does it mean "man's moral preoccupation with himself," in any psychological sense. The author's answer reads: "Ex-sistence, grounded in truth as freedom, is nothing less than exposition into the revealed nature of what-is-as-such (335). This queer usage need not detain us.

The outcome for man and history is noteworthy: "Only where what-is is expressly raised to the power of its own revelation and preserved there, only where this preservation is concerned as the quest for what-is-as-such, only there does history begin" (335 f.). Then there was no history in the remote past, or, in fact, before the emergence of philosophy. Reminiscent of the idealistic tradition is the author's statement that "only ex-sistent man is historical, 'nature' has no history" (336). Heidegger's "history" is as distinctive as his "ex-sistence," "freedom," and "truth"—and practically everything else, in his purportedly fundamentally new and original point of view. Thus he is able to assert that "the initial revelation of what-is-in-totality, the quest for what-is-as-such, and the beginning of the history of the West, are one and the same thing."

Speculative philosophers should be given unlimited freedom to reconstruct "absolutes" to their heart's content. But they should not be allowed to operate arbitrarily with regard to matters of fact, and especially history. One kind of history does indeed begin with the posing of the question of the nature of existence. But there are other kinds of history—economic, political, and on a larger scale, biological, geological, and astronomical. It is to be doubted, however, whether Heidegger's purposes could be served by such clarity of designation.

It is interesting to note, also, how Heidegger places certain terms in quotation marks—"time," "known," "subject," "object," etc. It tends to elevate the reader above such concepts, and to make him feel a partner in a frightfully searching inquiry. Heidegger was of course anticipated in this practice by Husserl, who questioned everything, all presumed existents being placed in quotation marks. For Husserl, however, it was a matter of an exactly defined method; whereas for Heidegger, in the present context, it is a matter of straining to get away from what he regards as ordinary, fallible, and naive meanings to an inexpressibly "deep" level.

For Heidegger, "freedom is not governed by human inclination"; and "man does not 'possess' freedom as a property," but, rather, "freedom, or ex-sistent revelatory *Da-sein* possesses man." It is evident that there can be no application of this conception of freedom to actual historical conditions, which abound in social conflicts and attempts to change social relations. For Heidegger, freedom is construed as "the letting-be of what-is," and it is supposed to "perfect the nature of truth in the sense that truth is the unconcealment and revealment of what-is" (336). The reader is reminded that truth is not the mark of a correct proposition, made by a human "subject" in respect of an "object." Truth is, for Heidegger, "the revelation of what-is, a revelation through which something 'overt' comes into force." But one cannot deny the legitimacy of the truth concept in connection with propositions, and the distinction between subject and object, or knower and known. That distinction is a real one, and no distinction is more important. It does not imply a metaphysical, or an ontological, difference. Whatever else the term "truth" may be taken to mean, it certainly has this application. In one sense, the knower is a finality, an irreducible fact. He has his ideas, and he is a proposition-making animal. His ideas may be good or bad, adequate or inadequate; and his propositions may be good or bad, true or false. If good, they express correctly the actual state of affairs concerned; if bad, they do not. One may say that a true proposition expresses the truth (more exactly, an instance of truth). It can also be said that some aspect or occasion of the real has been portrayed, rather than "revealed," in most propositions. One must be prepared, however, to allow for hypothetical, possible, and even unreal entities—even for impossible entities—in determining the truth or falsity of propositions.

Despite his nice words concerning truth as the revelation of what-is, Heidegger is compelled to recognize error. It would seem to be difficult to provide for human fallibility on his premises, but he has an effective means in the concept of freedom. Although historical man "lets things be," the author states that he "cannot really let what-is be just *what* it is and *as* it is." But he does not tell why historical man cannot do that. Is it because he does not like "what-is" in some respects, or that he wants to play a role more satisfactory to himself in the "what-is"? As the author states it, "what-is is covered up and distorted," and "illusion comes into its own" (337). His statement that man only ex-sists as the property of ex-sistent freedom, which is the essence of truth, is utterly incomprehensible as it stands. It is thus that he tries to account for man's being capable of history. With distortion and illusion, the essential negation of truth, its "dis-essence," appears. If freedom is not a property of man ("man only ex-sists as the property of this freedom and so becomes capable of history"), then neither is the dis-essence of truth a property of man. The latter cannot "simply arise *a posteriori* from the mere incapacity and negligence of man." In Heidegger's view, "untruth must derive from the essence of truth." Thus it turns out that freedom (Heideggerian freedom) must bear the burden of error as well as truth.

The clarification of "what-is-in-totality" proves to be revealing. It is not identical with the sum of known actualities. It is interesting to note that where few actualities are known, or where they are hardly known by science, "the manifest character of what-is-in-totality can operate far more essentially" than where the field of knowledge is endless. Heidegger speaks disparagingly of the "proliferation and standardisation of knowledge, this desire to know everything . . ." (339). The setting for irrationalism has been prepared therewith. In Heidegger's view, man's behavior "is attuned to the manifest character of what-is-in-totality." This "in-totality" is said to appear to us, however, "as something incalculable and incomprehensible." Although this "in-totality" is concerned as ceaselessly determining all things, it cannot, in the author's view, be understood in terms of what manifestly "is," and it remains indeterminable. It is "concealed." In each particular case of "letting be," something is revealed in its proper relationship, but what-is-in-totality is regarded as concealed therewith. Thus, the ex-sistent freedom of *Da-sein* involves "a dissimulation of what-is-in-totality," or concealment. This concealment is accorded a fundamental place: as an "authentic untruth," it is "anterior to all revelation of this or that actuality," and also to the letting-be of what-is, which, by revealing, conceals and thus establishes the dissimulation." This basis for irrationalism could only find a sympathetic welcome in anti-intellectualistic circles which had found the simpler bill-of-fare of Bergson no longer effective—if only because it was too easily understood.

The reader is now told that the "dissimulation of what-is-as-such" is a mystery, and that absolute mystery, or mystery as such ("the dissimulation of the dissimulated"), pervades the whole of man's *Da-sein* (341). In the great tradition, there has been a place for mystery, especially where theological considerations were involved; and it has been regarded as a mark of wisdom to know when to ward off all rational questions or objections. That "*Da-sein,* insofar as it ex-sists, reaffirms the first and most extreme non-revelation of all: authentic untruth" is no doubt best left as a mystery. Man errs, says Heidegger; he lives in error. But error is not something into which he occasionally falls; it is "part of the inner structure of *Da-sein,* in which historical man is involved" (345). The wrongness of a judgment, or the falseness of a perception, are regarded as only superficial ways of erring. Heidegger speaks of "the error in which historical man must always walk," and of error as dominating man "through and through by leading him astray" (346). What could "save" man, then, it is fair to ask: Heidegger's metaphysics— or possible future theology? Perhaps it may turn out that his being lost is the condition of being saved, and that the losing of the lost is another mystery. But, then, why should the present writer do Heidegger's theology for him? The point to be noted is that it is not too difficult to learn his style of inventing and manipulating a special jargon, and using words with firm connotations in other senses, with a final resort to mystery when the game has gone far enough.

When Heidegger speaks of Being, the reader is reminded of the peculiar use of the term "history." Those who have ears for this word (Being) are said to determine man's place in history. This cannot possibly refer to what is generally known as real history, or to real men, whether slaves or slaveholders, bourgeoisie, feudal lords, serfs, etc. They have their places in history, but they do not owe them to their having ears for the word "Being." Of course, this is not what the author is talking about, for he declares his attitude to history to be "fundamentally new" (351). He is at his best when dealing with a totality which involves mystery.

When the author inveighs against "all enslavement of philosophical thought" (349), he appears to be wearing the heroic garb of a defender of the rights of reason. His illustration corrects this impression, however, for he cites "the subterfuge of letting philosophy assert itself merely as an 'expression' of 'culture' (Spengler), as the ornament of a creative humanity" (349). Vulnerable though Spengler was, he had many concrete historical realities in mind. The author's objection to Spengler would apply to all scholars who recognize the actual part played by philosophies in history, and the ways in which the various cultural conditions—economic, political, scientific, etc.—act upon and determine philosophy. Such recognition does not necessarily lead to the abandonment of the view that there is a cumulative, constructive element to be discerned in much of the tradition of philosophy.

Taken as a whole, Heidegger's performance in his lecture on "The Essence of Truth" is rather clever and ingenious. He appears in the form of a philosopher, but his role is really that of a theologian. If he does not make philosophy serve theology outright—indeed, he purportedly makes it autonomous—that proves to be unnecessary, for the outcome is the same. There proves to be an ultimate mystery; man is fallible, and in effect condemned to err; there are concealment and revealment; and there are boundaries to possible scientific knowledge. In short, reason is circumscribed and undermined. Through it all there is an unsurpassed degree of pretentiousness and boldness, which is shown repeatedly in the display of verbal inventiveness. It is noteworthy that Heidegger could have written his lines centuries ago, with the same ease with which he is able to detach himself from the world and favor solitude rather than libraries. It is a curious fact that the reader is not likely to be aware of the complete absence of concrete illustrations or scientific references. Modern science and logic neither deter nor aid him in his attack on the German language. He appears in this lecture as a kind of dialectician who sets up contrasts and plays with opposites in order to exploit them. It is a furious attempt at originality, but is a miscarriage at best. A psychoanalytic type of interpreter would probably be tempted to speak of "the rage of intellectual (or scientific) impotence" as characterizing the style.

It is high time for Heidegger to emerge from his self-chosen role of philosopher and to declare himself. There may be a more appropriate place for him in the religious world. His characteristic language would make the step an easy one. There is a place in his system for a divine being, and original sin could have a metaphysical as well as an epistemological basis. That would give meaning and direction to his peculiar non-evolutionary conception of man.

These remarks are sure to be unpleasant to many of Heidegger's former students. Their self-feeling need not be injured, however. They could have done better in choosing a master, to be sure. It is never too late to acknowledge that fact and to reassess what they think they owe him. In some cases, the "transference" to Heidegger was too effective ever to be shaken by logical considerations, and one is reminded of the words, "Though he slay me. . . ." But the extensive influence of the man, now prominent in many countries, is to be explained culturally, in terms of the reasons for the receptivity of the times to irrationalism.

MINDING AS A MATERIAL FORCE

Howard L. Parsons

WHEN WE define "mind," we are confronted by three problems in linguistic usage. (1) "Mind" sometimes means the logical operations or calculations in intracranial space. The problem here is that "mind" in another sense means more than that, namely, sense receptors, an input and storage of information, and a bodily response to the environment. (2) "Mind," in a rationalist philosophical tradition, sometimes means consciousness, or clear and distinct ideas focused in an act of attention. This meaning, however, excludes the operation of an "unconscious" mind, i.e., activities that underlie conscious attention and influence it, such as dispositions and emotions. But we know now that the cerebrum is in the body in the world and is fed by impulses from the environment, senses, nerves, muscles, and viscera. (3) The very terms "mind" and "body" dispose us to seek separate, substantial entities and hamper us when we talk about the activity of minding which is neither identical with body, separate from it, nor predictable of it. Here we speak sometimes of a "minding body," but man is a single psycho-somatic process, and "mind" and "body" are abstract ways of characterizing him.

Definers of mind are moved by material interests. Amidst the ambiguity of Roman slave society, Lucretius wished to assert the power of a material orientation against the superstitious ideologies of a dissolving empire. But he ended by denying to mentality the power to change history. Hegel, the spokesman of the settled and rising bourgeoisie, exaggerated the power of mind beyond its material conditions and limits. Dualists like Plato, Aquinas, and Descartes were aware of the distinctions between mind and the forms of matter set over against it. But all had an interest in supporting the division of labor between oppressed workers who handled the things of nature, and "spiritual" men who read, wrote, talked, prayed, and

90

ruled. A contemporary definition of mind as "the processes inside the head that determine the higher levels of organization in behavior"[1] also has its class origins and ends. This kind of definition dates from the development of the physical sciences in the 17th and 18th centuries, which attacked mentalism, and from the rise of capitalism, which displaced its economic base, feudalism. Capitalists demanded that the restrictions of feudal economics and thought be swept away in favor of a laissez faire policy. For the purposes of the dominance of capitalist man over domestic and colonial workers, thinkers developed an ideology that individualized and sharply separated man from man and man from nature. Though Hobbes argued that men like the things of nature are power and are equal in power, he pictured men as essentially at war with one another, as individuals and nations, and at war with nature. Such a definition suited the vigorous capitalists exploiting the sea and land, robbing the wage laborers, and enslaving the Africans. Current positivist, analytical, existential, and phenomenological treatments of mind, instead of providing a fighting philosophy for capitalism, give it aid and comfort by passive, "neutral" accounts of the states, actions, words, etc. of subjects estranged from the objective world. They represent the pale evening-song of a dying capitalism.

Two considerations prompt us to seek a different solution to the "mind-body problem"—an ideological form of the class problem. The first is a practical one. In the last half-century one-third of mankind has become socialist, and national liberation movements are at work in many places. Increasingly, men have learned that minding activity is determined by the body's condition and that the body can be determined and liberated from exploitation by the guidance of thought; that the ruling class has controlled both their bodies and minds; that the new industrial and technological knowledge of the human mind is not the exclusive property of the ruling class to be used for its own benefit and the deprivation of the ruled; that such knowledge can and ought to be used for the good of all men; and that the way to unite men alienated in body and mind is a classless and cooperative society.

The second consideration is scientific. The recent theoretical work of the sciences—the Second Industrial Revolution, called by C. P.

---

[1] Donald Olding Hebb, *A Textbook of Psychology.* (Philadelphia and London: W. B. Saunders Co., 1958) p. 3.

Snow the Scientific Revolution[2]—has made vast advances in the development of automated machines such as computers. Computers are structures with input and output devices, arithmetic and control circuits, memory units, and a program of instructions. They interact with their environments through the exchange of information.[3] Automated machines, while processing and returning information to the environment, are characterized by feedback, i.e., continuous processing of the effects of their operations on the environment and comparing and adjusting these effects in relation to an ideal performance. Computers can be designed to set up goals, make plans, consider hypotheses, compare and evaluate, and recognize analogies—in short, to think. The fact that machines think does not mean that man, who thinks, is a thinking machine in the same sense, for man is a rational *animal*, and an animal, for all its similarities to a machine, is not identical with any machine that we now know or have made. Thus physical science in the form of cybernetics has revealed the structure and activity of minding as it can be constructed in machines which process information and regulate themselves.

In addition, experimental work in pharmacology and neurophysiology has demonstrated the physio-chemical basis of mental activities—perception, imagery, memory, inference, learning, mental illness, and the like. For example, a connection between the consolidation of memory and the manufacture of protein in the brain has been established;[4] and it is known that the molecule retinal ($C_{20}H_{28}O$) in the eye (of mollusk, arthropod, and vertebrate), when struck by quanta of light, changes shape and sets in motion the process of vision.[5]

Man's minding is an activity of a material body that evolved from the beginnings of the material earth 4½ billion years ago into living matter 3½ billion years ago, into a mammalian form nearly 200 million years ago, into a primate form 60 million years ago, into a walking ape 30 million years ago, and into a hominid one

---

[2]*The Two Cultures and the Scientific Revolution.* (New York: Cambridge University Press, 1961).

[3]For a survey of recent developments in the processing of information by computers, see *Scientific American*, Vol. 215, No. 3 (September, 1966).

[4]Bernard W. Agranoff, "Memory and Protein Synthesis," *Scientific American*, Vol. 216, No. 6 (June, 1967), pp. 115 ff.

[5]Ruth Hubbard and Allen Kropf, "Molecular Isomers in Vision," *Scientific American*, Vol. 216, No. 6 (June, 1967), pp. 64 ff.

million years ago. Here we mention only the highlights of the story of evolution of bodily structures serving specific functions in specific environments: arboreal life, increase in body size, length of life, and increasing available energy; developed hand and muscle-eye coordination; enlarged brain, sense of balance, touch, hearing; binocular eyes, color and detailed vision; year-round breeding; intimate community life, mutual grooming, facial forms and expressions, speech, communication; descent from the trees, upright posture, running, hunting, small monogamous family, intelligence and solicitude in care of the young, cooperation, development of voice mechanism; stretching out of brain development, consequent fetalization, nakedness, sensitivity; stone tools and fire-making. All these changes cumulated and culminated in a unique creature we call "intelligent," though only egoism or ignorance would lead us to deny our ancestors and living relatives their own kinds of intelligence.

Here, we take "minding" to be a material force arising in, conditioned by, and influencing environing forces. It is a human bodily activity (1) sensitive and responsive, (2) valuational and purposive, and (3) innovative and connective. (In what follows we shall treat these characteristics in turn.) Minding is not limited to brain, eyes, muscles, heart, viscera, or voice mechanism. Man's body acts as a unit, using all organs; his whole body is minded, for any impairment in an organ impairs his minding. Minding is the whole body's sensing and mediatively responding to other bodies, communicating and cooperating with other human bodies, to secure individual and social values.

The point of this definition is twofold. First and factually, man's minding body has evolved as bio-social-ecological; it is an interacting part in a larger system. Second, man's survival and fulfillment depend on his securing the right relation in this system, and minding is integral to man and that relation. If man is to master his current problems of war, population, poverty, pollution, and purposelessness, he will do so only if he acts intelligently.

I

"All things have wisdom and a share of thought," said Empedocles. Diderot's insight that all matter has the potentiality for sensing (the most elementary kind of knowledge) has been confirmed by observations and experiments demonstrating the material origin and character of all living forms. Excepting the small viruses and forms up to the large cellular bacteria, all organisms consist of certain molecular building blocks: nuclear DNA molecules, cytoplasm, RNA molecules, protein. DNA molecules "know" how to replicate themselves and, working together in a favorable environment of raw materials for food, temperature, oxygen, etc., all these molecules "know" how to produce a differentiated, integrated body of cells (one hundred million million in the case of man). In the nucleus of a single cell of a man the coded information consists of 340 million "words," the equivalent of 1000 printed volumes.[6]

There is still more to "the wisdom of the body." Homeostatic (negative feedback) systems keep the internal environment in balance. Needs provide information and drive toward the environment: who does not know when he is hungry, thirsty, or tired? The evolved systematized structures of the body (already mentioned) adapt it for survival. The whole system is geared to move dialectically in a universe of dialectical processes.[7] Organism and environment, instinct and learning (*a priori* and empirical, universal and particular) modify each other. The old philosophical puzzle of how mind can know matter is easily answered: minding is a material process that has evolved structures for coordinating its forms of action with those of the world. There is no other way to explain the great success of man remembering, predicting, controlling, and enjoying the patterns of nature.

All the particular, diversified forms and levels of matter are continuous in space-time, and we can trace the anticipations of human mentality in the behavior of simpler organisms. In the evolution of matter, the inorganic forms are sensitive (attractions and repulsions

---

[6]George W. Beadle, "The New Genetics: The Threads of Life," *Britannica Book of the Year 1964*. (Chicago: Encyclopaedia Britannica, Inc., 1964) p. 57.

[7]The outlines of a materialist-dialectical treatment of mind are given in Marx's *Theses on Feuerbach*, Lenin's *Philosophical Notebooks*, and Mao Tse-tung's works. It may seem that these formulations, which stress the unity of theory and practice, or "practical-critical activity," have not always been consistently adhered to. For example, Engels defined mind as "a function of the brain", *Socialism: Utopian and Scientific*. Translated by Edward Aveling. Introduction to the First English Edition. (New York: International Publishers, 1935, p. 11), and Lenin offered the same definition (*Materialism and Empirio-Criticism*, Moscow: Foreign Languages Publishing House, 1952, p. 233.) This definition, however, aimed at correcting idealism. To Marx, Engels, and Lenin, and Mao the brain is in the nervous system, the nervous system is in the body, the body is in society and nature, and its action is always dialectical.

of subatomic particles, valences of atoms, bondings of molecules); organisms are sensitive, with emerging purpose; and higher animals are sensitive, purposive, and symbolically innovative. W. H. Thorpe has pointed to the disposition of animals to explore and to constitute their worlds' perceptually;[8] C. Judson Herrick has observed the directive and novelty-making activity of all living things.[9] Even at the level of very simple organisms, there is a diminutive adumbration of mental purpose and learning.[10] Insects incorporate elaborate systems of knowledge (the wasp laying its eggs in appropriate larva or spider, the sequences in metamorphosis, the sign-interactions of ants and bees); birds and social primates communicate and some use tools. Evolutionary man epitomizes similar sensitivities, instincts, purposes, and powers of communication. But his additional large brain and nervous system, voice mechanism, and hand help to create a syntactical and social system of signs that make his "mind" unique.[11] In arbitrarily limiting the term "minding" here to man's socialized, linguistic bodily action, however, we keep in mind those very old and stable forms of his bodily knowing that subtend and impel man's "higher" mind. Man is a late arriver on the evolutionary scene, an orchestration of variations on prior themes. Moreover, while man often thinks that it is he as a conscious, free, and unique individual who "thinks," most of his thinking is an unconscious, determined, and generic process carried out by the massively unified molecular activities of his body in a social and ecological context. His conscious and controlled cerebral processes release or inhibit that. Minding is the functioning of individual bodies, but the full minding process is the whole human species interpenetrating its activities with non-human nature.

8*Learning and Instinct in Animals.* (Cambridge: Harvard University Press, 1956.)

9"A Biological Survey of Integrative Levels," in *Philosophy for the Future.* Edited by Roy Wood Sellars, V. J. McGill, Marvin Farber. (New York: The Macmillan Co., 1949) pp. 222-242.

10W. E. Agar, *A Contribution to the Theory of the Living Organism.* (New York: Oxford University Press, 1943). H. S. Jennings, *Behavior of the Lower Organisms.* (New York: Columbia University Press, 1906.) Ralph Lillie, *General Biology and the Philosophy of Organisms.* (Chicago: University of Chicago Press, 1945.) See also Charles Hartshorne, "Panpsychism," in *A History of Philosophical Systems,* ed. Vergilius Ferm. (New York: The Philosophical Library, 1950) pp. 442-453.

11D. O. Hebb, "The Problem of Consciousness and Introspection," in *Brain Mechanisms and Consciousness.* Edited by J. F. Delabresnaye. (Springfield, Illinois: Charles Thomas, 1955.)

Minding is an activity of living matter, i.e., of a special organization of matter. It involves a degree of sensitivity and responsiveness to influences that less developed activity does not display. It arises by reason of a prior substrate activity of matter which is a peculiar combination of changeability and stability. This is protoplasm, one of whose properties is irritability. Protoplasm moves in the presence of mechanical, chemical, electrical, and other stimuli. Its flow passes from place to place within the organism, via cytoplasmic bridges or specialized nerve conductors. Or it passes out toward the environment in the form of preferential and avoiding behavior. The capacity for internal flow, produced by stimuli at the surface, may be called sensitivity or receptivity. The capacity for external movement may be called responsiveness.

This double movement, now plain enough in comparatively large, one-celled organisms, and obvious in the higher animals, is analogous to the interchange of materials with the surroundings called metabolism. Like metabolism, it maintains the activities of the organism in an equilibrium in the midst of a changing environment. By means of its capacity of receptivity, the organism can be affected by environmental changes at a distance or at its surface, and can respond accordingly. By analogy with our own behavior we may suppose that as any organism is moved by action upon its receptors, and by consequent effector action, it registers an impression or proto-feeling that *is* to it the stimulus. That is the *way* in which it is receptive: affect is the organismic way of being affected. Through such a stimulus the organism is led to respond to the environment in a primitive taking-account-of the environment. Thus a Paramecium responds to light in a series of trials until it finds an optimum position with respect to light.[12] This mode of adjustment lays the basis for sign-behavior and for symbols in man, for once the stimulus-response mechanism, with its conditioning, is established, a spatial and temporal world begins to swell into being through signs. And when substitute signs (like sounds and marks) are produced by organisms and function socially, the domain of symbols—i.e., mind in the human sense—has emerged.[13]

In order to respond and hence adjust to its environment an organism must have some way of registering information about changes

---

[12]H. S. Jennings, *op. cit.*

[13]The distinction here between signs and symbols follows Charles Morris, *Signs, Language and Behavior.* (New York: Prentice-Hall Inc., 1946.)

in that environment. Protoplasm (organic compounds) appears to have a generalized capacity to do that, a capacity which is differentiated as the specialized sense receptors are developed. The skin of a wide variety of animals has been found to respond to flashes of light with sharp discharges of electric current.[14] Skin, bone, hair, and other human tissues exhibit a piezoelectric effect, i.e., they generate electric charges when put under pressure in certain directions.[15] Thus organisms are "put in touch" with their worlds and messages are transmitted through them to memory and processing centers for appropriate action. Lucretius long ago recognized that this "touching" of common elements in the environment and the body is necessary to any kind of knowledge of the world.[16] It is in this primitive affective prehension of the world that all organismic knowledge begins. This sensitivity of members of species evolved in a favorable environment, so that the Gestalts, reflexes, and instinctual responses that exist in them today are the accumulated results of prolonged adjustments. The tendency to form inductive generalizations, patterning past events and projecting the pattern into the future, and the tendency to engage in deductive reasoning, are habits that have been acquired as organisms have interacted with their environments over a period of 3 billon years or more. Minding is an evolved habit of bodily adjustment flexibly adapted to the requirements of the environment.

In the higher vertebrates, affect serves an important function in the orientation of the organism. It stands between the stimulus-object and the response and thus mediates between them: it signifies the import of the object and elicits response. It prepares the organism, in Cannon's words, for fight or flight.[17] It may also, in thinking animals, prepare a mindful response, becoming a sign itself, or causing the organism to invoke signs as a way of dealing with an environment whose presence has been conveyed in the way most immediately possible, namely, through affect or feeling.

The differences between living matter and non-living matter are quantitative and these together effect a qualitative difference. The

---

[14]By Richard A. Cone and Heywood Eric Becker, as reported in *The New York Times,* December 15, 1966.

[15]As discovered by Morris Shamos and Leroy S. Lavine, and reported in *The New York Times,* February 10, 1967.

[16]*De Rerum Natura,* Book IV.

[17]See also Charles Darwin, *The Expression of the Emotions in Man and Animals.* (London: Watts & Co., 1934.)

range and variety of stimuli to which organisms are sensitive and responsive are considerably wider than they are for non-living matter. Protoplasm is highly labile, highly responsive to relatively weak stimuli. It is plastic and deformable. It is probable, writes a biologist, "that all the cases normally regarded as involving true irritability involve the release of energy in amounts disproportionately large compared with the energy of the stimulus."[18] Living matter is matter that is greatly impressed by—vividly feels—its environment. It has a tendency to over-respond to that environment. This surplusage of responsive power is, in the case of man, delayed and channelled off into deliberation.

Living matter has a certain litheness and clever elusiveness about it. It is resilient. It resists the destruction of outside influences, like non-living matter; but unlike the latter it does so by absorbing their influences and bouncing back. Correspondingly, the secret of the success of the minded body is obedience to the law, "He who fights and runs away may live to fight another day." Bodily minding succeeds by detaching itself from battle and considering a strategic employment of its forces. Minding is moving and being moved; it is capacity to prepare for what lies beyond the present or presented; it is a taking account of that larger world by choosing among possible responses or innovating new ones. "Choice" at this level is definable as a certain relatively low probability of a given response to a given stimulus. For example, the probability that an amoeba will respond in a given way (advancing or withdrawing) to an iron wire is lower than the probability that a wire will respond in a given way to a magnet. Now minding is an extension of this capacity of choice. It is more than an extension. It introduces the elements of self-produced symbols. It is living process guided by symbolic processes.

Now matter is not just a resistive power that stands in the way of living process guided by symbols. There is a continuity between material process and mental process, whereby material that is non-minded is transmitted—"communicated" in the broad sense—to what is minded. How is this possible? A materialist will refer to the transmission of energy; an idealist, to the transmission of form or idea; a vitalist, to the vector of a feeling (Whitehead). But all agree that

---

[18]George Evelyn Hutchinson, "Biology II. The Living Organism as a Natural Body," *Encyclopedia Britannica*, Vol. 3. (Chicago, London, Toronto: Encyclopedia Britannica, Inc., William Benton, Publisher, 1959), p. 609.

what are called mind and matter have something in common in this process. A mind attending to a snowstorm is surely different from a mind attending to the hot sands of a desert. The content, the data, are different; and they are internal to the mind. This difference is due to the fact that minding involves a sensitive material medium that records in its own way the effects of material bodies and forces acting on it in the mode of qualities, forms, and relations. The assertion by Lucretius (and before him, Democritus) that mind is very fine matter anticipates what we now know of the material basis for the acuity and rapidity of the action of the nervous system.[19] Minding action has in it the capacity to pick up in a subtle way some of the characteristics of the material world. Minding as a material force is in the world of other material forces, some minded and some not; and they likewise interpenetrate minding.

How does matter get across to mind? This traditional way of putting the issue falsifies the facts, prevents a correct answer, and betrays man's egoistic belief that exaggerates his mind's differences from external matter. Minding occurs in the place where life takes place and is implicated in events both living and non-living. Conversely, non-mental matter enters into organizations of minding activity, providing the materials of thinking, as Locke said.[20] James' view that a thing is material stuff in one sequence of events, mental stuff in another, and thus can be counted "twice over"[21], while suggestive, misleadingly separated minding from physical (external) and organic (internal) processes. Berkeley's question of how body can act on mind becomes answerable, not in Berkeley's terms, but because minding is a way of nature's events, in and among other ways of nature, and because every minding is a functioning of the individual body and is thus continuous with the other bodies, minded or not, which it affects and is affected by.

Given this prior continuity of minding matter with not-so-minding matter, how does mind make that kind of connection with matter which we call "minding" or "knowing"? We are immediately aware of "the flux of our sensations."[22] If an allegedly existent thing has not been or cannot be particularized or materialized itself to us in

---

[19]*De Rerum Natura*, Book III.

[20]*An Essay Concerning Human Understanding*, Book II, 1, 2.

[21]Lecture I, "Does Consciousness Exist?" *Essays in Radical Empiricism*. (New York: Longmans, Green and Co., 1912.)

[22]*Pragmatism*. (New York: Longmans, Green and Co., 1907) p. 244.

this way, we may be skeptical of its existence. Phenomenologically, matter is known as structured percepts—percepts, as Berkeley observed, of primary and secondary qualities. But matter is not just percepts; it is what can or does make itself felt: it is the external source of the perceptually given element in experience. A material thing is what impresses us; it is something which, like a person who impresses us, has "character" and "substance." Moreover, what impresses us from the material world is not limited to that which leaves an effect in the modes of the refined sensa—colors, sounds, odors, etc. Science demonstrates that a vast number and variety of impulses are continuously pouring into the human organism and that, while not recorded as refined sensa, they affect minding. Overexposure to sun's rays can produce unconsciousness, and certain kinds of food and radiation affect order and disorder in thinking. We have all had insights into people and situations which contained more information than that given to us through our eyes and ears. The body has a generalized power to feel the causal forces of the material environment.

External matter does not just object to our mental intentions. It resists our efforts to come at it, but it also offers something in the bargain. It presents us with data. But a datum is ambiguous. It is a gift but it is also a demand. What is demanded is consideration, decision, action. It is not enough for an organism to stand there and feel; it must do something. It is driven by its own internal demands— hunger, bodily safety, and association with those of its kind. Thus external matter is not only matter of fact; it is matter for consideration. Akin to the matter out of which our own minded bodies are made, it is beneficent and supportive: we breathe its air, drink its water, eat its food, enjoy its colors and forms and sounds. But environing matter is also hostile: it threatens, deprives, sickens, and kills. Hence our own minded bodies must exert their material force against external bodies; they must choose between good and evil, acting so that both they and their seed may live.

II

Minding activity is valuation. To mind is to regard, to pay attention, to be concerned, to care, to take care. It is to express preference—and to do so by means of signs or meanings in action. To be mindful is to be alertly observant, to perceive with care, to sense and respond in a polarized way to things, to divide what is relevant from what is irrelevant with respect to what is perceived, prospectively, as value. Thinking that proceeds without some sense of importance is a routine chore, and easily falls into errors of perception and of reasoning. It ceases to that extent to be thinking. The presumed thinker ceases to be mindful of his business. He does not attend because he does not tend values; he is not careful because he does not care.

To mind is to engage in symbolic activity that aims at obtaining, making secure, or increasing what is considered of value. Minding is emphasizing and clarifying valuings. Just as there would be no point in mind if there were nothing for it to serve, so the quest for values which seems to go on throughout nature would tend to be canalized and blind to the extent that there are no sign-processes to bring them to light and direct them to their proper ends.

Minding can facilitate responses of valuing because of its projective and prospective character. To mind something is to take it as a sign of something else, and to produce and connect signs in certain determinate ways. An organism with a limited degree of mind responds with a limited degree of freedom to the influences that affect it. It tends, moreover, not to go out and recreate its environment; it remains more or less subject to it. But a minding response foresees a variety of possibilities as following from what it is immediately confronted by. Moreover, it helps to create those possibilities by reconstituting its environment. To mind a thing is to care about it, not merely for itself but for its consequences. These consequences are foreseen in imagination. In the case of man they are indicated by self-produced signs, stimulated by the store of previously symbolized experiences relevant to the immediate. To minded response, a thing is valuable or not valuable—*capable* of producing this or that consequence which is then appraised. A thing or a piece of matter, therefore, is not for mind something simply and obviously given. It is the immediate percepts *plus* all the possible percepts, as well as all the possible values which these, in the context of action toward and upon their events, are conceived to have or confer. To mind a thing is to consider what potential properties of it *could* be actualized and to judge in anticipation which of those *could* be satisfactory and which not.

Valuation involves a directional or purposive aspect of mind. To think is to have one's mind *on* a goal or outcome. Minding is envisaging what is indicated as capable of having value. It is having something in mind—an image, in imagination—that pertains to what is not now physically present. What is in mind stands as a symbol of what is absent, disposing present behavior to that as what is valued and chosen, presenting itself as a candidate for such valuation and choice.

Minding is purposeful; the organism in which it arises is a valuing creature. The creature values; it is needful and incomplete. It cannot supply its own energy. Its material system is open and dynamic. It must obtain that energy from outside itself. Unless it does it will cease to be. It chooses to be—which is to say, it casts about for sources of energy. To say that an organism has a purpose is to say it does what increases its chances of obtaining energy and of surviving. One may state this less operationally and say that it has a will to live. The organism, in short, is moved by an impulse to live and fulfill itself. Mind is instrumental to the purpose of life. When it does not act so, whatever else it may do, we rightly call it undeveloped, arrested, deranged, or moribund.

The organism—biological processes, if we may speak more accurately—is that place[23] in nature that is peculiarly subject to influences but it also capable of subjecting the environment to the requirements of its needs. It stands between one environment and another. It is not a substance; it is a transition. It mediates between two worlds —the past and the future, the settled and the to-be-settled, the valued and the valuable. Organic matter has inherent in it this minding capacity. It is selective and valuational process. It does not just take things as they come. It strains and transforms and bends them to its own naturings and completions. As a means to certain completions, it acts to secure certain states of things and shuns others.

The minding organism is continuously reconstitutive of its own state through a reconstitution of its material world. Ideas (things as signified) emerge at those points where the drives of the organism intersect the settled and brute things of nature and become unsettled. They are reflexes of blocked action. Reflection, carried on in symbols, is the world of events reflecting itself and reflecting upon itself. An idea is a proposal for action, a means of possible extrication. It is the product of mind in focus. It is a way of initiating reconstitution. Minding in its total process is a way for living process,

---

[23]"Hence the Platonists are justified in calling the soul the place of forms . . ." Aristotle, *Psychology* (*De Anima*), trans. Philip Wheelwright. (New York: The Odyssey Press, 1951) p. 142.

using symbols, to carry on certain modes of activity so that things are related one to another and other things are gotten around in order to get at other things. It is a way of coping with obstacles to survival, of subjecting objects to control. The final object of thinking is a consummatory relation with what living process goes for. It is the upsurge of external matter against organismic purpose that evokes ideas. And it is external matter that ideas, intervening in habitual living process, must ultimately come to terms with and be about.

"Matter" in the objective sense refers to what stands over against some other activity—some *Gegenstand* that resists and objects to what is other than itself. Matter has or is what the physicists used to call substance and now term mass (inertia or energy). It has or is the capacity to do work. It is a stuff that underlies, like a substratum, the play of qualities and forms. Moreover, it does not just stubbornly resist what comes in the way of it. It exerts a causal efficacy itself. It is what does or can make a difference to what is in its environment. To know that a thing makes a difference is to know that "it matters."

With this concept of matter, men have easily passed over to the view that matter is what *is*. It comprises part or all of the *real* world. Matter, whatever it may be, has for some answered to that "external permanency"[24] which Peirce took to be the object of science and the only way of settling disputes in a scientific way. And if the criterion of the real is what is independent of our thinking,[25] as Peirce also held, matter would seem to fill the bill. A material thing objects both to other material things and to our own subjective purposes. It is something materialized or materializing; it is a particular formation of energy, either a thing or a process; and its materiality is its specific and measurable impact.

If minding is a means to the fulfillment of living need, be it biological or psycho-biological, then external matter is a means of mind. As what is passive and potential (hylê) it is something to be molded by the minding body's activity on things and events. As providing us with, or stimulating for us, the stuff to be formed by mind, external matter is for mind-as-symbolic the percepts of experience, the contents of propositions, the stuff to be manipulated and organized by minded organisms aiming at impressing their ideal forms on material things. External matter supplies us with the

---

24*Collected Papers of Charles Sanders Peirce*, V. 384. Edited by Charles Hartshorne and Paul Weiss. (Cambridge: Harvard University Press, 1931-1935.)
25*Ibid.*, 405.

materials of thinking; experience is this materialization in us. On the other side, such matter is the comparatively plastic medium that lends itself to the impress of mental purpose. It is responsive to the treatment of minding activity. Descartes thought it solely the means of mind. Aristotle conceived of it as passive and indeterminate. Taken literally, this is mistaken; if Aristotle had known more of experimental physics, he might have changed his mind about matter. Nevertheless, external matter does yield itself to some degree to the determination of the minding force of our bodies. The artifacts of human culture, and all the processes by which the things and landscapes of nature are transformed to suit our human purposes, are evidences of this.

For minding is a material force in its own right. It stands over against other material things and makes its own demands. It does its own work and it makes a difference in the world of material things in which it moves. Minding as a material force has fully as much "external permanency" as any stone or star; it is there at work whether or not it or another minding process becomes aware of itself. It was only when men like Marx and Engels began to understand this that scientists were on their way to a science of human history. When minding is taken to be subjective, then all history becomes an illusion or a mystery explainable in some non-material, i.e., fantastic way.

Objective matter is what minding is about. It is the *terminus ad quem* of mind. We have got to think *about* matter if we want to do something *with* it. Matters of fact, factual matters, must occupy us as ends of inquiry if they are to be transformed into useful means. It has been said that we do not think about matter but instead think about ideas. This is a half-truth. Only in special and comparatively rare pursuits do we think exclusively *about* ideas—as in logic or grammar, where our subject matter is comprised by the ideas used by ordinary men in reasoning or knowing processes. Commonly, deduction has its final reference and testing point in the context of existential inquiry where it has its origin. In any case, we think *with* ideas; ideas are the mode in which our thinking occurs. What the thinking is all *about* are the conditions, the brute facts and frictions, that occasion inquiry and in terms of which inquiry must be terminated.

What a thinking being ordinarily has in mind is not merely the reference of its sign-behavior but also what "would permit the completion of the response-sequences to which an interpreter is disposed because of a sign."[26] It has in mind, in short, *what* will satisfy

---

[26]*Signs, Language and Behavior*, p. 347.

its impulses. This is something material. When a man wants to write, and finds that his pencil is broken, what his whole being gropes toward and consequently what he thinks about (if he thinks) is that set of presentations that constitute his difficulty and obstruction, as well as that set of presentations that would comprise the restoration of his interrupted activity. These presentations, to be and to continue to be of concern to him, must converge toward what he has in mind as a final end, namely, a state of things in which his want is achieved. To that end, however, he does not manipulate his presentations; he manipulates the things in virtue of which presentations arise and are related in determinate ways. To guide his manipulations, he employs inferences that are intended to carry him from one presentation to another by way of action on things. The material object is what *does* make a difference to our experience and the content of our inference. It is also what *could* make a difference to experience. The difference that material things make to minding are of two kinds: those that evoke sign-behavior and problem-solving response, and those that satisfy, complete, and terminate that. What the minding inquiry of the body aims at, therefore, is not merely satisfaction of interest but a state of material things in and by which satisfaction is secured. It aims at a satisfactory matter. Unless the minding body is thus about the way things are, it is judged as demented. This judgment is not just reflective of a society's norms of sanity. It is reflective of the fact that mind is an instrument of survival and its proper function is to take account of things, their properties, and their relations, and to adjust the organism to them in accordance with its demand for value.

III

As purposive, a minding organism is also innovative activity. The more irritable, mobile, and freed from habit it is, the more it must rely on innovation. It must innovate or die.

Minding is an instrument of permanent and changing features. It retains a constancy of form through a variety of operations. It is a tool that is involved in the production and improvement of all tools, including itself. It is this in virtue of its power of innovation. It is an abiding power of change, changed for the better or for the worse in this regard by its own operations. Minding innovates by insight. What it innovates is ideas—dispositions to respond as induced by self-produced signs. Insofar as such dispositions are colored by emotional preference and purpose as they always are, they are ideals that hold forth the lure of possibility. Ideals thus emerge in material process. As Marx said, "the ideal is nothing else than the material world reflected by the human mind, and translated into forms of thought."[27] Such reflection is not passive, however. It transforms the raw data of the world by the force of decision, purpose, and action.[28] Ideals are efficacious in imagination until they prove or do not prove themselves effective in satisfying the demands that initiated them, or until interest flags or some other interest supersedes them in their claim upon attention and action.

We could not mind new ideas, new meanings could not emerge, unless our minding processes were flexible. To flex sensitively with the impact of conditions is a prime characteristic of minding matter; to reflect is no less characteristic. Minding processes move with their situation; else they have failed to function, or have been petrified in habit. To have a change of mind is the most natural function of minding. But mind could not change, it could not shift its focus and pace, unless it possessed some relatively abiding identity and direction. A mind that sticks with its purposes we regard as sound and genuine. But a mind that flits about is suspect. It is not composed, it is not of one mind, it has lost force and character.

What distinguishes minding matter from relatively mindless matter is just this level of flexibility of mental behavior. The permanence of mind is the deposit of experience. It is the system of meanings (or symbolic dispositions) which have been accumulated through learning, which are implicit in every act, which are continuous, and which form the rich and unconscious background of potential responses that any given conscious act draws on. This permanence of individual mind is conferred because the meanings of social institutions are cumulative, continuous, and more or less permanent.

Sensitive, responsive, and reflective toward changes in the environment, minding process also is the pivot and clearing house for such processes. It stands *between* them and some selected outcome (cf. "intelligence," "intellect"). It stands between nature as actual, efficacious, and settled, and nature as prospective, ideal, and to-be-settled. It thus guides and directs the changes of nature to its own selected ends. Were it merely changeable, it would soon go to pieces

---

[27]*Capital.* Vol. I. Afterword to the Second German Edition. (Moscow: Foreign Languages Publishing House, n.d.) p. 19.

[28]Cf. V. I. Lenin, *Philosophical Notebooks*, Vol. 38 of *Collected Works.* Moscow: Foreign Languages Publishing House, 1961, p. 212: "Man's consciousness not only reflects the objective world, but creates it."

in a riot of responsiveness. Were it merely permanent, it would no more be affected by external change than would a rock. But it moves through changes, rejecting or assimilating them and transforming them to its own uses. Minding is in the midst of plural nature. To be natured (natura) is to be born, to happen, to become an event. And minding is a process by which certain (symbolic) events intervene in other events or births and bring them to a selected predetermined, or purposed eventuation. As such, minding is novelty-producing.

In contrast to non-mental matter, minded matter is a way of behavior more effective in controlling the future. Things follow from one another, according to laws man can mind and discover; but the things themselves do not follow their course at one remove as minding does. Minding possesses a repetitive, imitative, and economic power: we remember that the bodies we have seen do fall. But because minding is remembering brought up into symbolization, it is not only seeing but also foreseeing, and hence supervenes upon unmindful events and exercises domination over them. But minding does not supervene upon things as something alien or utterly disparate. Rather it can be about celestial bodies, crystals, viruses, plants, and animals because, though different, it is continuous with them. The immediate points of contact it has with bodies are its own bodily receptors. The minding-body is one among innumerable bodies. It has grown up out of a common matrix with them. It is sensitive to their impact, which generates a continuing if fading train of qualities and forms. These are the external material world making their mark in material mental process. Minding in its fullness organizes them selectively and symbolically, and employs symbols for the cultivation of its own free artistic, theoretical, or practical activity. Minding transcends its world because it is first immanent in nature; its transcendence consists in a certain free play and control of forces focused in the body and, to less degree, in other bodies lending themselves to manipulation. Minding nature is innovative because it is first capable of following the habits of nature's events; its free, innovative activity is itself a habit for getting around among and controlling the other habits of nature. Minding is matter transmuted into an open system of system-making: its openness is the sensitivity of the biological organism that transforms physical cause into mental data; its tool is symbols; and the systems it creates are those of the arts, sciences, philosophies, religions, and other modes of human expression.

Nature prior to minding nature exists in its own right, but the only way in which mind can know nature is its way of operating in and on the things of material nature. If and as objective matter appears regular and stable, that is in part because minding finds or by experiment fixes those features and utilizes them in its journey toward securing its ends. If matter appears contingent and variable, that is in part because minding is capable of taking different viewpoints toward material things; because it can fluctuate in response to the flux of nature; and because, in its pursuit of a given fixed end through inquiry, it may decide to use as a means some thing or property or relation that was, in another context, an intrinsic part of its fixed end. Minding varies in its attitudes toward and operations on nature precisely because it is capable of adopting fixed ends or goals. And it seeks the unchanging in nature precisely because it needs to count on what is reliable in the midst of its changeable and changing goals.

Minding as innovative is a combining and connecting process. Once minding as a permanent and cumulative funding of meanings makes impact upon the obstructions of matter, and recoils, the only possible responses are those of brute habit, unstructured confusion, or innovation. The former—the blind habit and the confusion we see in mental illness—are unthinking responses. But innovation which then moves on to introduce a new strategy of acting into the situation is characteristically mental. The new strategy involves a reorganization of behavior and of the world. To think is to pause for reflections, to stop and think. It is to take account, to count, to calculate, to add things up until they make sense—i.e., to discriminate and relate sign, signified, and signifier so as to produce meaning. To think is to "see" the situation, perceptually and conceptually, in a new way. And it is to plan a new way of behaving and of having things, and to test that out. Insight, deductive planning, and experiment are the integrative side of mental activity.

Innovating and connecting processes constitute the creativity of thought. A new idea is a new set of sign-connections or meanings; a new disposition, a change of mind. Deductive elaboration of such meanings is a way of explicating the connections of signs one with another and with their referents in things and the relations of things. Such elaboration may uncover additional novelties. A new idea is a proposal of a new connection among material things. It is tentative and provisional. To be a vital element in thought it must assume the form of a plan of action and go over into action in the form of new and experimental connections. New insight, symbolic elaboration, and experiment do not exist full-blown and antecedent to inquiry. They evolve into life. Mind, in Aristotle's expression, "has no actual existence before it thinks."[29] Inquiring is questing; thinking is creative movement. It is the establishing of new connections that ultimately stand or fall as they prove or do not prove viable in the material economy of the creature and its society.

Mental innovation can have relevance and effect because it grows out of experience. Experience constitutes a permanent substratum out of which ideas emerge and in which they are tested. Just as the seeds of plants will germinate only under special conditions of light, temperature, moisture, etc., because their germinating capacity has evolved and proved adaptable to similar conditions *in the past;* so ideas that emerge in present minding become useful in adaptation to the extent that they are drawn from similar conditions in the past. (Operationally, "the past" means a usable similarity of the environment from time to time.) "Learning," says a psychologist, "is a change of behavior (increase of response strength) as a function of experience and in the direction of a predetermined criterion."[30] With human beings, learning is vastly increased by their power of imagery and symbols. Imagery is a retained impress of things experienced in the past. It represents and preserves the quality of the past; it is an element for meaning to work over and connect, a fragment lifted out of past contact with things to be used in guiding future contacts. It becomes fixated by abstract images, ideas, and the enhancing effect of symbols. Memory is thus a storing and abstracting process which makes available, to minding as anticipatory and creative, the record of past experience. The latter can innovate and can be freed from the constriction of its problem to the degree that its repertoire of plans and choices, carried over from the past, is wide and varied. To innovate, to have something in mind as a purpose, is to have it in mind, at least in part, as memory. This is the basis for the Platonic doctrine of mind as reminiscence.

The continuity of minding, therefore, lies in this bridging power. Its growth is a twofold affair of remembering or holding constant accumulated meanings and a process of creating new meanings modi-

---

[29]*Psychology.*

[30]James Earle Deese, *The Psychology of Learning.* (New York: McGraw-Hill Co., 1952) p. 351.

fying the accumulated fund. All organisms are open systems,[31] and what we call minding in man is simply an extension of this openness and dynamic equilibrium. A moribund mind neither remembers nor innovates very well. On the other hand, a lively mind neither remembers everything it experiences, nor does it become victimized, like the pallid intellectual, by an excess of ideas and choices. Its fund of remembered meanings undergoes (within limits) changes proportionate to the demands made by immediate material situations.

Like metabolizing, minding assimilates selectively, breaks down and then builds up anew the materials of its environment. It analyzes and synthesizes. It internalizes a portion of the environment. It externalizes these changes, reorganizing a wider area of nature after the patterns that have evolved in its own small area of solitude. In individual cases, this pattern can be identified by the recurrence of certain meanings or dispositions. But these are slowly changing, just as are the protein materials of that metabolizing we falsely identify with a substantival piece of protoplasm.[32] A mind is what it is known as, namely, meanings in operation—responses to substitute stimuli some of which are producible by the respondent. Potential minding is potential disposition to such response. The biological organism of *Homo sapiens* possesses this capacity or tendency. Mind *grows* into being as symbolic response emerges and becomes habitual. Thus, as we can know living matter only by observing certain responses, so we can know mind only by observing certain responses, and, from their habitual character, by predicting them.

Inferring, as Dewey has observed, is a carrying across, a transition movement.[33] A child near the fire feels its warmth and infers a future burning. A young Galileo observes the moving of the cathedral pendulum, and infers a law. A philosopher observes the world and infers an ultimate principle, a world hypothesis. Minding involves the anticipating of something to be done. It is the place where the future or possibility comes into being, and affects present activity by calling on it to move in a proposed direction. All speculative activity, for all its freedom, must ultimately come to this empirical pay-off, or become, in Bacon's language, "idle" and "fantastic."

---

[31]Ludwig von Bertalanffy, "The Theory of Open Systems in Physics and Biology," *Science*, III, 23 (1950).

[32]Garrett Hardin, "Meaninglessness of the Word Protoplasm," *The Scientific Monthly*, 82, 3 (1956).

[33]*How We Think*. Revised edition. (New York: D. C. Heath and Co., 1933.)

The present as human is nothing distinctive unless it is a presentiment of what is to come. Like other creatures with eyes, man sees what is before him; but he also foresees. Man as minding has envisagement and prevision. Minding is a special and powerful way of securing that provisional activity that is so commonly evidenced in the activities of living things.[34] In minding we see what does not meet the eye; this seeing or foreseeing is "the mind's eye," or symbolizing behavior. This is a special kind of response to stimulus, a delayed, deflected response. Interrupted in the pursuit of its interests, the human creature retreats and begins to mind its business, to control its inferences. It surveys its situation. It becomes a witness in the Hindu and classical philosophical sense. It speculates or sees. But such seeing cannot be indefinitely its own end, if the person is to survive. It must become fore-seeing. It must penetrate into the problematic obstructions and conditions. It must provide a map, a plan, a proposed itinerary through and forward among material events. Minding as living process is a peculiar reconstituting activity. It recoils from blockage, shock, lesion, and rupture—and goes on. Its characteristic feature is finding a new way. Its way is to find new ways by means of meanings that probe the future. Its habit is the habit of symbolic creativity. If some men have powers of clairvoyance and prevision they illustrate and do not refute the general principle of mind.

Minding as innovative and integrative is social. "Social" for human beings means "associated symbolically." A symbol is a self-produced sign used inter-subjectively. Thus, as Mead so carefully showed, mind and society arise together, through the use of the significant symbol.[35] Minding is not something substantial behind its meanings; it *is* those meanings in use or in disposition to usage. It is as public as any natural activity, and in principle it can be found out by appropriate operations and observations as the hardness of a diamond can be found out by scratching and looking. Gilbert Ryle,[36] among others, has recently called our attention to this public character of mind. Precisely as the meanings that comprise a mind are open to observation they are social. To be public and social, meanings must

---

[34]Frederick J. E. Woodbridge, *Nature and Mind*. (New York: Columbia University Press, 1937.)

[35]*Mind, Self and Society*. Edited by Charles W. Morris. (Chicago: University of Chicago Press, 1934.)

[36]*The Concept of Mind*. (New York: Barnes and Noble, Inc., 1949.)

be enacted and embodied—in a word, materialized. As I speak my mind, my speaking is my minding; but it is not only I who hear with meaning. The symbol evokes a communal response of meaning. If I wish to make my mind or that meaning clear, I must, as Peirce said,[37] act it out, or have it acted out, or speak it out, so that what I inwardly intend can be observed or vividly imagined (imported into disposition) by myself and others. When Peirce defined clarity in this way, he implicitly meant something public and social. A "clear mind," in the full sense of mind, is grammatically tautologous. Non-mental matter as such can never be social in this sense; it can never express or body forth a meaning; it simply *is*.

As mind is social, truth is social. I cannot know what is in or on my mind, and certainly no one else can, unless that mental content is expressed. For to "know" anything, be it matter or mind, is to be aware of things and to shape them into meaningful connections. Merely to assert that I know, or have my mind on something in a way that is faithful to it, i.e., in a way that claims truth, and not to *show* or *demonstrate* that I do, is a contradiction for others and a deceit to myself. For a meaning to be tested for its truth-value it must first be expressed in material acts and made public. Full expression, moreover, is not just a verbal act; it carries out bodily what the verbal expression indicates. Truth cannot be just verbal agreement or a consensus that pertains to the meanings of certain terms and their rules of transformation. It is instead the result of the collaborative performances of a plurality of minding bodily activities, corroborating one another. This is the way in which reference is made to material things. Unless symbols or minds ultimately move into this mode of reference, they remain subjective and any claims to truth they make are unfounded.

In a conversation my minding or symbolic expression initiates sign-vehicles (usually sounds) but these take on meaning only as they become meaningful or symbolic elements in the minding activity of myself and another. He in turn initiates what sets off meaning in my experience and becomes part of my minding. In this way minding in us becomes something more than just individual activity, though it is carried through individuals and transforms them. Minding becomes informed by a creativity working through the mutual stimu-

---

[37]"How to Make Our Ideas Clear," *Collected Papers of Charles Sanders Peirce*, V. 388-410.

lating and responding of individuals through symbols.[38] In such association minding becomes an inter-individual system of activities, an "open system," a system of emerging and integrating meanings. The old claim of a super-individual, group, or absolute and all-embracing mind was destined to remain unsupported so long as "mind" was thought of in substantival terms. But when mind is seen as symbolic process involved in sociality and interaction with other such processes, it becomes intersubjective, objective, and social in a way that preserves the autonomy and novelty of individual minding but also accounts for its relatedness to other mindings and certain of its transformations. The individual mind depends on a constantly varied input of sensory stimuli; lacking this, it begins to deteriorate.[39]

Finally, as we have observed, the minding human being is an ecological creature and its survival and fulfillment depend on continuous and mutually reinforcing transactions with its environment of living creatures and physical things. During the relatively recent period of agrarian and urban life (15,000 years) the human species has realized climactically some of the potentials of its biological equipment. By reason of its techniques of creating an expanding food supply and expanding population, it has become a dominant species on earth. By reason of its energetic and systematic knowledge of its natural world, it has constructed industrial and technological civilizations, unlocked the power within the atom, and probed into the molecules that determine life. These triumphs of minded man have produced also the misery of hunger, illness, and meaninglessness among half or two-thirds of mankind and the threat of nuclear, chemical, and bacterial destruction of all life on the planet.

Something then is wrong with man's minding activity—wrong with his knowledge and wrong with the way it is used. First, the creation and distribution of food and other life-necessities have consequences for societies and nature; unplanned, unmindful, they produce a ruined nature and congested swarms of people which become breeding grounds of disease, poverty, alienation, violence, and other pathologies. Physical and biological knowledge are not sufficient. Man lives in a planetary environment, and to be adequate his knowledge must be ecological. Second, knowledge in most contemporary societies is

---

[38]Henry N. Wieman, *The Source of Human Good.* (Chicago: University of Chicago Press, 1946.)

[39]D. O. Hebb, "The Problem of Consciousness and Introspection."

controlled and applied by a military-industrial-political-scientific elite using it primarily to maintain its own power rather than to benefit all members of society. That elite at the top of a class structure in feudal and capitalist societies manipulates its knowledge to control both the basic economic processes and ideas of the men in the society. (The emergence of elites in socialist societies is a problem of a different order.) Such an elite requires exploitation, poverty, pollution, and war to perpetuate itself. Its science is turned to its own ends. It can use knowledge to send men to the moon, since that secures profits for itself and circuses for the people. But it cannot understand or apply the ecological knowledge that would transform a class society into a classless society, an elite world into a people's world, a world of exploitive and selfish knowledge into a world of liberating and cooperative knowledge, a society of destruction into a society of creation.

The force to achieve this transformation belongs to the masses of people who have the most to gain by it. It belongs to the people disposed to a social and ecological perspective in dealing with man's problems. That force is the force of men themselves, the force of materialized and socialized minds thinking and acting together to achieve mankind's survival and fulfillment.

Part III

SOCIAL PHILOSOPHY

THE CRISIS OF THE 1890'S AND THE SHAPING
OF TWENTIETH CENTURY AMERICA

Robert B. Carson

ALTHOUGH the afterglow of later achievements has tended to obscure the fact, the United States entered the twentieth century with the spectre of chaos hanging heavy over the land. The closing decades of the nineteenth century had been marked by a series of social and economic ruptures which to many contemporary observers seemed to augur not only the demise of the old political and social system, but the ultimate collapse of order in general. The threats seemed to come from all sides. For one thing, the values men lived by for so very long seemed not to work in an increasingly complex urbanized and industrialized society. New consumer products, new communications media, new types of jobs and working conditions, new immigrants, and wild, new ideologies dizzied the head of anyone steeped in the traditions of an earlier, predominantly agrarian, way of life. While these external threats generated an atmosphere pregnant with anxiety and concern, the real threat to order lay within the system itself, in its obvious inability to function well.

The country's economic performance, despite the vaunted growth of new industries, such as railroads, steel, and oil, and the steady westward expansion of the nation, was simply quite disappointing. Between the close of the Civil War and the end of the century, the economy had suffered five major depressions and during 23 of these 35 years, the United States found itself in straitened economic conditions.[1] Successively, the economic crises appeared to be deeper and more protracted as the economy seemed to show an ever-accelerating tendency toward stagnation.

---

[1]Herman E. Krooss, *American Economic Development* (Engelwood Cliffs: Prentice-Hall, 1966), p. 11.

By the 1890's, the incipient decline had begun to produce great rifts in the social system and could no longer be dismissed as the familiar boom-bust-boom rhythm of a capitalist economy. In the face of the rising crisis, the traditional philosophy of economic and political liberalism seemed wholly incapable of dealing with the growing disenchantment with American institutions and values.

In agricultural areas, the brushfires of populism were raging out of control, producing a radicalism heretofore unique among American farmers. Farmers were urged to "raise more hell and less corn," to fight against the railroad, farm machinery, and marketing combinations which seemed to be the cause of their depressed prices and high costs.[2] In industry, as wages tumbled and short work-weeks grew more common in the 1890's, the labor movement, which had been characterized by a growing radicalism and commitment to industrial violence since the 1870's, adopted increasingly militant postures. Throughout 1892, 1893, and 1894, a rash of violent strikes staggered the economy. At Homestead, Pennsylvania, Cour d'Alene, Idaho, Buffalo, New York, and Pullman, Illinois, it was necessary to call in military units to put down the strikes, and, successively, the strikes seemed to be worsening.[3] Whereas, only 8,000 Pennsylvania National Guardsmen had been needed to force the Carnegie steelworkers back to their jobs at Homestead, the implied power of the entire United States Army had to be employed by President Cleveland in 1894 to break the back of the Pullman strike and boycott. Meanwhile, by early spring of 1894, an army of unemployed men were marching from a number of points about the country toward Washington to demand that the government create a $500 million program of public works to provide jobs.[4] Although Coxey's army disintegrated rather timidly at the Capitol steps when its leaders were arrested for trespassing, the spectacle of Washington under siege was not to be passed off lightly.

The loss of faith in the American economic system was by no means limited to laboring groups. As business failures mounted after the panic of July, 1893, the normal optimism of the business community,

---

[2]See J. D. Hicks, *The Populist Revolt* (New York: 1931).

[3]Ray Ginger, *Eugene V. Debs: A Biography* (New York: Collier, 1962), pp. 101-167.

[4]See D. L. Murray, *Coxey's Army* (New York: 1929); and Thorstein Veblen, "Army of Commonweel," *Journal of Political Economy*, Vol. II (1894), pp. 456-71.

which usually prevailed even in the worst of economic conditions, began to vanish. A few men, like J. P. Morgan, who was appalled by the fact that more than one-third of the American railroad network lay in bankruptcy and that steel and other industries were similarly threatened, talked openly about the need to reform American economic institutions so that they were no longer vulnerable to the economic fluctuations associated with a *laissez faire* market organization.[5] To this end, Morgan set the pattern for other business and financial leaders and for other industries by attempting to establish a banker hegemony over American railroads which would have replaced the usual excessive competition and periodic instability with central direction and control.

Confused and incredulous at the wave of events, the dyspeptic Henry Adams managed to be relevant for once and probably spoke for many of his countrymen, both intellectuals and ordinary people, as he observed to a friend in 1894:

> "We don't know what is the matter with us, yet we all admit that we have had a terrific shock of some sort. We see no reason at all for assuming that the causes, whatever they are, which have brought about the prostration, have ceased, or will cease, to act. On the contrary, as far as we can see, if anything is radically wrong, it must grow worse, for it must be in our system itself, and at the bottom of all modern society. If we are diseased, so is all the world. Everyone is discussing, disputing, doubting, economizing, going into bankruptcy, waiting for the storm to pass, but no sign of agreement is visible as to what has upset us, or whether we can cure the disease. That the trouble is quite different from any previous experience, pretty much everyone seems to admit; but nobody diagnoses it. . . . We want to know what is wrong with the world that it should suddenly go to smash without visible cause or possible advantage. Here is this young, rich continent, capable of supporting three times its population with ease, we have had a million men out of employment for nearly a year, and the situation growing worse rather than better."[6]

The depiction of anxiety and despair in American life became the persistent theme in American literature after the early nineties. A

---

[5]Frederick Lewis Allen, *The Great Pierpont Morgan* (New York: Bantam, 1956), pp. 62-76.

[6]Letters of Henry Adams to Charles Gaskell, April 28, 1894, in W. C. Ford, ed., *Letters of Henry Adams, 1892-1918* (Boston: Houghton Mifflin, 1938), pp. 46-47.

generation of writers, from Howells and Mark Twain to Dos Passos and Sinclair Lewis repeated Henry Adams' lamentations about the aimlessness and drift of American life, as the old values and the old ways became incredibly irrelevant in actual practice. As Ray Ginger has pointed out in his *Age of Excess,* repeatedly the novels of the nineties dealt with the emotional disorientation of individuals, and, strikingly, this disorganization all too frequently terminated in suicide.[7] America was a land of dreams, but the dreams were being smashed; and, like Dreiser's Sister Carrie, America "had learned that in this world, as in her own present state, was not happiness. Though often disillusioned, she was still waiting for that halcyon day when she could be led forth among dreams become real."[8] But real conviction in the belief that the society could rebuild itself was usually lacking. As Twain observed to Howells, "we all belong to the nasty stinking little human race. . . . Oh, we are a nasty lot—and to think that there are people who would like to save us and continue us. It won't happen if I have any influence".[9]

However, the apparent disorder and chaos invoked by the crisis of the 1890's did not always produce despair. While the old order of social relations no longer worked, this only pointed out to some men the necessity of creating a new order, one that would prove less fragile and more adaptable. One among many of different pursuits and talents who labored on this problem was Harvard University philosopher William James. To James, the answer was to jettison all of the old philosophies and political theories which supported the image of a world in which there were unchanging truths and values. Men were instead to determine their own truths as the test of performance proved them successful or "practical." In short, James argued for an activist's philosophy in which men could, in fact, manage and manipulate their own lives and institutions for their own improvement. Writing in the *New York Times* some years after his pragmatic philosophy, or "radical empiricism" as he preferred, had gained wide appeal, James outlined his creed:

> "Our minds are not here simply to copy a reality that is already complete. They are here to complete it, to add to its importance by their own remodeling of it, to decant its contents

[7]Ray Ginger, *Age of Excess* (New York: Macmillan, 1965), p. 304.

[8]Theodore Dreiser, *Sister Carrie* (New York: Modern Library, 1900), p. 557.

[9]Letter of Mark Twain to William Dean Howells, April 2, 1899, in H. N. Smith and W. M. Gibson, eds., *Mark Twain-Howells Letters* (Cambridge: Belknap Press, 1960), Vol. II, p. 692.

over, so to speak, into a more significant shape. In point of fact
the use of most of our thinking is to help us *change* the world.
. . . Thus we seem set free to use our theoretical as well as our
practical faculties . . . to get the world into a better shape, and
all with a good conscience. The only restriction is that the world
resists some lines of attack on our part and opens herself to
others so that we must go with the grain of her willingness, to
play fairly. Hence, the *sursum corda* of pragmatism's message."[10]

Not all James' words were always to be remembered, and the
"tough-mindedness" he referred to was to be replaced by some
practitioners of pragmatism with simple hard-headedness, but his call
for activism and experimentation and his faith in progress was
appealing for it seemed to offer a way out of the desperation of the
1890's.

The political and economic analogue to James' pragmatism was,
of course, "progressivism." Although the term usually is applied
rather narrowly to a specific political philosophy or movement falling
within the time period roughly bounded by the presidential adminis-
trations of Theodore Roosevelt and Woodrow Wilson, progressivism
has been more than just a relatively short-lived category of political
thought or period in American history.[11] Progressivism was a new
way to look at the problems of political economy. It was both a
method of analysis and a policy. Moreover, it was, in terms of
analysis and policy, the dominant theme in twentieth century
American politics, not simply an ideology narrowly associated with
any one particular political party or special group of reformers. While
it has been handy to use the term "progressive" in contrast to "conservative" in our simplistic categorization of American politics, this
has only obscured the fact that few real differences in political
philosophy ever developed in American politics in this century and
that the whole corpus of theory and policy as it developed was
essentially progressive.

In the same way that James' pragmatism sought to restore order
and meaning to fields of philosophic inquiry, progressivism, in all
its various forms, attempted to reconstruct the American economic
and political order so as to provide purpose and rationality to social
relations and institutions. Progressivism at the minimum required
only an unshakable belief that the American social system could be

---

[10]*New York Times*, November 3, 1907.

[11]For representative writings of these years, see Otis Pease, ed., *The Progressive
Years* (New York: Braziller, 1962).

manipulated to maintain a steady economic development with its attendant general happiness, without a radical reconstruction of the institutional arrangements or ideology of the society. Lest such a definition of progressivism be considered so amorphous as to be meaningless, it should be pointed out that one of the striking characteristic of American political thought in this century has been the general agreement among its leaders on means by which economic and social progress was to be attained. Moreover, it has been this inclination to study only the relatively minor differences in political theory and policy and the tendency to expand these differences out of all sense of proportion that has confounded serious attempts to study and explain modern American history. Progressivism in one form or another pervaded all layers of American society and politics. It made Republicans and Democrats or labor leaders and businessmen more alike than different on the really crucial questions of how the society should be organized and governed.

This consensus on goals and means doubtless contributed to the quite remarkable political continuity and economic stability of the nation in the twentieth century. The consensus was also self-supporting. As stability and continuity seemed to be the by-products of a progressive system, it was possible to accept as a fundamental dogma of American political thought the euphoric belief that the system could not really have any unsolvable problems. As social and economic difficulties inevitably arose, it was understood that any and all could be resolved without radically altering the social system.

While at the very minimum progressivism demanded a belief in the pragmatic manipulation of American institutions, there were more rigorous articles of faith. In particular, progressivism presumed that traditional values of economic individualism and private property relations were to be preserved. As Professor William Appleman Williams has observed:

> "Only the anarchists and a few doctrinaire laissez faire spokes-men seemed willing to accept the possibility of chaos. Arguing that it was both necessary and possible, most Americans re-formulated and reasserted their traditional confidence in their ability to choose and control their fate . . . given a consensus on the sanctity of private property, and confronted by the in-creasingly obvious failure of laissez faire, this faith could be verified only by controlling the marketplace."[12]

---

[12]William Appleman Williams, *The Contours of American History* (New York: World, 1961), p. 356.

The system that eventually developed along these lines was a regulated capitalist economy which has been given a variety of names. To Williams, it was "corporate capitalism." Others have labeled it variously, "political capitalism," "the mixed economy," "corporate liberalism" and a sundry collection of other terms.[13] But terms or labels are really of little importance; the fact remains that the economic and political system as it was understood in the 1890's needed to be reordered, and it was, but along lines consistent with traditional economic and political beliefs.

In simplest terms, the fundamental flaw in the old political and economic organization which had been discovered in the crisis of the 1890's was the system's capacity to produce more than it was able to consume. This led, in turn, to chronic fluctuations in prices and employment, diminished assurity of markets and profits for business ventures, and the prospect, and to some degree, the reality, of social and political collapse which Marx had brilliantly postulated as the attendant manifestations of the later stages of capitalist disintegration.

On the burning question of what to do about the problem of excess productive capacity, two lines of policy gradually developed. First, industrial competition, which excess capacity too frequently triggered, was to be replaced by monopolistic or oligopolistic market arrangements. Through industry regulation, the periodic price wars and diminished profits were to be eliminated. At first, regulation was largely of a private nature with businessmen expected to act, according to J. P. Morgan, "ably and with wisdom and restraint."[14] But, when private regulation proved incapable of controlling private profit-seeking motives, it was gradually understood that federal regulatory machinery would be erected and employed to correct market imperfections. Moreover, this concept of regulation was eventually expanded to mean not only rational decision-making and cooperation between firms, but also the construction of a rational and regulated relationship between business and its traditional protagonist, labor.

The second technique for eliminating excess capacity problems was to expand the market. By the mid and late 1890's, this was accepted by practically all American economic groups to mean expansion of world markets. Professor Frederick Jackson Turner had proclaimed

---

[13]See Gabriel Kolko, The Triumph of Conservatism (New York: Free Press, 1963).

[14]Lewis Corey, The House of Morgan (New York: Grosset & Dunlap, 1930), p. 145.

in 1894 that ". . . now, four centuries from the discovery of America, at the end of one hundred years of life under the constitution, the frontier has gone, and with its going has closed the first period in American history."[15] Turner's words were a threat or provocation as much as a statement of fact. To a nation whose economy had always seemed to depend on the constant expansion of the market, the closing of the frontier and the economic difficulties of the 1890's appeared to be connected events, and during the 1890's, a growing number of business, agricultural and labor leaders urged that America's new economic frontier should be the world.[16]

The always sanguine Theodore Roosevelt spoke more directly to the question of American expansion than did most of his contemporaries. To Roosevelt, opportunities were there for those strong and courageous enough to pick them up. For America, facing "very serious social problems" at home, it was essential that opportunities to develop foreign markets and overseas economic penetration be seized and exploited. "America," he noted, "has only just begun to assume that commanding position in the international business world which we believe will more and more be hers."[17]

It is noteworthy that both of these basic themes in twentieth century American development have generally been misrepresented or neglected by conventional historical writing. The rationalization of a highly regulated domestic economy has been wrongly depicted as a victorious struggle by progressive or liberal elements, who sought to curb the power of financial or business interests, over willful, self-centered groups bent on exploiting the rest of society. America's emergence as a world power similarly has been misinterpreted, viewed as the position taken by a nation reluctantly thrust into international leadership.[18]

The twin progressive policies of market regulation and market expansion, of course, did not suddenly emerge as full-blown and complete programs. Consensus on both the means and goals was by

---

[15]Frederick Jackson Turner, *The Frontier in American History* (New York: 1947), p. 38.

[16]See Walter LaFeber, *The New Empire* (Cornell University Press, 1963), pp. 153-196.

[17]President Roosevelt's Annual Message to Congress, December 3, 1901; in William Appleman Williams, ed., *The Shaping of American Diplomacy* (Chicago: Rand McNally, 1956), pp. 486-487.

[18]Representative of this view, see Arthur Schlesinger, Jr., *The Vital Center* (Boston: Houghton Mifflin, 1949), pp. 219-242.

no means total by the turn of the century, and serious differences of opinion existed into the early years of the twentieth century; but, to emphasize the diversity among men and ideas and the apparent inconsistency of many actual policies undertaken is misleading. There was substantial agreement on the broad outlines of these two programs by virtually all important economic and political groups, and a pattern for consensus was being laid down which would be the framework of American action and thought for the next half-century or more.

To obtain this consensus, serious contradictions in American economic and political theory and practice had to be resolved. Regulation and expansion presupposed the centralization and nationalization of economic and political power. For a society which broadly acclaimed the principles of individualism and which had not been noted in the nineteenth century for its singlemindedness and unity, the fairly speedy acceptance of uniformity and strong methods of internal control might have seemed impossible. However, Americans proved themselves equal to the task, and centralization and control became not only attributes of public affairs, but nationalization pervaded all levels of American life, so that the society created not only strong national markets and federal agencies, but also a national culture and national tastes and values. Most important, this nationalization was accomplished without admitting that the older values now stood as irrelevancies. After 1900, the public and private rhetoric in praise of individualism and freedom never wavered and, if anything, became louder and more ponderous, while the actual practice of politics, economics, and everyday life evidenced greater control and conformity. In a process of massive, national self-deception, Americans constructed for themselves illusory institutions and ideologies to create the effect but not the substance of a democratic society.

The progressive administration of Theodore Roosevelt set the pattern of pretense for twentieth century domestic politics. While arguing for reform to protect consumers, small businessmen, farmers, and laborers, economic and political power was steadily centralized into instruments over which these groups had no effective control. The Meat Inspection Act and the Pure Food and Drug Act of 1906, while ostensibly attacking such ills as those pointed out in Upton Sinclair's *The Jungle*, in reality were devices used for the elimination of small food processors whose competitive zeal had posed a threat to market stability. The cleaning up of conditions of meat and food preparation was really only a guise to effectively control these producers. Meanwhile, the whole point of Sinclair's muckraking, the work conditions of the employees of the meat plants, was ignored.[19] Similarly, the Elkins and Hepburn Acts, frequently cited as progressive attempts to strengthen Interstate Commerce Commission control over the railroads, in fact, provided the rate setting stability and non-competitiveness for the rail industry which it had never been able to obtain by itself. Even Roosevelt's reputation as a "trust-buster" was a pose, for he did not halt the steady acceleration in mergers nor did his forty-four anti-trust indictments interfere with his tennis playing with banker friends or their continued financial contributions to the Republican Party. In fact, Roosevelt's dependence upon the financial oligarchy was made quite apparent when he had to seek out the leadership of J. P. Morgan to solve a major banking crisis in 1907.[20]

No administration after Roosevelt radically altered this pattern of business-government relations. Disagreements occasionally raged over the selection of means, but the proposition that it was government's and business's responsibility to maintain a strong, centrally-managed economy was not seriously challenged. The Wilson administration, with all its posturing for a "New Freedom" for the ordinary citizen, defined that freedom only as a by-product of a strong, business-dominated economy. The creation of such agencies as the Federal Reserve System and the Federal Trade Commission, popular mythology notwithstanding, was with the general concurrence of business, for they were understood as attempts to replace market instability with rational guidelines for banking and business behavior.[21] The Republican years of the 1920's further demonstrated the non-partisan appeal of the progressive ideology. Coolidge's apt observation that the "business of America is business" was translated into policy at the Department of Commerce by a man both political parties had considered for the presidency in 1920. For all his well-known belief in the tonic of a philosophy of "rugged individualism," Herbert Clark Hoover, as Secretary of Commerce and as President, saw no inconsistency with making all of the machinery of government available for business's use.[22] "Business organization," he noted, "is

---

[19]Kolko, op. cit., p. 107.
[20]Ibid., pp. 153-158.
[21]Ibid., p. 273.
[22]See Joseph Brandes, Herbert Hoover and Economic Diplomacy (University of Pittsburgh Press, 1962).

moving strongly toward cooperation. There are in this cooperation great hopes that we can even gain in individuality . . . and, at the same time, reduce many of the great wastes of over-reckless competition in production and distribution."[23] To Hoover, any cooperation which government might encourage would thus strengthen business, and, thereby, strengthen America.

The crisis of the 1930's, rather than producing a serious reappraisal of the directions of American political economy, only pointed up the need for further tightening of central control. Franklin Roosevelt's early New Deal programs, such as the National Industrial Recovery Act, the Public Works Administration, and the use of the Reconstruction Finance Corporation were devices to give direct aid to business. In fact, the short-lived NIRA virtually suspended anti-trust legislation in allowing price-setting and output collusion. Meanwhile, the WPA, the Social Security Act and legislation giving unions broader powers served to blunt any popular radical assault upon the system.[24]

The depression also brought forth an important addition to orthodox economic theory. In the writings of British economist, John Maynard Keynes, there seemed to be a way to forestall economic depressions and recessions.[25] According to Keynesian economics, the chronic instability of capitalism, quite as Marx had pointed out sixty years before, was the natural tendency of the economic system. To Keynes, it could only be eliminated by central government actions which would maintain high levels of consumer and investment demand for goods and services. Keynes called for new roles to be played by the government through its monetary and fiscal policy to stimulate and maintain high levels of demand and offset the system's basic tendency for production capacity to outrun consumption. While supporters of the older, more conventional, economic theories were initially uncomfortable with Keynes' direct appeal for greater government control and direction of the economy, it was gradually understood that there was little in Keynesian economics which attacked established property relations and concentrations of economic power. Indeed, it was a brilliant move to protect these arrangements.

Much of the opposition to the vast expansion of federal economic control necessitated by the Great Depression and legitimated by

---

[23]Herbert Hoover, *American Individualism* (New York: 1922), p. 44.
[24]Williams, *Contours*, pp. 439-440.
[25]See John M. Keynes, *The General Theory of Employment, Interest, and Money* (New York: Harcourt, 1935).

Keynesian economics was erased during World War II and the post-war years. First of all, the war required virtually complete control of the nation's economy by the government. Secondly, with the coming of peace in 1945, many economic and political leaders feared a return to the depression conditions of the thirties, and, as a testament to their belief that *laissez faire* was now dead, the Congress enacted the Employment Act of 1946, committing to governmental responsibility the maintenance of high levels of employment, stable prices, and economic growth.

Although the acceptance of Keynesian devices for managing the economy were at first only haltingly tried and frequently challenged by dissenters, the "new economics" was victorious by the 1960's. The 1964 presidential election had in some respects been a referendum on this issue, and it had seen large numbers of business leaders desert their traditional party in support of the clearly Keynesian economic policies of the Johnson Administration. Indeed, consensus on the proper economic policy seemed so broad that the President's Council of Economic Advisers could confidently report in 1965:

> "The role of the Federal Government changed in the New Deal of the 1930's, and in World War II. The Government accepted responsibility for assuring a minimum of economic well-being for most individuals, for many special groups, industries, and agriculture. It undertook the task of stabilizing the economy against the destructive power of the business cycle. . . . After years of ideological controversy, we have grown used to the new relationship among Government, householder, business, labor, and agriculture. The tired slogans that made constructive discourse difficult have lost their meaning for most Americans.
>
> "It has become abundantly clear that our society wants neither to turn backward the clock of history nor to discuss our present problems in a partisan spirit."[26]

The Annual Report of the council then proceeded to enumerate the unfinished economic problems facing the society—urban decay, inadequate education, poor health, poverty, and inequality of economic opportunity. It was a measure of the self-deceptiveness of American political and economic thought that no one seemed to see the irony or contradiction in such a bombastic pronouncement of the victory of progressive ideas on the one hand, and the tacit admission of failure on the other. The "success" of a political philosophy obviously did not depend on whether it really worked.

---

[26]*The Economic Report of the President, 1965,* p. 145.

The victory of the progressive program for an integrated and controlled domestic economy was complemented by the political acceptance of the necessity to expand and protect overseas markets. And again, the process of self-deception was important. Expansion was couched in terms of duties and responsibilities as well as economic necessity when it was initially discussed in the 1890's. It took on a strong moral and religious flavor, becoming a way of doing the Lord's work as well as America's. To Rev. Josiah Strong, that indefatigable proponent of picking up the white man's burden, it was nothing short of a God-given responsibility for the "Anglo-Saxon," of which the United States was the only strong representative, ". . . to exercise the commanding influence in the world's future."[27] Senator Albert Beveridge meanwhile intoned that "God has not been preparing the English-speaking and Teutonic peoples . . . for nothing. . . . He made us the master organizers of the world to establish a system where chaos reigns . . . that we administer government among savages and senile peoples."[28]

The pattern for American overseas expansion, what William Appleman Williams has called "Imperial Anti-Colonialism," had been laid down in Secretary of State Hay's Open Door notes of 1899.[29] While the notes seemed specifically addressed to the problem of keeping China open to trade and halting the growth of European spheres of economic interest on the China mainland, the real thrust was to state America's intention to keep all world markets open to free commerce, meaning our commerce as well as anybody else's. The Open Door became the basic theme of American foreign policy in the twentieth century. America never really sought to acquire an empire in the eighteenth or nineteenth century meaning of the word and what overseas possessions we had always proved embarrassing to us. America eschewed taking others' land in favor of the real or imagined benefits of penetrating their markets, and the nation would go to any lengths to keep world markets open to American products and investment.

The internationalism of Theodore Roosevelt, Taft, and Wilson, with its erection of a virtual hegemony over the Caribbean, economic

---

[27]Josiah Strong, *Our Country* (New York: The Home Missionary Society, 1885), p. 168.

[28]Senator Albert Beveridge (1899), in Williams, ed., *The Shaping of American Diplomacy*, pp. 433-434.

[29]William Appleman Williams, *The Tragedy of American Diplomacy* (New York: Delta, 1962), p. 16.

penetration into South American, Asian, and even European markets, and eventual involvement in World War I (which Wilson justified largely in terms of freedom of the seas and freedom for commerce) is a well-known tale, hardly needing recounting. However, this period of vigorous, often ruthless, overseas expansion is sometimes depicted as an exception to later developments. The twenties and the thirties are frequently shown as "isolationistic" and the post-World War II period as humanitarian internationalism. In viewing themselves in this way, Americans have come to think of their country as a reluctant internationalist thrust into the world for the world's sake. The facts reveal, however, quite a different story.

First of all, America never was isolationist except in the irrelevant domestic political poses of the 1920's and 1930's, which were sheer self-deception. From a theretofore all time high of $2.4 billion in exports in 1913, the United States exported $4.9 billion in 1925 and $5.2 billion by 1929. Between 1920 and 1933, overseas United States private investment grew by more than $10 billion and income on these investments averaged about two percent of the gross national product, perhaps not an awesome figure by itself, but enough to make the difference between profit and loss for many firms.[30]

The rejection of the Treaty of Versailles and the League of Nations did not indicate a withdrawal from the world, but the assertion that America should remain free to act without the possible interference of a super-government it might not yet have been able to dominate. As the world's leading creditor and industrial power, America perceived few benefits in such an organization. Meanwhile, at the newly organized Department of Commerce, Herbert Hoover labored to induce American businessmen to tap foreign markets. His agency produced a flood of propaganda publications through the twenties, broadcasting the potential return on foreign investment. It published detailed analyses of the economic and political conditions of possible investment areas and unmistakably hinted that the full political and military power of the nation would be utilized to protect wisely undertaken investment.[31]

The international economic collapse during the thirties and World War II clearly illustrated the weaknesses of attempting to maintain the "open door" through our own individually initiated arrangements. Moreover, the war cleared away any remaining sympathy for a

---

[30]U. S. Department of Commerce Publications.
[31]Brandes, op. cit., pp. 151-169.

"little America" line of policy and induced practically all Americans to accept what most businessmen and all twentieth century presidents had understood since the turn of the century—that America must, for its own sake and that of the world, act as the dominant international power. The United Nations seemed to be the device by which the "open door" would become the basis for post-war international arrangements. By the logic of its charter and by the fact that America dominated the Allied wartime alliance, it seemed that American principles would have to prevail.

But, as the war closed, Soviet Russian Communism failed to collapse as many supposed, and its implied threat of world revolution raised a new spectre which had to be dealt with. The world was to be divided between the free half which was dominated by American economic and political power and the communist half which was understood as a constant threat to any sensible man's concept of freedom. Through the 1950's, America, by a maze of confusing economic and military alliances, tied the "free world" to herself. The "free world," of course, was that which had institutions or held political views which opened it to our commerce or our political leadership, that part which subscribed to the "Open Door." Communist nations, with their anti-capitalist ideology, by definition were threats to the international capitalist economic apparatus that the United States conceived as essential for its and the "free world's" continuation. Most Americans, meanwhile, understood the cold war treaties and aid programs not as devices to expand and strengthen the business economy, a justification which might have had dubious appeal by itself, but as necessary means to halt the spread of anti-democratic communism, a way to protect our freedom as well as other people's. Meanwhile, the government poured more than $120 billion in aid into receptive countries and business accumulated $60 billion in overseas investment by 1964.[32] That this overseas investment for the sake of freedom did not always produce freedom for the people of the recipient nations, or that American business penetration generally produced greater economic dependency rather than growth or self-sufficiency was usually overlooked. The simple arithmetic which showed that America returned in profits about two dollars for every one directly invested abroad during the 1950's

---

[32]U. S. Department of Commerce, Office of Business Economics, *Balance of Payments* and *Survey of Current Business*.

and 1960's was rarely seen as connected with the rising tide of social revolution and its growing anti-American bias.

The illusion of world markets and their relation to the domestic economic security of America became the reality of garrisoning the "free world" and intervening in the affairs of both weak and strong nations.

In 1898, Senator Albert Beveridge had observed:

> . . . "The rule of liberty that all just government derives its authority from the consent of the governed, applied only to those who are capable of self-government. We govern the Indians without their consent, we govern our territories without their consent, we govern our children without their consent. . . . We cannot fly from our world duties: it is ours to execute the purpose of a fate that has driven us to be greater than our small intentions. We cannot retreat from any soil where Providence has unfurled our banner; it is ours to save that soil for liberty and civilization."[33]

The tragedy of American relations with the rest of the world lay in the fact that such an outlook more aptly described American foreign policy in the 1960's than it had at the beginning of the century.

Once perceiving the political and economic directions laid down by progressive dogma, a student of American affairs is left with the burden of explaining just how such a monstrous ideology of international expansion and internal control was ever acceptable to the nation. Indeed, there does not seem to be an easy answer.

Ordinary people appear to have been relatively easily deceived into believing that the liberal or progressive philosophy really worked. In the labor movement, for instance, radical alternatives died away, not, as it would be easy to believe, because of repression or opposition from the authorities (there was plenty of that, of course), but mostly through the real improvement of the laboring classes' economic condition. Real wages continued to climb after 1900, and, while the business cycle still unsettled the economy periodically, there was enough belief in the continued progress of the system to offset a small radical upsurge during the depression of the thirties.

Paternalism by government and business improved real working conditions and steadily eradicated old miseries imposed by unem-

---

[33]Beveridge, in Williams, ed., *The Shaping of American Diplomacy*, p. 434.

ployment, sickness, injury and old age. In the absence of real conditions of economic and social repression, there was little popular support for a radical ideology. An indication of the lack of radical content to the American labor movement can be seen in the fact that while Samuel Gompers, the recognized leader of labor at the beginning of the century, might disagree with Judge Gary and other capitalists on unionist philosophy or the desirable bargaining strength of workers and employers, all could agree that Eugene Debs or the radical I. W. W. were a threat to the nation. Indeed, unionists proved to be more active than capitalists in purging radical ideas from the labor movement.

American working classes recognized considerable economic mobility for themselves and greater social mobility for their sons and daughters in a society dominated by business institutions and middle-class sensibilities.[34] Changes in the structure of American industry and government, with the growth of more white collar jobs, usually jobs with titles and status, seemed to make nonsense of proletarian identifications. By mid-century, American social scientists were able to celebrate the abject failure of Marxian prognostications by pointing to the "salariat's" replacement of the proletariat in the capitalist scheme.[35] The United States Information Agency could propagandize the world about "People's Capitalism," in which there were no robber barons, only little people, working, saving, and being the real owners of enterprise. Thus, workers did not hew to a radical political alternative, and as Veblen had recognized a long time ago, they became the staunchest supporters of the system and its values.

By no means all Americans were able to participate equally in the rising abundance. For black Americans, economic conditions only improved during the two world wars, and, between the wars and after World War II, they returned to the position of economic irrelevancy they had occupied since the end of slavery. There were other pockets of poverty and disadvantage, too—in rural Appalachia and New England, in Pennsylvania and West Virginia steel and coal towns, and other forgotten places. For these people, the system held out no rewards, but their racial and geographic isolation and their pathetic hopefulness and belief in the American Dream set aside until the 1960's any latent radical political tendencies.

That ordinary people deceived themselves about the workings of

---

34Williams, *Contours*, p. 431.

35See C. W. Mills, *The White Collar* (New York: Oxford, 1951).

a progressive ideology is not surprising; that the intellectuals should be equally easily deluded is another matter. Nevertheless, the fact remains that there never developed an intellectual tradition which might have seriously challenged progressivism. As Randolph Bourne observed of American intellectuals during the first World War, they "identified themselves with the least democratic forces in American life. They . . . assumed the leadership for war of those very classes whom the American democracy has been immemorially fighting. . . ."[36] To Bourne, an unreconstructed radical all his life, this defense of war and the general failure of American intellectuals to respond to real social issues showed that they had "substituted simple syllogism for analysis." In the search for pragmatic truths, the intellectual "regresses to ideas that can issue in quick, simplified action." His thought "becomes an easy rationalization of what is actually going on or what is to happen inevitably tomorrow."[37] The intellectual was not a mover and shaper of his culture; he was its apologist.

Generally, the experience of academic life as a training ground left few intellectuals prepared to question their society and to develop radical alternatives. University life itself was virtually without a radical tradition in America. Even more than in Europe, it tended to be very middle-class in its perspectives and social consciousness. The individual intellectual, located on or off the campus, who drifted off into radicalism, had few emotional crutches to help him. In university life he was either a pariah or an interesting deviant. Off the campus, he rarely could act politically, for there was no radical movement among workers, farmers, or poor people after the collapse of the radical political activity during World War I. Consequently, as Bourne concluded, intellectual radicals "became the most despicable and impotent of men. . . . Either support what is going on, in which case you count for nothing . . . or remain aloof, passively resistant, in which case you count for nothing because you are outside the machinery of reality."[38]

"Reality" after 1900 was mostly a growing, booming nation. There were, of course, dismal sides to this reality, the cities, the oppression by big business, and the ever-present poor; and, these problems

---

[36]Randolph S. Bourne, *War and the Intellectuals* (New York: Harper & Row, 1964), p. 5.

[37]*Ibid,* p. 11.

[38]*Ibid.,* p. 13.

attracted intellectual attention and produced a degree of radical scholarship and thought. But, there was always the iridescent dream in the background of a progressing and improving America, able to deal with any social and economic problem and still better than any other place in the world. To offer critiques or ideologies which suggested that there were basic flaws in the system was difficult going, hard to prove empirically or intuitionally. To be sure, America produced a few radical intellectuals, but all too frequently their radicalism was only a phase in their lives, not a style of life. Men like John Dewey, Walter Lippman, James Burnham, and Sidney Hook drifted back to the "conventional wisdom" after youthful fancies. As Christopher Lasch points out in his *The New Radicalism,* many others who remained strong in their radical commitment found themselves wholly isolated from politics and life, and their radicalism often became withdrawn into weird personal aberrations and fetishes.[39]

Even the temporary breakdown of the system in the 1930's produced no lasting radical intellectual movement. Although, proportionately more radicals may have appeared in and at the fringes of academic life than in labor unions during this period, they had all but disappeared by the late 1940's and early 1950's. Post-war "subversive activity" investigations and witch-hunts must be counted as a factor in this dissipation of radical intellectualism, but most of the intellectuals of the 1930's, including such strong types as Arthur Koestler, Granville Hicks, and John Dos Passos had become extremely dissillusioned with their flirtations with communism and socialism and had quite voluntarily moved to the right. During the McCarthy era, dozens of old radicals testified before various investigating committees about their own and their former comrades' communist ties, not simply out of fear for their jobs, as is too commonly believed, but because of their own change of conscience. As Granville Hicks explained his actions, ". . . as an anti-communist, I was not opposed on principle to the investigation of communism."[40] With a vengeance, many turned their considerable intellectual talents, in the university and outside it, against any attempt to nurture radical intellectual activity. Shamelessly, the ex-radicals and the ex-communists served the CIA and the United States Information Agency to alert Americans and the world of the perils of communism and the virtues of liberal

---

[39]See Christopher Lasch, *The New Radicalism in America, 1889-1963* (New York: Knopf, 1965).

[40]Granville Hicks, *Where We Came Out* (New York: Viking, 1954), p. 4.

America.[41] The ex-communist anti-communists had no peers in their unswerving loyalty to the American economic and political system.

Meanwhile, the mainstream of American intellectual life during the 1930's and after remained liberal or progressive. It accepted the enlargement of government in the economy as necessary, and it justified the expansion of America into the world as duty. Thus, America was to remain a stable and free society at home and was to bring freedom to the rest of the world. By the 1960's, Arthur Schlesinger, Jr., a prototype of the liberal intellectual, could describe liberalism as "humane, experimental, and pragmatic" with "no sense of messianic mission and no faith that all problems have final solutions."[42] A few years before, a fellow historian, Walt Whitman Rostow, quoted a colleague in describing his own liberal faith: "It does not prefigure ends or final results," he noted. "It awaits the arrival of the new occasion before supplying the new duties."[43] Yet, within a short time, both men had contributed materially as presidential advisers to an inflexible foreign policy which brought America "eyeball to eyeball" with Russia over Cuba. And, within a few more years, Schlesinger had renounced his former presidential employer over the handling of the Viet Nam War, and Rostow remained with the administration as the chief architect of his nation's massive military intervention in Southeast Asia. Such were the strange fruits of the pragmatism of the liberal intellectual establishment.

Through the 1950's and 1960's, when intellectual effort was not justifying anti-communism and praising a modified welfare capitalism, or actually formulating and implementing policy to these ends, it tended to wander off into the fancies of what C. Wright Mills called "The Great American Celebration," assuring Americans that everything was going along fine. Academic social scientists, for instance, busied themselves with attempts to apply scientific techniques to social situations, producing simulation models and other studies which supposedly gave insights to the functioning of American society and economy. Typically, these studies, financed through enormous private and public programs for research, saw few crises in America's present and future development. Representative of

---

[41]Christopher Lasch, "The Cultural Cold War," *The Nation*, Vol. 205, No. 7, September 11, 1967, pp. 198-212.

[42]Schlesinger, *op. cit.* (1962 preface), p. XV.

[43]W. W. Rostow, *Stages of Economic Growth* (Cambridge University Press, 1962), p. 165.

this cheery view of America, one researcher, writing on the development of American business institutions, observed in 1962 that ". . . with so few signs of domestic upheaval at the beginning of the 1960's any elite could take pride in the record of American business leadership."[44] The dangerous irrelevance of this type of scholarship has been pointed out by two Marxist critics of America, Paul Baran and Paul Sweezy, who have argued that none of the crises of the mid and late 1960's were predicted by such research efforts. They observed, "one can say that social scientists, assuring us for so long that all was for the best in what they took to be the best of all possible worlds, did what they could to keep us from looking reality in the face."[45]

A few liberal intellectuals were able to see the direction their society was heading and were frankly appalled. By 1967, John Kenneth Galbraith, a scholar and presidential adviser and briefly a government official, surveyed the apparatus that had been constructed to manipulate people and to maintain the economy and social order and opined that very possibly in the future people's lives will be even increasingly directed "to the ends of the industrial system."[46] Despite the affluence and freedom which might be possible for all Americans if technology and productive ability were properly utilized, Galbraith, for all his attempts to be hopeful, concluded that the present course was not toward this end, but rather toward the building of a more manipulated society and that "will not be freedom."[47] In the last analysis, Galbraith and other thoughtful, liberal intellectuals could only talk vaguely about a "chance for salvation" for the American social system, but, beyond such intuitive speculation and hopefulness, their minds seemed immobilized.

As the progressive or liberal ideology began to flounder in the mid-1960's on the frustrating failures of American foreign policy and emerging racial strife at home, radical assaults upon society became, predictably, more frequent and shrill. A "New Left," drawing its strength mostly from academic sources, jolted the calm of the campuses, but the new radicals remained, as usual, largely ineffective

---

[44]Robert H. Wiebe, *Businessmen and Reform* (Harvard University Press, 1962), p. 224.

[45]Paul Baran & Paul Sweezy, *Monopoly Capital* (New York: Monthly Review Press, 1966), pp. 1-2.

[46]John K. Galbraith, *The New Industrial State* (Boston: Houghton Mifflin, 1967), p. 398.

[47]*Ibid.*, p. 399.

and isolated from political power, "the most impotent of men," as Randolph Bourne had said.

Looking back over more than seven decades, the progressive resolution of the crisis posed in the 1890's must be considered, in terms of specific goals, successful—but at the price of creating a kind of Frankenstein monster. In the world, the United States by the 1960's has found both markets and highly profitable sources of investment; but, it also has emerged as the chief supporter of political and economic reaction, attempting always to head off truly revolutionary social movements by use of its enormous wealth, its notorious support of friendly repressive regimes, and, when all else fails, its willingness to commit its vast resources and young men in wars of opposition to radical social change, even when such efforts are threats to its own economic well-being. At home, the material abundance, easily attributed to the successful development of a carefully rationalized and directed market system, can be seen everywhere. But, equally obvious is the evidence that for all its abundance, the society has not provided, nor shows much sympathy for providing, solutions to many crucial problems. The gross inequities of being black in white America, which have built a lengthening legacy of civil disobedience and disorder, the scarred and disfigured countryside, with its polluted water and air, the ugly cities and the uglier suburbs are also outgrowths of the internal system Americans created.

The "success" of the progressive ideology now seems scarcely bearable. The spectacle of a great nation sharply divided within itself over the conduct of its foreign policy and torn at home by racial warfare, its educational, familial, and religious institutions increasingly threatened by internal disaffection, and its culture reflecting bizarre flirtations with psychedelic paraphernalia and other devices to escape reality currently projects an atmosphere of anxiety and tension certainly as great as any felt in the 1890's. Ordinary citizens everyhere have become stupendously confused and concerned, and there is a growing, haunting feeling afoot in the society that existing political institutions are simply out of control and unable to deal with the problems of America. By the late 1960's, the spectre of chaos hangs over the land once again, the shining progressive vision of building a great nation seems to be turning to ashes.

In the reconstruction of the American political economy after the crisis of the 1890's, Americans had chosen not to question the traditional property relations and power arrangements of their society. Rather than viewing the crisis of the system as basic to the organization of the society itself, as Marx and some home-grown heretics had argued, Americans decided only to reform their social and economic institutions by doing everything possible to strengthen them. By concluding that crisis in America could be headed off only through the construction of a regulated capitalist-type economy, Americans had never come to grips with the question of what kind of life-style to build. The "quality of life" for the society, therefore, could never be a seriously pursued line of inquiry so long as all discussions started from the proposition that the American system was necessarily committed to maintaining essentially capitalist economic, political and social institutions. The quality of life was really the by-product of whatever was necessary to keep such a system going, and, to keep it going, it became necessary to be increasingly expansionistic in the world and ever more tightly controlled at home.

There was never any serious challenge to this line of policy after the 1890's. Radical interpretations of American development simply never gained any serious attention. Indeed, this lack of a radical tradition or theme in American thought and politics made the emerging crisis of the 1960's all the more difficult to understand and to deal with. America had deceived itself into believing that the traditionally cherished values of individual freedom and identity depended upon the continuation of a capitalist social system and it had, indeed, become a wealthy and strong nation. However, by the 1960's, this wealth and power seemed to threaten both the lives of its citizens and the rest of the world. The new American crisis now lay in resolving this paradox, for very much as Engels had once observed while traveling by train through the countryside of his native Germany, "What a lovely land, if only one could live in it!"[48]

---

[48]In Edmund Wilson, *To the Finland Station* (New York: Doubleday, 1940), p. 337.

IDEOLOGY, SCIENTIFIC PHILOSOPHY, AND MARXISM*

John Somerville

WHOEVER speaks today about the interrelations of philosophy and ideology should first specify the sense in which he is using the key terms, because many of our present problems in this connection arise out of vagueness, ambiguities and confusions of language—what Francis Bacon called "Idols of the Market Place." These idols generate unnecessary controversies over unreal issues, and thus prevent a useful meeting of minds. Let us therefore begin with the semantic aspect of our theme.

Most of the increasing and important discussion of ideology today either centers on Marxism or includes Marxism, so that one of our primary concerns is with the Marxist definitions of ideology and philosophy, and the corresponding conception of their interrelations. In approaching the matter from this side, we are immediately confronted with the fact that the meaning of both terms—ideology and philosophy—has undergone a significant evolution within Marxism since the time of Marx and Engels, so that anyone who tried to undertake a critique of present-day Marxism in connection with the philosophy-ideology theme, limiting himself to the sense in which these terms were employed by Marx and Engels, would be tilting at windmills, under the impression that none of the battles, none of the issues, none of the conditions had changed its nature or vanished, that the whole scene had somehow remained the same. But the scene is quite different. Moreover, that Marxism itself as a doctrine should undergo change and development, that key terms should take on new content in the light of new conditions, new develop-

---

*Paper read at the XIVth International Congress of Philosophy (Vienna, 1968).

140

ments, new problems, is a fact that ought to occasion no surprise, since the cardinal emphasis of Marxism throughout is dialectical, i.e., upon change, development, evolution at all levels of existence, including the cognitive.

Thus it may be said to be a requirement of Marxist methodology itself that, in order to understand its own conceptions, to see the point of its own definitions, an historical approach must be taken. The terms "ideology" and "philosophy" are cases in point; let us consider them in order. It is interesting to note that before Marx and Engels came upon the scene the word ideology was being used in the sense given it by eighteenth-century thinkers like Destutt de Tracy (the author of a multi-volume treatise entitled *Éléments d'idéologie*), Volney and Cabanis, who were interested among other things in what we call the body-mind problem, and who took the very radical position, for those days, that the whole process of having ideas takes place by virtue of the operation of man's observable physiological system, and not by virtue of the alleged operation of an unobservable spiritual substance. In other words, they insisted that the epistemological question be decided empirically, by means of what we call scientific method, and the term ideology had for them the direct connotation of a science which studies ideas in terms of their causes and effects. These men belonged mainly to the materialist trend of the Enlightenment, and were influenced by Locke, Condillac, Helvétius and similar thinkers.

From the standpoint of Marx and Engels this approach to the problem of ideas represented only the beginning of a critique of the prevailing conception of mind as independent of body, of mind as spiritual substance, and the like. It did not succeed in introducing into its critical picture the socio-historical dimension central to man's thought and life. In other words, taking for granted the fact that there is a physiological basis for the individual's process of thinking, Marx's point was that this physiological basis could not explain the *history* of *idea-systems*, i.e., the important changes that take place in ethical systems, codes of law, political theories, religions, art, and other such fields. Therefore, when Marx and Engels criticized ideology and ideologists, it was not to quarrel with the thesis that thinking as a process has physiological causes, but to insist that its general content and direction have social causes. They also wanted to criticize the prevailing notion that, in terms of genesis, social institutions are mainly effects of the ideas in men's minds. To sum up the situation, their contention was that almost all thinkers who had dealt with these matters suffered from two serious shortcomings: 1) they were unaware of the sense in which changes and developments in systems of social thought have been responses to or effects of changes and developments which antecedently took place in the economic foundations of society, in the forces and relations of production; 2) they assumed that changes in social ideas, in ways of thinking, are the main cause of changes in social institutions (including, of course, economic institutions). These two points comprise what Marx and Engels specifically called the ideological process, i.e., the belief that ideas, as independent forces, are the chief determinants of social institutions, of social practice generally.

Thus, in a well-known letter to Mehring in 1893 Engels says, quite sharply: "Ideology is a process accomplished by the so-called thinker consciously, indeed, but with a false consciousness. The real motives impelling him remain unknown to him, otherwise, it would not be an ideological process at all. . . . It is, above all, this appearance of an independent history of state constitutions, of systems of law, of ideological conceptions in every separate domain, which dazzles most people."[1] It is important to note that Engels is not saying that the ideas involved in his ideological process must necessarily be false, as doctrines. What is false is the conception of their genesis, motives, causal roots. That is, the thinker does not realize that his own doctrines and others' doctrines have in any vital sense been conditioned by the prevailing mode of economic production and exchange, i.e., the character of the technological powers and sources of economic production, and the legally enforced economic relations which implement these powers, but which can lag behind their development and begin to obstruct them, thus generating life-and-death struggles within society. This is very similar to the situation in which a person may not be aware of the sense in which certain of his conscious preferences, value judgments, standards of beauty and the like, are conditioned by the sexual dynamics within himself. It is similar also in the further fact that the operation of such a conditioning process does not imply that the judgments or standards in question are necessarily bad or false, or necessarily beyond rational determination as to goodness or badness, truth or falsity. These remain open questions.

---

[1]*The Selected Correspondence of Marx and Engels, 1846-1895* (New York: International Publishers, 1942), p. 511.

Thus, even under Engels' sharp conception the classification of doctrines as ideological was not decisive as to their truth-status; at most, it indicated the given thinker's ignorance of the actual antecedents of the doctrines, together with an exaggerated impression of the degree of their strength as causes of fundamental changes in social institutions. In this connection it is also significant that Engels had to emphasize, in 1890, in his famous letter to Bloch, that while he and Marx always held the economic factor to be the major determinant of the course of history, they recognized that ideas, doctrines, traditions and other such factors also acted as causes, only not as the main or decisive cause, which was the most important key to the problem as a whole. Moreover, Engels added: "Marx and I are ourselves partly to blame for the fact that younger writers sometimes lay more stress on the economic side than is due it. We had to emphasize this main principle in opposition to our adversaries, who denied it, and we had not always the time, the place or the opportunity to allow the other elements involved in the interaction to come into their rights."[2]

No doubt all these considerations played a part in bringing Lenin and others to the view that, on the whole, it would be more useful to employ the term ideology to designate all systems of social doctrine whatsoever, irrespective of the views of their authors or believers on the question of their causal antecedents and the degree of their power to bring about societal changes. Then attention would be focused directly on what are, after all, the questions of chief importance: which doctrines are objectively true, and which false? which ideological systems are scientific and which unscientific? In other words, Marxism itself, and every other system of social thought or of philosophy in general, is termed an ideology. This is the approach followed by the great majority of Marxists today.

A wider understanding on the part of non-Marxists of this evolution which the term ideology has gone through would obviously have a constructive effect towards clarifying the real issues, as distinguished from those imaginary ones which arise out of confusions about language. This applies not only to the term ideology, but equally to the term philosophy, in respect to which we are, in fact, confronted with a very similar historical evolution. That is, just as the term ideology had, for Marx and Engels, certain pejorative connotations, so also did the term philosophy. Put bluntly, what was pre-

---

[2]*Ibid.*, p. 477.

dominantly associated in their day with the word philosophy was the metaphysical approach, especially strong in Germany, of course, in terms of the influential system of Hegel. Although, as Marx and Marxists have always emphasized, there were some very valuable elements contained in this system—elements pertaining to dialectical methodology—it contained also the claim found in so many older systems of philosophy, that it possessed a truth not grounded in any material, natural or empirical source, yet capable of deciding the most important question concerning things material, natural, and empirical.

In making derogatory comments about philosophy in general, or suggesting that it would fortunately die out, Marx and Engels clearly had in mind that kind of philosophy, not what we today call scientific philosophy. Their work as a whole clearly shows that this derogatory evaluation did not apply to the kind of philosophy which created the special sciences, nor would it apply to future philosophy which would carry scientific method into further special fields, nor to the task of summing up and generalizing in a responsible way the results of the special sciences. It is obvious that Marx and Engels respected materialist philosophy as the empirical foundation of science, both historically and methodologically, and felt that they were adding to it those dialectical elements which would enable it to give rise to better science and new sciences, especially in social fields. But the term philosophy still had too many anti-scientific associations.

Here again a semantic development has taken place since the days of Marx and Engels, a development similar to what occurred in the case of the term ideology. That is, philosophy as a term used by Marxists lost its pejorative associations; like ideology, it became simply a blanket term. And, just as in the case of ideology, the problem then was to distinguish between true and false philosophy, scientific and unscientific philosophy, not between what was to be called philosophy and what was to be called something else. Marxist philosophy itself is considered a science, the most general science, not in the classical metaphysical sense of a body of generalizations gained by some method independent of and allegedly higher than the method by which truth is gained in the special sciences, but, as pointed out above, in the sense of generalizing and synthesizing the results of the special sciences, and building up new sciences.

In the light of what has been said so far, it is clear that if we today raise the direct question: what, according to Marxism, is the relation between philosophy and ideology? The answer is that all philosophy, including Marxist philosophy, is a part of ideology. But of course, in itself this statement settles only a semantic aspect of the matter. Though that aspect is not without its importance, as we have seen, there are other aspects more fundamental in the substantive sense. We have touched upon some of them from time to time in the preceding account; let us here try to draw them together in a more systematic way.

Put very bluntly, I think the main substantive questions are: What is the nature of the basic problem Marx poses? What is important about the kind of solution offered by him? In relation to the first question the first thing to be borne in mind is that Marx's main problem is not to account for ideas, but to account for history. While these two problems overlap, they must be distinguished, and kept in perspective. The history of ideas is, of course, part of history as a whole, so that, as far as philosophy or any other idea-system is concerned, the question takes the form: how does Marx's general theory of history apply to the particular field of ideas? To understand the answer to this, we must of course be clear on what his general theory does and does not say. Let us therefore refresh ourselves with a brief statement of it, which is often quoted, and deservedly so, from Marx's *Contribution to the Critique of Political Economy*:

"The general conclusion at which I arrived and which, once reached, continued to serve as the leading thread in my studies, may be briefly summed up as follows: In the social production which men carry on they enter into definite relations that are indispensable and independent of their will; these relations of production correspond to a definite stage of development of their material powers of production. The sum total of these relations of production constitutes the economic structure of society—the real foundation on which rise legal and political superstructures and to which correspond definite forms of social consciousness. The mode of production in material life determines the general character of the social, political and spiritual processes of life. It is not the consciousness of men that determines their existence, but, on the contrary, their social existence determines their consciousness. At a certain stage of their development the material forces of production in society come into conflict with the existing relations of production, or—what is but a legal expression for the same thing—with the property relations within which they had been at work before. From forms of development of the forces of production these relations turn into their fetters. Then comes the period of social revolution. With the change of the economic foundation the entire immense superstructure is more or less rapidly transformed. In considering such transformations the distinction should always be made between the material trans-formation of the economic conditions of production, which can be determined with the precision of natural science, and the legal, political, religious, aesthetic or philosophic—in short, ideological forms in which men become conscious of this conflict and fight it out."[3]

It is important to recognize at this point that Marx is not saying a number of things he has frequently been accused of saying. He is not saying that the social philosophy of the individual philosopher is necessarily a deliberate rationalization of the economic interest of the class to which the philosopher happens to belong; nor is his thesis so interpreted by the great majority of Marxists, though every movement has had what William James once called its "lunatic fringe," and, we might add, its one-track minds. Marx is also not say-ing that the social philosophy of the individual philosopher is neces-sarily an *unconscious* rationalization of the interest of the class to which he happens to belong. Marx recognizes that a philosopher might be completely dedicated to the interest of a class to which he does not belong. (He did not forget that neither he nor Engels was proletarian by class membership.) Nor is he saying that the individual thinker's philosophy, to whatever class interest it may be related, must have the character of a rationalization in the bad sense of that term, in the sense of a doctrine or thesis which is false.

What Marx is saying, so far as these matters are concerned, is that the individual's philosophy, whether true or false, and whether the individual is aware of its social antecedents and role or not, bears an important relationship to class interests, to the struggle of classes, and to the whole economic process which, in the history of civilization up to now, has motivated and necessitated the struggle of classes. This process, as we have just seen, centrally includes de-velopments in the technological forces and powers of production, developments which sooner or later compel adaptive changes in the legally enforced relations of production, which, however, cannot be changed without also bringing about radical changes in the pre-vailing legal codes, theories and forms of government, moral codes, religious interpretations—in short, without a socio-cultural revolution, violent or peaceful. As Marx sees it, that has been the central dynamic

---

[3]Pp. 10, 11. Chicago: Kerr, 1904.

of the historical process as it has taken place during the last ten thousand years or so. History has been basically formed by struggles between classes over control of the way of life, which has necessarily meant control over the means of life, i.e., control over the means of production.

This whole drama has, in a sense, turned on the fact that there have been shortages in the means of life, a condition which could hardly help but generate the tragic sense of life, if one looks upon the shortages as an eternal condition. But Marx took history seriously, and saw, a hundred years ago, what almost anyone can now see— the dynamics of technological development capable of eliminating shortages. And in all we are today doing and not doing in response to that, in all the struggles and conflicts, violent and non-violent, we are going through in relation to the increase of technological powers, their control and their relative distribution among classes, nations, geographical areas, and the impact of all that on existing politics, national and international, on forms of government, systems of philosophy, interpretations of religion, are we not behaving in the main as Marx said we would? His predictions were not accurate in all respects, of course. But the question remains: did anyone in the middle of the nineteenth century predict with as much accuracy as Marx the basic course of history for the hundred years following? If anyone did, and did it in terms of a body of doctrine still open to use and development, let us give him, as a social philosopher, as much attention as we are giving Marx.

But it is difficult to put this whole picture in historical perspective, or to see clearly the part played in it by the history of ideas if one approaches it from the side of the specific ideas held by an individual philosopher, as if the problem were to try to explain why X holds just the particular views he happens to hold. This would miss the point in much the same way that the point would be missed by one who, hearing the play *Hamlet* called beautiful, would fasten one some single line, or some one word, and ask to be shown the beauty. If beauty is there, in the sense meant, it is an aspect of the drama as a whole, a function of the dynamic interrelationships of its parts. Just so, if there is truth in a theory of human history, it cannot be found by looking very closely at a single person; and if there is truth in a theory about the history of ideas, it cannot be found by looking very closely at a single idea. The truth can only emerge as an aspect of the theory as a whole, as a function of the interrelationships of the parts.

Thus in his theory concerning the history of ideas, Marx is trying to explain not the genesis of any single idea, but rather why a given age, epoch or historical period has the kind of prevailing and pre-dominant ideology—systems of doctrine in philosophy, law, govern-ment, religion, morality, education, science and the like—that it does have, and why these systems of doctrine undergo the basic, large-scale changes that they do undergo in the course of time. As we have seen, Marx's explanation is that, in response to human needs in process of development, changes take place in the tools, sources and methods of production (which he calls the economic base), and changes take place in such a field as philosophy (which is part of what he calls the superstructure), and that the interrelations between these two levels of change are such that it is the philosophy which changes in response to new developments in the economic base far more and far more strongly than it is the other way around. Causation runs both ways; but it runs far more powerfully one way than the other. For example, it was much more a case of the economic system, in response to new technological developments, changing from a slave or serf basis more and more to a wage-labor basis, and that change inducing changes in the prevailing moral, legal and religious principles (from justification of slavery and serfdom to condemnation of them) than it was a case of new moral ideas concerning slavery and serfdom bringing about a new economic system (one which replaced slavery and serfdom with wage-labor). Can this be doubted today?

Consider for a moment a theory of history diametrically opposite to that of Marx in regard to its position on the role of ideas. I refer to the theory of one of Marx's older contemporaries, Auguste Comte, which he sets forth in the first chapter of his *Positive Philosophy*. Comte writes: "It cannot be necessary to prove to any-body who reads this work that Ideas govern the world or throw it into chaos; in other words, that all social mechanism rests upon Opinions. The great political and moral crisis that societies are now undergoing is shown by a rigid analysis to arise out of intellectual anarchy. . . . But whenever the necessary agreement on first prin-ciples can be obtained, appropriate institutions will issue from them without shock or resistance."[4] There, in its dazzling purity, is the ideological process of which Engels wrote. This is the kind of thesis Marx is denying when he says what we quoted above: "It is not the consciousness of men which determines their existence, but on

---

[4] Martineau translation.

the contrary it is their social existence that determines their consciousness." Who today could defend Comte's position from the
charge of naiveté?

At the same time, Comte was a very great mind, who, like Hegel,
made an immense contribution at the methodological level—in Comte's
case, especially in relation to the building up of systematic social
science. Both Comte and Hegel, like Marx, was pervaded, through
and through, by the historical sense, the feeling for the centrality
of history in all things. Yet, is not something significant revealed in
the fact that when we look back upon the actual predictions made
by Comte and Hegel concerning the course history would take, they
seem incredibly naive, whereas Marx's predictions, in spite of the
particulars in which he went wrong, sound like the world we live
in? Comte predicted that by the middle of the twentieth century
the world would be divided into a number of "positivist republics,"
each about the size of Belgium, and each governed by a committee
of benevolent bankers taking advice and counsel from a Priesthood
of Humanity whose members would unite scientific sociology with
a naturalistic religion of love. But how was all this to be brought
into being? Comte's grand strategy consisted in going directly to the
heart of the matter as he saw it: change the ideas of the present
rulers. Accordingly, he sent copies of his works explaining the merits
of his new system to such personages as the Tsar of Russia and the
Sultan of Turkey with covering letters pointing out, quite seriously,
how glad they would be to abdicate thrones and give up empires
once they had digested the ideas basic to the positivist social order.
In contrast, does not the strength of Marx's realism consist precisely
in the fact that he took the measure of the economic factor as a
determinant, and saw that the history of idea-systems taken as a whole
could not possibly be independent of such a factor?

Let us examine somewhat more closely the nature of this dependence, the character of the interrelationships between philosophic
ideas and economic facts. An important aspect of Marx's thesis might
be formulated in this way: The general kind (in terms of content
and form) of world view, moral code, system of law, political theory
and religious interpretation which is *predominant* in a given period
(meaning, which has most influence, is given most opportunities
for development, which is most respectable, most widely disseminated
and implemented in practice) must be such that, a) it does not
condemn, or pronounce as illegitimate, the existing system of production and exchange (or be so taken), and b) it can and does exercise

a cooperative function in relation to the needs of this system as a going concern. If a) and b) were not the case, either the predominant philosophy would cease to be predominant or the existing system would cease to exist. (The point on which everything turns is that the history of ideas is not independent, but conditioned.)

Perhaps we should re-emphasize that these objective conditions within which philosophy, taken as a public, shared enterprise has to operate, do not necessarily condemn the individual thinker to hypocrisy, cowardice, intellectual dishonesty or error. An individual thinker can serve the interests of some existing system, consciously or unconsciously, without being hypocritical, cowardly, dishonest or mistaken; it all depends on the nature of the system, the stage of its development, and the character and intelligence of the individual. One thing I think we can all agree on: a given social system is not necessarily worthy of one's approval simply because one was born under it. We might also agree that on the issue as to whether the existing system is worthy of approval and support, silence usually counts operatively as tacit approval and a form of support. While there is a temptation to imagine that silence and inaction constitute neutrality, and even to associate such neutrality with moral purity, he who would derive any comfort from this must firmly close his mind against analysis, even of the simplest kind. Is it not clear that on the important issues of human life genuine neutrality is objectively impossible? How is one to be neutral about whether he is living in the right way, about whether the present system should be changed, about whether his government should be permitted to go on pursuing the foreign policy it is at present pursuing? Since the issue is whether to change something or not, the decision to do nothing is obviously a decision that favors one side rather than the other, for which we are held accountable. If a person throughout his life has avoided any discussion of marriage and any action in that direction, and dies a bachelor at the age of eighty, was he in fact neutral in relation to matrimony? At most, he might have *thought* of himself as neutral, but that is merely subjective, like the "false consciousness" Engels wrote about.

Here we see the basis of the contemporary Marxist conception of ideological partisanship. That is, for example, if there is any such thing as a ruling class and a ruled class, each in a concrete context of conditions, no one can be objectively neutral about whether the situation should be changed. One either accepts it or not, and one's work either includes a judgment about it, or avoids any explicit reference to the whole matter. In either case, non-partisanship is impossible; silence and inaction are votes in favor of the existing order, and these votes, irrespective of the causes that have led up to them, and the subjective consciousness which accompanies them, have objective consequences. They play a certain role and exert a certain influence in relation to the social struggles which are going on, which means, in relation to the course of history as it is developing. To *take* a side in the struggle between classes is a matter of subjective consciousness, which one can avoid. To further the interest of one side as opposed to the other is a matter of objective effect, which one cannot avoid. One tries to be clear about the sides, and to place one's net effect on the side of one's values.

In this connection it is not usually noticed how profoundly partisan science is, how pervaded with value judgments, first of all in favor of man, as opposed to the rest of nature. If microbes could think, could they be expected to think that microbiology is non-partisan? Or parasites that parasitology is non-partisan? Is medicine neutral as between health and disease? Are astronomy, physics and chemistry neutral on the question whether man ought to increase his power over nature? For the scientist to imagine himself as simply neutral or non-partisan, as free from value judgments, is clearly naive. He is free from partisanship and value judgments only in one respect: once he has chosen a problem, he regulates his conclusions about it strictly by use of a method which depends on confirmable evidence, not on his wishes, hopes or fears. But is not his choice of that method a commitment to the value of human power, a humanly fortunate partisanship? Man is not yet in a position to say that he wants truth just for truth's sake, that he wants or loves any piece of truth whatever, just because it is true. He wants truth, of course, but a certain kind of truth, a kind that has certain relationships to man, or to a God that has certain relationships to man.

There is sometimes even a question of when and where involved. Suppose in Nazi Germany there had been a proposal to publish a book entitled "The Crimes of Jews against Children," in which every word would be true, and every loathsome crime committed by a Jew against a child for centuries back would be fished up from the records and set forth in every documented detail. How many of us who were not anti-Semites would have said: "Fine; we want and love every piece of truth. By all means publish the book in Nazi Germany"? And those who would have objected could not consistently have done so simply on the ground that this book was not "the full truth," for no book is ever the full truth. The fact is that the sciences abound in special studies of every kind (including studies of special crimes of special groups) to which no one objects, because there is no immediate danger of monstrous injustice being perpetrated as a result of their publication. But to allow justice to enter means that we are involving ourselves in value judgments; and to decide in favor of the oppressed means we must abandon the claim to neutrality.

Of course, every period and every existing system has its protesters, its disbelievers and rebels, all of whom suffer various persecutions, and a good many of whom (some of the best) are put in prison or put to death, or both. Everyone knows this, and sees it around him on a large or small scale, so that there is a certain pressure which everyone feels. But precisely what or who is it that exerts this pressure? We use terms like "the existing system" or "the establishment," but these are blanket terms. On closer inspection Marx sees the power of the state enforcing those standards and preventing transgression beyond those limits, which the prevailing mode of economic production and exchange, the major concentration of property-power, the existing ruling class (these are three expressions for the same thing) needs to have respected in order to continue as the prevailing mode of production, major property-power, ruling class. Political conflicts are thus seen as chiefly about control of the means of life, and those who have controlled them as a class have always tried to prevent the dissemination of ideas which they consider a serious threat to their power, to their way of life. This is what is involved in the Marxist formulation to the effect that the ruling ideas of a given period are the ideas of its ruling class.

But a key question here arises: If there is a ruling class, and it has the major power in terms of its control of the prevailing mode of production, how can it ever be dislodged and its idea-systems replaced with contrary idea-systems? This can happen because the mode of production can undergo changes beyond the control of the given ruling class, changes which result in greater and greater productive power being placed in the hands of another group, representing a different mode of production, a different class. This is what took place in the transition from the predominantly agricultural system of feudalism to modern industrial capitalism, in which transition the feudal nobles were displaced as the ruling class by big capitalists; and the laws, forms of government, concepts of morality, systems of philosophy, interpretations of religion and religious authority that went with feudalism were necessarily displaced by those that went with industrial capitalism—by new concepts of individual private property, freedom of movement of the worker, freedom from the bonds of serfdom, freedom to act in a new way, freedom to think in a new way, freedom from the old authorities, freedom to work out a new kind of philosophy (which comes to be called science) capable of radically increasing human power over nature.

If feudalism had been able to hold on, these new idea-systems would not have been allowed to grow. But why was feudalism unable to hold on? Was it because these new ideas won a victory in the battle of ideas, and then, having changed men's opinions, as Comte would have it, the men involved changed their social institutions and way of life accordingly—from feudalism to capitalism? Did it happen mainly that way, or did it mainly happen, as Marx would have it, because a different form of production, based on manufacture, improved machinery, new sources of raw materials and new markets, aided by bankers with growing cash reserves to lend or invest—the form of production we have come to call capitalism—grew to the point where its productivity, hence its power, was greater than that of feudalism, so that feudalism with its ideas was forced to give way?

It will be recognized that what we have here said represents but the barest sketch of an extremely complex pattern of interrelated factors, a pattern which, as Marx saw it, constituted the central dynamic, the strongest determinant, the major causal agent of the historical process as a whole, within which we must locate, and to which we must relate, the history of ideas. This pattern in its fullness is seen, of course, not only in the transition from medieval feudalism to modern capitalism, but in all large-scale historical transitions. Before leaving this part of our theme a comment should perhaps be made on a sort of wholesale challenge which in our day has been directed against the very effort underlying this whole line of thought, the effort put forth not only by Marx, but by Comte, Hegel and others, to deal with history as a whole rationally or scientifically. Karl Popper has called this effort "historicism," and has summarized the chain of argument against it as follows: "1) The course of human history is strongly influenced by the growth of human knowledge; 2) We cannot predict, by rational or scientific methods, the future growth of our scientific knowledge; 3) We cannot, therefore, predict the future course of human history. This means that we must reject the possibility of a historical social science that would correspond to *theoretical physics*. There can be no scientific theory of historical development serving as a basis for historical prediction." Popper adds: "The decisive step in this argument is statement 2. I think that it is convincing in itself: if there is such a thing as growing human knowledge, then we cannot anticipate today what we shall only know tomorrow."[5]

But that is exactly what we can do: we can anticipate today that we shall know something tomorrow (e.g., enough about the composition of the moon's surface to determine what types of construction it can support) without thereby claiming to know today what we shall only know tomorrow. In other words, Popper fails to see that there is a difference between predicting *that* something is going to be proved, and predicting *how* it will be proved, that is, the content and details of the proof. He fails to make any distinction between predicting the *growth* of knowledge and predicting knowledge, though he uses both terms. The growth of knowledge is predictable (probabilistically, of course) on the basis of past experience relating to such factors as volume of research, developments in related fields, and improvements in instruments and techniques of observation and experiment: instances abound. It is also important in this connection to note that an idea, in Marx's view, does not necessarily affect the course of history just by being proved. The stage reached by the development of social institutions must be such that the newly proved idea can be functionally absorbed and implemented. Otherwise, nothing comes of it at the time. The further fact that we can identify many of the conditions that make a given idea functionally implementable facilitates the predictive process.

Francis Bacon once said that scholars, in dealing with their respective fields, should not only report accurately the existing facts, but should recognize a special obligation to point out any important misimpressions current among the public or in learned circles concerning the matters being dealt with. Let us here follow Bacon's admonition, and direct attention to some extremely important misimpressions pertaining to Marxism as an ideology, misimpressions which have gen-

---

[5]Both quotations from *The Poverty of Historicism* (New York: Harper & Row, 1964), pp. vi, vii. Italics of original. Parenthetical comments omitted.

erated, and continue to generate, unfounded hostilities and tensions of the most serious nature. These hostilities and tensions involve the arrest and imprisonment of individuals, the intellectual distortion of educational systems, and have even been, and are being, put forward as a justifiable cause of armed warfare between powerful states possessed of thermonuclear weapons. Has not "ideological warfare" become in our day a common expression, often used in connection with the possibility of World War III? Considering the existing facts as a whole, the plain truth is that in all previous history, and in all the previous history of ideas, it is impossible to find any situation of greater human gravity, of greater danger in regard to the very survival of mankind, than the present one.

What specific misimpressions about Marxism are capable of playing such a fateful role? They have to do with the subject of violent revolution and armed warfare, that is, with the teachings and doctrines of Marxism concerning these subjects. The predominant impression, or, rather, misimpression in my country—and this is probably true of most other capitalist countries—is that Marxist doctrine teaches: 1) that the working class may hope to attain social justice only through violent revolution; 2) that the Marxist parties and leaders are justified in calling for violent revolution against capitalism at any time and under any conditions; 3) that, so long as there are both capitalist states and communist states existing in the world together, war is inevitable between them. These misimpressions about Marxism as an ideology are not only current among the general public, but represent the predominant orientation found in the educational system as a whole, in the popular arts and mass media, and in the minds of the vast majority of government officials—legislative, executive and judicial.

One result of this in the United States has been the passage of a whole corpus of legislation, from the Smith Act to the Communist Control Act, designed to put Communists in jail and deprive them of various civil rights because they believe in Marxist doctrine—all of this on the assumption that Marxist doctrine teaches the three propositions just set forth. Under the Smith Act alone (a sedition law which punishes speech, teaching and published doctrine) dozens of leaders of the Community Party have served prison sentences of from two to five years. It is necessary to emphasize that all this was done on the basis of alleged conspiracy to teach ideas, not on the basis of alleged conspiracy to take any overt action. No Communists in the United States were ever accused, let alone convicted, of any actual attempt to overthrow the government, or of any conspiracy to engage in such an attempt.

The legislation referred to began to appear in the late thirties, and reached a point where the historical tradition of American freedom of speech, thought and teaching, the tradition of Jefferson, was brought almost to the brink of death in the country of its birth, though it continued to flourish elsewhere, and, we hope, may once again be restored to health in its own house. The irony of this is at once exquisite and grim: the very doctrine that Thomas Jefferson put in the center of the Declaration of Independence, universally recognized as the best expression of the ideology on which the United States of America was founded—the doctrine that all people have the right of revoluion when they believe their government has become a tyranny—is the very doctrine that is made a criminal offense under the Smith Act. Is there any better explanation for such a development in the realm of ideas than the one Marx offers—that the history of ideology is essentially a response to the history of power developments, to the situation and the struggles at the economic base?

The doctrine of the right of revoluion is, of course, a direct corollary of the doctrine of the sovereignty of the people; and it should be clear that the Marxists did not invent either of these doctrines. When Marx and Engels came upon the scene these concepts were already established in explicit and systematic doctrine worked out by English, American and French social thinkers of the seventeenth and eighteenth centuries, and implemented in historical practice by the English, American and French Revolutions. This was the source from which Marx and Engels took the concept of the right of revolution—not their socio-historical explanation of the fact of revolution (that was their own creation), but the political-moral concept of the right of revolution. Those who profess to accept the doctrine of the right of revolution as found in Locke and Jefferson, but not as found in Marxism, usually seem to imply that the earlier thinkers restricted the justifiability of armed revolution to those cases where it had the support of a majority of the people, whereas Marxism allegedly makes no such restriction, and justifies armed revolution against capitalist governments at any time or place, irrespective of whether the revolution has majority support. But the facts are, as I have tried to document in detail elsewhere, that in the classic works of Marxism which explicitly treat of this question, especially works of Lenin, it is insisted, over and over again, that no armed revolution is justified, or is to be undertaken, unless there is clear evidence that such action has the support of the majority.[6]

This position is worked out in much greater detail and concreteness by Lenin than by either Jefferson or Locke. The Marxists have accordingly developed a whole literature around these matters, in which it is pointed out, among other things: 1) that it is possible to have majority support for a revolution without the revolution being justified, since there might not yet exist what Lenin called the "subjective" preconditions, i.e., a disciplined political organization and competent leadership; 2) that it is possible to have a tyrannical government without having majority support for revolutionary action, in which case such action would also not be justified; 3) that there are times and places in which a peaceful revolution is possible, a peaceful transition from capitalism to socialism, which is always to be preferred to a violent transition. In connection with the issue of violence it should be recognized by all that Marxism, unlike such an ideology as Fascism or Nazism, contains no doctrinal evaluation of war as higher or nobler than peace, and does not regard armed warfare as an eternal social phenomenon, or as a form of conduct ineradicably rooted in human nature. In the great majority of countries where there are powerful Marxist movements the predominant view taken is that war between capitalist and communist states is not inevitable in any absolute or fatalistic sense, and can be avoided if capitalist states are willing to compete peacefully on a basis of equal rights in the international community.

These problems take us into the most important aspect of the whole theme—its relation to war and peace. For the fact is that the misimpressions listed above are being used in the most powerful capitalist states as the justification for a foreign policy which proceeds from the premise that communism as a socio-political movement, because of its acceptance of the Marxist ideology, constitutes essentially a criminal conspiracy, which gives to non-communist governments the right to deal with it more or less as the police deal with the underworld. In other words, communist governments do not have equal rights with ours; they can and should be "contained," but, of course, they have

---

[6]John Somerville, *The Communist Trials and the American Tradition: Expert Testimony on Force and Violence* (New York: Cameron, 1956), chapter. 2-7. This book contains the official record of the writer's testimony and cross-examination as a non-Communist expert witness on Marxist doctrine in three of the Smith Act trials.

no right to "contain" us; we have the right to line their borders with our military bases and installations, but, of course, they have no right to line our borders with their bases and installations; we have the right to give any amount of military equipment and assistance to small countries in their immediate neighborhood who are friendly to us, but of course, they have no right to give military equipment or assistance to small countries friendly to them in our immediate neighborhood; and so on, and so on, closer and closer to the final thermonuclear confrontation which will be called World War III in the unlikely event that its aftermath should include the presence of any linguistic phenomena.

Here again, is not Marx's explanation the best that has been offered? Are not these ideological issues, and the struggles we see arising over them, a response to technological-economic developments and the power consequences of such developments? But technological or economic developments as such, and ideas as such, do not drop bombs. There is a human, international struggle involving economic forces and involving ideas only because there are people—with specific needs, powers and potentialities, conditioned by the situation in which they find themselves. Our first human need is the need to live. Therefore, our first human right is the right to live, the right to live out our normal span. Another way of putting the point is to say that a necessary precondition of human values is human life. Thermonuclear war today threatens not only all existing human values; it threatens the very possibility of creating any further human values to replace them. It threatens to commit a crime for which there is not even a name: to extinguish the human future.

Is it not true that this is the enemy of all of us, no matter to what school of thought we may belong? Let us disagree about everything else; but let us agree to reject and resist, in theory and practice, this ultimate madness. From whatever standpoint we may approach philosophy, be it metaphysics, theism, idealism, materialism, rationalism, phenomenology, existentialism, logical analysis, linguistic analysis, or any other standpoint, let us recognize this common task, and let each make to it the contribution that it is possible for him to make.

MARX AND CRITICAL SCIENTIFIC THOUGHT

Mihailo Marković

M ARX CREATED a theory which is both scientific and critical. However, in most interpretations and further developments of his thought one of these two essential characteristics has been systematically overlooked. Among those who speak in the name of Marx or consider themselves his intellectual followers some accept only his radical criticism of the society of his time, some lay emphasis only on his contribution to positive scientific knowledge about contemporary social structures and processes.

To the former group belong, on the one hand, various apologists of post-capitalist society who develop Marxism as an ideology; on the other hand, those romantically minded humanists who consider positive knowledge a form of the intellectual subordination to the given social framework and who are ready to accept only the anthropological ideas of the young Marx.

To the latter group belong all those scientists who appreciate Marx's enormous contribution to modern social science, but who fail to realize that what fundamentally distinguishes Marx's views from Comte, Mill, Ricardo and other classical social scientists, as well as from modern positivism, is his always present radical criticism both of existing theory and of existing forms of social reality.

The failure of most contemporary interpreters of Marx to grasp one of the basic novelties of his doctrine has very deep roots in the intellectual climate of our time and can be explained only taking into account some of the fundamental divisions and polarizations in contemporary theoretical thinking.

I

The development of science and philosophy in the twentieth century has been decisively influenced by the following three factors:

(1) accelerated growth of scientific knowledge which gave rise to a new technological revolution characterized by automation, use of huge new sources of energy and new exact methods of management; (2) discovery of the dark irrational side of human nature through psychoanalysis, anthropological investigations of primitive cultures, surrealism and other trends of modern arts, and above all, through unheard of mass eruptions of brutality from the beginning of World War I until the present day; (3) the beginning of the process of destructuralization of the existing forms of class society and the rapidly increasing role of ideology and politics.

As the result of a rapid technological development and of an increasing division of work in modern industrial society, the rationality of science has gradually been reduced to a narrow technological rationality of experts interested only in promoting and conveying positive knowledge in a very special field. In an effort to free itself from the domination of theology and mythology, modern science has from its beginnings tended to get rid of unverifiable theoretical generalizations and value-judgments. As a consequence, a spiritual vacuum was created which, under the given historical conditions, might have been filled only by faith in power, faith in success in all its various forms. This philosophy of success, this obsession with the efficiency of means, followed by an almost total lack of interest for the problem of rationality and humanity of goals, are the essential characteristics of the spiritual climate of contemporary industrial society.

By now it has already become quite clear that while increasing power over nature, material wealth, and control over some blind forces of history, while creating new historical opportunities of human emancipation, material form of positive science—industry has neglected many essential human needs and has extended possibilities of manipulation of human beings. The universal penetration of technology into all forms of social life has been followed by the penetration of routine, uniformity, and inauthenticity. Growth of material wealth did not make men happier; data on suicide, alcoholism, mental illness, juvenile delinquency, etc., even indicate a positive correlation between the degree of technological development and social pathological phenomena.

Obviously, positive science and technology set off unpredicted and uncontrollable social processes. The scientist who does not care about the broader social context of his inquiry loses every control over the product of his work. The history of creation and use of nuclear weapons is a drastic example. Another one is the abuse of science for ideological purposes. The most effective and, therefore, most danger-ous propaganda is not one which is based on obvious untruths, but one which, for the rationalization of the interests of privileged social groups, uses partial truths established by science.

Science would be helpless against such abuses if it were atomized, disintegrated, disinterested in the problems of wholes and neutral with regard to such general human values as emancipation, human soli-darity, development, production according to the "laws of beauty," disalienation, etc.

However, the most influential philosophy in contemporary science is positivism, according to which the sole function of science is to describe and explain what *there is* and, if at least some laws are known, to extrapolate what there *might probably* be. All evaluation in terms of needs, feelings, ideals, ethical, aesthetic and other stand-ards—are considered basically irrational and, from the scientific point of view, pointless. The only function of science, then, is the investiga-tion of the most adequate means for the ends which have been laid down by others. In such a way science loses power to supersede the existing forms of historical reality and to project new, essentially different, more humane historical possibilities. By its indifference to-wards goals it only leads to an abstract growth of power, and to a better adjustment within a given framework of social life. The very framework remains unchallenged. So behind this apparent neutrality and apparent absence of any value orientation one discovers an im-plicit conservative orientation. Even a passive resistance to the re-duction of science to a mere servant of ideology and politics is ac-ceptable to the ruling elites because pure, positive, disintegrated knowledge can always be interpreted and used in any profitable way: ultimately society would be devoid of its critical self-consciousness.

II

Positivism and other variants of philosophical intellectualism, con-formism, and utilitarianism are facing nowadays a strong opposition among all those philosophers, writers and artists who prefer "the logic of heart" to "the logic of reason," and who rebel against the prospect of an impersonal, inauthentic life in an affluent mass society of the future. They see clearly that power and material wealth in themselves do not help men to overcome their anxiety, loneliness, their perplexity, boredom, uprootedness, their spiritual and emotional poverty. New experiences in political life, modern art, and science indicate a general lack of order and stability in the world and the presence of a basic human irrationality. Thus they strengthened the feeling that after all successes of positive sciences and technology a fragile, unreasonable and suicidal society emerged.

As a reaction to the spirit of the Enlightenment (which had to some extent survived in the form of positivism) a powerful anti-Enlightenment attitude is gaining ground among intellectuals. The world does not make sense, there is no rational pattern by which the individual can hope to master it, no causal explanation which would allow him to predict the future. There is no determination and progress in history; all history of civilization is only the history of growing human estrangement and self-deception. Human existence is absurd and utterly fragile. Confronted with a universe in which there is pure contingency, lacking any stable structure of his being, man lives a meaningless life full of dread, guilt, and despair. There are no reasons to believe that man is basically good; evil is a permanent possibility of his existence.

Such an anti-positivist and anti-Enlightenment philosophy (which has been most consistently expressed in *Lebensphilosophie* and various forms of existentialism) is clearly a critical thought, concerned with the problems of human individual existence. However, this kind of rebellion against "given" and "existing" tends to be as *immediate* as possible and to avoid any mediation by positive knowledge and logic. The basic idea of this obviously anti-rationalist form of criticism is the following: to rely on empirical science already means to be caught up within the framework of the given present reality. On the other hand, as neither historical process nor human being has any definite structure preceding existence, all general knowledge is pointless. Nothing about the present can be inferred from the past, nor can the future be determined on the basis of the knowledge of the present. All possibilities are open. Freedom of projection is unlimited.

This kind of romantic rebellious criticism is entirely powerless. Postulated absolute freedom is only freedom of thought; as already Hegel in *Phänomenologie des Geistes* has shown, it is the imagined freedom of a slave. Real criticism must start with the discovery of concrete forms of slavery, with the examination of human bonds and real practical possibilities of liberation. Without such concrete practical examination, which requires the use of all relevant social knowledge and the application of scientific method, a criticism is only an alienated form of disalienation.

III

In an historical epoch of fundamental social transformation a theory which expresses the needs and acceptable programs of action of powerful social forces becomes one of the decisive historical determining factors.

The theory of Marx has been playing such a revolutionary role for the whole historical epoch of human emancipation from alienated labor. It has been and still is the existing theoretical basis for every contemporary form of active and militant humanism.

The critical thought of Marx is the fullest and historically the most developed expression of human rationality. It contains, in a dialectically superseded form, all the essential characteristics of ancient Greek *theoria*: a rational knowledge about the structure of the world by which man can change the world and determine his own life. Hegel's dialectical reason is already a really creative negation of the Greek notion of *ratio* and theory: here the contradictions between static, rational thinking and irrational dynamics, between positive assertion and abstract negation have been superseded *(aufgehoben)*. The theory and method of Marx is a decisive further step in the process of totalization and concretization of the dialectical reason: it embraces not only change in general but also the specific human historical form of change: *praxis*. The dialectic of Marx puts the question of rationality not only of an individual but also of society as a whole, not only rationality within a given closed system, but also of the very limits of the system as a whole, not only rationality of praxis as thinking but also of praxis as material activity, as mode of real life in space and time. There is a dialectical reason in history only to the extent to which it creates a reasonable reality.

This theoretico-practical conception of man and human history, has not been further developed by Marx's followers as a totality, but underwent a far-reaching disintegration into its component parts: various branches of social science, philosophical anthropology, dialectics, philosophy of history, conception of proletarian revolution and socialism as a concrete program of practical action, etc.

Science without dialectic and humanist philosophy incorporated in its *telos*, in all its assumptions, criteria and methods of inquiry, underwent in socialist society a process analogous to the one in capitalism: it developed as partial, positive, expert knowledge which informs about the given but does not seek to discover its essential inner limitations and to overcome it radically. The connection with philosophy remained doubly external: first, because it assimilates the principles of Marxism in a fixed, completed form as something given, obligatory, imposed by authority, abstract, torn out of context, simplified, vulgarized; second, because these principles externally applied do not live the life of science, are not subject to the process of normal critical testing, re-examining, revising, but become dogmas of a fixed doctrine.

That is why Marxist philosophy became increasingly more abstract, powerless, conservative. This part of it which pretended to be a *Weltanschauung* looked more and more as a boring, old-fashioned, primitive *Naturphilosophie,* and the other part which was supposed to express the general principles for the interpretation of social phenomena and revolutionary action assumed increasingly the character of pragmatic apologetic which was expected to serve as a foundation of ideology and for the justification of the past and present policies.

This temporary degeneration was the consequence of several important circumstances:

—of the fact that the theory of Marx became official ideological doctrine of victorious labor movements.

—of the unexpected success of revolutions just in the underdeveloped countries of East Europe and Asia where, in addition to socialist objectives the tasks of a previous primitive accumulation, industrialization, urbanization have to be accomplished.

—of the necessity, in such conditions, to give priority to accelerated technological development, to establish a centralized system and to impose an authoritarian structure on all thinking and social behavior.

Thus a return to Marx and a reinterpretation of his thought is needed in order to restore and to further develop a critical method of Marx's theoretical thinking.

IV

The essential theoretical and methodological novelty of Marx's conception of science is constituted by the following features:

First, by moving in the process of research from unanalyzed given concrete phenomena (such as population, wealth, etc.) towards abstract universals (such as commodity, labor, money, capital, surplus-value, etc.) and from them back towards (this time) analyzed empirico-theoretical concreteness Marx succeeds in overcoming the traditional dualism between the empirical and the rational (speculative) approaches. There is no doubt that he makes great efforts in order to support each of his contentions by as ample evidence as possible. All his major works have been preceded by years of studying data, establishing facts. But, in sharp contrast to empiricism, Marx's science neither begins with brute facts nor remains satisfied with simple inductive generalizations from them. His real starting position is a philosophical vision and a thorough critical study of all preceding relevant special knowledge. Initial evidence is only a necessary component of the background against which he builds up a whole network of abstract scientific concepts endowed with an impressive explanatory power. This elaboration of a new conceptual apparatus (new not so much in the sense of introducing new terminology as in the sense of giving new meanings to already existing terms) is the most important and most creative part of Marx's scientific work.

Second, according to Marx, science should not be primarily concerned with the description of details and explanation of isolated phenomena but with the study of whole structures, of social situations taken in their totality. That is why Marx's new science does not know about any sharp division into branches and disciplines. *Das Kapital* belongs not only to economic science, but also to sociology, law, political science, history, and philosophy. However, although the category of totality plays such an overwhelming role in the methodology of Marx, this is not a purely synthetical approach. Marx knew that any attempt to grasp totalities directly without analytical mediation leads to myth and ideology. Therefore, a necessary phase of his method is the analysis of initial directly grasped wholes into their components, which in the final stages of inquiry have to be brought back into various relations with other components and conceived only as moments within a complex structure.

Third, some variants of contemporary Marxist humanism which are mainly interested in diachronic aspects of social formations, and structuralism which pays attention only to their synchronic aspects are degenerated, one-sided developments of certain essential moments of Marx's method. However, in Marx's new science these moments are inseparable. A totality cannot be fully understood without taking into account its previous development and the place it has in history. A socio-economic system becomes a meaningful structure only as a crystallization of the past forms of human practice and with respect to historically possible futures. On the other hand, what is historically possible cannot be grasped without taking into account determinant structural characteristics of the whole given situation. Marx has discovered self-destructive forces within the very structure of the capitalist system; without establishing the law of decreasing average rate of profit and other laws of capitalist economy, he would not have been able to establish real historical possibility of the disappearance of capitalist society. But on the other hand, had he not had a profound sense of history, had he approached capitalist society in the same ahistorical way as Smith, Ricardo and other bourgeois economists—as the permanent natural structure of human society, he would hardly have been able to look for and find out all those structural features which determine both relative stability and ultimate transformation of the whole system.

Fourth, true sense of history implies a *critical* component not only with respect to all rival theories but also with respect to the examined society. Marx's dialectics is essentially a method of critique and of revolutionary practice. He himself had expressed this fundamental characteristic of his method by saying that dialectics arouses anger and horror of the bourgeoisie because it introduces into positive understanding of existing states the *understanding of its negation,* of its *necessary destruction;* because it conceives every existing form in its change, therefore as something in *transition;* because it does not let anything impose upon it, and because it is fundamentally critical and revolutionary (see Marx, *Capital,* Afterword to the Second German Edition). This thought was expressed much earlier in "Theses on Feuerbach": the basic weakness of traditional materialism was construing reality only as object, not as *praxis.* This praxis is critical and revolutionary. Thus man is not just the product of social conditions, but the being who can change these conditions. He lives in a world full of contradictions, but he can resolve and practically remove them. The main objective of philosophical criticism should be the "real essence" of man; however, this essence is not something ahistorical and unchangeable but the totality of social relationships. In short, what really matters is not just the explanation but the transformation of the world.

What must follow from such activistic assumptions is a new conception of the function of science. According to this conception, science does not only provide positive knowledge but also develops critical self-consciousness. It does not only describe and explain the historical situation but also evaluates it and shows the way out. It does not only discover laws and establish what are the possibilities and probabilities of the future, it also indicates which possibilities best correspond to certain basic human needs. Thus critical scientific thought does not remain satisfied by showing how man can best adjust to the prevailing trends of a situation and to the whole social framework; it expresses a higher level idea of rationality by showing how man can change the whole framework and adapt it to himself.

Two examples would suffice to illustrate this conception of critical science.

In his economic writings Marx has thoroughly examined structural and functional characteristics of capitalistic society. He had done that in an objective way in accordance with all requirements of the scientific method of his time. But a critical anthropological standpoint is always present; this is the standpoint of man as "generic being," as a potentially free, creative, rational social being. From the point of view of what man already *could be*: how he already *could* live in a highly productive and integrated industrialized society, Marx shows how utterly limited and crippled man is in a system in which he is reduced to his working power, and his working power is being bought as a thing, and regarded not as a creative power, but as merely a quantity of energy which can be efficiently objectified and sold at the market with a good profit. The message of Marx's theory is not that the worker could better adjust to the situation by demanding a higher price for his labor power; in so far as his labor power is a mere commodity, he already receives the equivalent for it. The implication of Marx's theory is that the worker should reject the status of a thing, of a commodity, and change the whole social framework in which his labor is so alienated.

Another example. In his criticism of Hegelian philosophy of law, Marx pointed out that the general interest of a human community could not be constituted by the abstract conception of an ideal, rational state. So far as in "civil society" there is *bellum omnium contra omnes* and each individual and social group pursues only one or the other particular interest, general interest of a truly human community has not yet been constituted. The Hegelian state, construed as a moment of objective spirit, exists only in abstract thought. What exists in reality is alienated political power *beside* and *above* all other individual and particular interests. The form of this alienated political power, which treats society as the simple object of its activity is the state with its bureaucracy. Now, Marx's explanation of the nature of professional politics, state, and bureaucracy does not lead to the conclusion that man could be freer if he merely makes the state more democratic or increases control over bureaucracy. Without disregarding the temporary importance of such modifications, Marx opens up the prospects of a radical human emancipation by altogether abolishing the state and political bureaucracy as forms of social organization. This, according to Marx, is possible if organized labor, the only class whose ultimate interests coincide with those of mankind as a whole, practically removes economic and political monopoly of any particular social group. The atomized, disintegrated world of the owners of commodities would, in such a way, be superseded by an integrated community of producers. The state would be replaced by the organs of self-management, i.e., by institutions composed of the true representatives of the people who have been elected by a general free vote, who are immediately responsible to and replaceable by their voters, and who do not enjoy any privileges for the duties they perform.

V

The nature of the key concepts in Marx's anthropology and philosophy of history best shows the character of his theoretical thought. These concepts are not only descriptive and explanatory but also value-laden and critical.

Thus Marx's criticism of fetishism of commodities in *Das Kapital* can be understood only under his assumption of a truly *human production* in which man affirms himself and another in a double way:

—by objectifying his individuality and experiencing his personality as an objective, sensate power;
—by an immediate awareness that by his activity and by the use of his product a need of another human being would be satisfied;
—by mediating between the other man and generic human being: his activity has become a part of the other human being and has enriched and complemented it;
—this mediation allows man to immediately affirm and fulfill his own true generic being (*Marx-Engels Gesamtausgabe*, I, Bd. 3, S. 546). Alienated labor is labor which lacks these qualities.

In a similar way the concepts of *social man, human needs, history, freedom, state, capital, communism, etc.*, always imply a distinction between actual and possible, between factual and ideal.

Social man is not just the individual who lives together with other individuals, or who simply conforms to the given norms of a society. Such a person can be very far from reaching the level of a social being. On the other hand, a person may be compelled to live in isolation and still profoundly need the other person and carry in his language, thinking, and feeling all essential characteristics of human generic being.

In this sense Marx distinguishes, for example, between man who regards woman as "prey and the handmaid of communal lust," "who is infinitely degraded in such an existence for himself," and man whose "natural behavior towards woman has become human" and "whose needs have become human needs." This "most natural immediate and necessary relationship" shows to what extent man "is in his individual existence at the same time a social being" (*Economic and Philosophical Manuscripts [Marx's Concept of Man]* by Erich Fromm, New York, 1961, pp. 126-127).

Furthermore, *history* is not just a series of events in time—it presupposes supersession of "the realm of necessity" and full emancipation of man. That is why Marx sometimes labeled the history of our time as "prehistory."

Freedom never meant for Marx only choice among several possibilities or "the right to do and perform anything that does not harm others." Freedom in Marx's sense is ability of self-determination and of rationality controlling blind forces of nature and history. "All emancipation is restoration of the human world and the relationships of men themselves" (Marx, "On the Jewish Question," *Writings of the Young Marx on Philosophy and Society,* ed. by Loyd Easton).

State is not just any social organization which directs social processes and takes care of order and stability of the society. The typical feature of the State, according to Marx, is its coercive character as an instrument of the ruling class. The state is institutionalized alienated power. Therefore, Marx very definitely held the view that the labor movement must abolish the institution of the State very soon after successful revolution and replace it by the associations of workers.

Capital is not only objectified, stored-up labor in the form of money or any particular commodity. It is the objectified labor which at the given level of material production appropriates the surplus value. The objective form of capital conceals and mystifies a social relationship beyond it; the object mediates between those who produce and those who rule.

There is no doubt that both in early and mature writings the concept of *communism* does not only express a possible future social state, but contains also evaluation of that society. In his *Economic and Philosophical Manuscripts* there are even three different descriptions and evaluations: [1] "crude communism" in which "the domination of material property looms so large that it aims to destroy everything that is incapable of being possessed by everyone as private property;" [2] communism "(a) still political in nature, (b) with the abolition of the state, yet still incomplete and influenced by private property, that is by alienation of man;" [3] communism "as positive abolition of private property, of human self-alienation" (*op. cit.*, p. 127). But even when Marx in *The German Ideology* denies that communism is "an *ideal* to which reality will have to adjust," he says, "we call communism the *real* movement which abolishes the present state of affairs" (*Writings of the Young Marx on Philosophy and Society*, p. 426). Here the adjective "real" clearly is a value term.

Therefore, any attempt to determine the nature of Marx's scientific thought should lead to the conclusion that it is both a knowledge and a vision of the future. As knowledge, it is vastly different from the idea of knowledge of any variant of empiricist philosophy because, among other things, for Marx our future project determines the sense of everything in the present and the past, and this preliminary vision of the future is more the expression of a revolt than a mere extrapolation of the present trends established in an empirical way. And still, no matter how bold and pervaded by passion was this vision of the future, it is not merely an arbitrary dream or a utopian hope. The future is not a logical inference from the present situation, it is really not the result of a prediction made according to the methodological standards of empirical science, it is also not divorced from the present and the past. In the beginning of inquiry it is a relatively *a priori* projection (based more on preceding theory than on empirical data). But, when at the end of inquiry it was shown that the preliminary is by all available evidence about actual trends in the present reality, then *a posteriori,* this vision of the future becomes part of a meaningful knowledge.

This dialectic of the future and the present, of the possible and the actual, of philosophy and of science, of value and fact, of *a priori* and *a posteriori,* of criticism and description is perhaps the essential methodological contribution of Marx to contemporary science—one which so far has not sufficiently been taken into account even by the followers of Marx themselves.

VI

In order to clarify and further elaborate the contention about the critical character of Marx's scientific thought the following further qualifications should be made:

(1) Criticism is present in all Marx's works at all stages of his intellectual development. To distinguish sharply between a value-laden humanist utopia of the young Marx and value-free scientific structuralism of the mature Marx would be a grave error indicating a superficial study of his work. To be sure, there are some important differences in methodology, in richness, and concreteness of the conceptual apparatus used, in the extent to which theory is supported by empirical evidence. However, the fundamental critical position is the same. There is often only a change of vocabulary or substitution of specific terms applicable to capitalistic society for general terms applicable to society in general. For example, what Marx calls "alienated labor" in his early writings (e.g., in *Economic and Philosophical Manuscripts*) will be expressed in *Capital* by the "world of commodities." Or, in his criticism of Hegel's philosophy of the state Marx says that "the abolition of bureaucracy will be possible when general interest becomes a reality" and "particular interest really becomes a general interest." In *Capital* and in his analysis of the experience of the Paris Commune, Marx is much more concrete and explicit; associated producers will do away with the state and take control over exchange.

(2) Marxist criticism is radical although not destructive in a nihilistic sense. Without understanding the Hegelian concept *aufheben* the nature of this criticism can hardly be grasped.

In spite of the differences between Hegel's and Marx's method, the idea of dialectical negation contains both a moment of discontinuity and of continuity: the former in so far as the given cannot be accepted as it is (as truth in Hegel's logic, as satisfactory human reality in Marx's interpretation of history); the latter in so far as a component of the given must be conserved as the basis for further development —it is only the inner limitation which has to be overcome.

Most Marxists are not quite clear about the nature of Marxist criticism—which is not surprising taking into account how few have to interpret him in the context of the whole intellectual tradition to which he belongs. However, a good deal of misunderstanding is of an ideological character. Thus in order to develop a militant optimism or to express a natural revolt against market economy tendencies in underdeveloped socialist countries, some Marxists tend to underestimate the importance of those forms of civilization, of political democracy, of educational, and of welfare institutions which have been developed in western industrial society. Marx took into account the possibility of such a primitive negation of private property and called it "crude" and "unreflective" communism, which "negates the per-

sonality of man in every sphere . . . sets up universal envy and level-
ling down . . . negates in an abstract way the whole world of culture
and civilization," and regresses to "unnatural simplicity of the poor
and wantless individual who has not only surpassed private property
but has not yet even attained to it" (*Economic and Philosophical
Manuscripts*, p. 125). Thus, there can hardly be any doubt that for
Marx a true negation of class society and alienated labor is possible
only at a high level of historical development.

Such a negation presupposes abundance of material goods, various
civilized patterns of human behavior (which arise in the process of
disappearance of scarcity), and, most important of all, it presupposes
an individual who, among other things, has overcome at least elementary, rudest forms of his greed for material objects.

While in this respect some Marxists appear as too radical critics
who fail to realize that certain features of advanced capitalism are
necessary conditions for any higher level forms of society, they, on
the other hand, in some other essential respects, give the impression
of mere reformers who remain quite satisfied with certain initial
changes and who too soon become predominately interested in preserving the *status quo* instead of persisting in their revolutionary role
and striving for further and deeper structural changes.

What present day socialism offers as the practical solution of the
fundamental problems of alienated labor and political alienation is a
far cry from a really radical criticism, from real supersession of alienation in capitalist society.

Thus the essential source of exploitation and of all other aspects
of economic alienation lies in the rule of objectified, stored-up labor
over living labor (*Marx-Engels-Archiv*, Moscow, 1933, S. 68). The
social group disposing of stored-up labor is able to appropriate the
surplus value. The specific historical form of this structure in Marx's
time was the disposal of capital on the grounds of private ownership
of the means of production: however, private property is not the
cause but the effect of alienated labor. Abolition of the private ownership of the means of production is only abolition of one possible
specific form of the rule of dead labor over living labor. The general
structure remains if there is any other social group such as, for example, bureaucracy, which retains monopoly decision-making concerning the disposal of accumulated and objectified labor. Therefore, only
such criticism might be considered radical and truly revolutionary
which puts a definitive end to exploitation and which aims at creating

conditions in which associate producers themselves will dispose of the products of their labor.

Another example. If the state, as such, is historically a form of alienated political power, the abolition of the *bourgeois* state is only the important step in the process of disalienation of politics. This step, according to Marx (and Lenin in *State and Revolution*), must be followed by a transition period of gradually withering away of any coercive state apparatus. Unless such an apparatus is replaced by an entirely different social organization which issues—all the symptoms of political alienation, such as apathy, distrust, lust for power, need for charismatic leaders and for ideological rationalization, use of all available techniques for manipulating masses, etc., would be reproduced.

In so far as in man there is a profound Faustian need to rebel against any permanent historically determined limitation in nature, society and in himself, he will strive to supersede practically such limits, to develop further his human world and his own nature. Such an activistic attitude towards the world will always need a philosophical and scientific thought which would be a bold radical criticism of existing reality.

EXPERIMENTALISM EXTENDED
TO POLITICS*

Ernesto Guevara

THIS IS a unique Revolution which some people maintain contradicts one of the most orthodox premises of the revolutionary movement, expressed by Lenin: "Without a revolutionary theory there is no revolutionary movement." It would be suitable to say that revolutionary theory, as the expression of a social truth, surpasses any declaration of it; that is to say, even if the theory is not known, the revolution can succeed if historical reality is interpreted correctly and if the forces involved are utilized correctly. Every revolution always incorporates elements of very different tendencies which, nevertheless, coincide in action and in the revolution's most immediate objectives.

It is clear that if the leaders have an adequate theoretical knowledge prior to the action, they can avoid trial and error whenever the adopted theory corresponds to the reality. The principal actors of this revolution had no coherent theoretical criteria; but it cannot be said that they were ignorant of the various concepts of history, society, economics, and revolution which are being discussed in the world today. Profound knowledge of reality, a close relationship with the people, the firmness of the liberator's objective, and the practical revolutionary experience gave to those leaders the chance to form a more complete theoretical concept.

The foregoing should be considered an introduction to the explication of this curious phenomenon which has intrigued the entire world: the Cuban Revolution. It is a deed worthy of study in contemporary world history: the how and the why of a group of men who, shattered by an army enormously superior in technique and equipment, man-

---

*Reprinted by permission from *Studies on the Left*, Vol. I, No. 3, 1960, pp. 75-85.

aged first to survive, soon became strong, later became stronger than the enemy in the battle zones, still later moved into new zones of combat, and finally defeated that enemy on the battlefield even though their troops were still very inferior in number.

Naturally, we who often do not show the requisite concern for theory, will not run the risk of expounding the truth of the Cuban Revolution as though we were its masters. We will simply try to give the bases from which one can interpret this truth. In fact, the Cuban Revolution must be separated into two absolutely distinct stages: that of the armed action up to January 1, 1959, and the political, economic and social transformation since then.

Even these two stages deserve further subdivisions; however, we will not take them from the viewpoint of historical exposition, but from the viewpoint of the evolution of the revolutionary thought of its leaders through their contact with the people. Incidentally, here one must introduce a general attitude toward one of the most controversial terms of the modern world: Marxism. When asked whether or not we are Marxists, our position is the same as that of a physicist or a biologist when asked if he is a "Newtonian," or if he is a "Pasteurian."

There are truths so evident, so much a part of people's knowledge, that it is now useless to discuss them. One ought to be "Marxist" with the same naturalness with which one is "Newtonian" in physics, or "Pasteurian" in biology, considering that if facts determine new concepts, these new concepts will never divest themselves of that portion of truth possessed by the older concepts they have outdated. Such is the case, for example, of Einsteinian relativity or of Planck's "quantum" theory with respect to the discoveries of Newton; they take nothing at all away from the greatness of the learned Englishman. Thanks to Newton, physics was able to advance until it had achieved new concepts of space. The learned Englishman provided the necessary steppingstone for them.

The advances in social and political science, as in other fields, belong to a long historical process whose links are connecting, adding up, molding and constantly perfecting themselves. In the field of social and political sciences, from Democritus to Marx, a long series of thinkers added their original investigations and accumulated a body of experience and of doctrines. The merit of Marx is that he suddenly produces a qualitative change in the history of social thought. He interprets history, understands its dynamics, predicts the future, but in addition to predicting it (which would satisfy his scientific obligation), he expresses a revolutionary concept: the world must not only be interpreted, it must be transformed. Man ceases to be the slave and tool of his environment and converts himself into the architect of his own destiny. At that moment, Marx puts himself in a position where he becomes the necessary target of all who have a special interest in maintaining the old. . . . Beginning with the revolutionary Marx, a political group with concrete ideas establishes itself. Basing itself on the giants, Marx and Engels, and developing through successive steps with personalities like Lenin, Stalin, Mao Tse-tung and the new Soviet and Chinese rulers, it establishes a body of doctrines and, let us say, examples to follow.

The Cuban Revolution takes up Marx at the point where he himself left science to shoulder his revolutionary rifle. And it takes him up at that point, not in a revisionist spirit, of struggling against that which follows Marx, of revising "pure" Marx, but simply because up to that point Marx, the scientist, placed himself outside of the History he studied and predicted. From then on Marx the revolutionary could fight within History. We, practical revolutionaries, initiating our own struggle, simply fulfill laws foreseen by Marx the scientist. We are simply adjusting ourselves to the predictions of the scientific Marx as we travel this road of rebellion, struggling against the old structure of power, supporting ourselves in the people for the destruction of this structure, having the happiness of this people as the basis of our struggle. That is to say, and it is well to emphasize this once again: the laws of Marxism are present in the events of the Cuban Revolution, independently of what its leaders profess or fully know of those laws from a theoretical point of view. . . .

Each of those brief historical moments in the guerrilla warfare framed distinct social concepts and distinct appreciations of the Cuban reality; they outlined the thought of the military leaders of the Revolution—those who in time would also take their position as political leaders.

Before the landing of the "Granma," a mentality predominated that, to some degree, might be called "subjectivist"; blind confidence in a rapid popular explosion, enthusiasm and faith in the power to liquidate the Batista regime by a swift, armed uprising combined with spontaneous revolutionary strikes, and the subsequent fall of the dictator. . . .

After the landing comes the defeat, the almost total destruction of the forces and their regrouping and integration as guerrillas. Characteristic of those few survivors, imbued with the spirit of struggle, was the understanding that to count upon spontaneous outbursts throughout the island was a falsehood, an illusion. They understood also that the fight would have to be a long one and that it would need vast *campesino* participation. At this point, the *campesinos* entered the guerrilla war for the first time. Two events—hardly important in terms of the number of combatants, but of great psychological value—were unleashed. First, antagonism that the city people, who comprised the central guerrilla group, felt toward the *campesinos* was erased. The *campesinos*, in turn, distrusted the group and, above all, feared barbarous reprisals of the government. Two things demonstrated themselves at this stage, both very important for the interrelated factors: to the *campesinos*, the bestialities of the army and all the persecution would not be sufficient to put an end to the guerrilla war, even though the army was certainly capable of liquidating the *campesinos*' homes, crops, and families. To take refuge with those in hiding was a good solution. In turn, the guerrilla fighters learned the necessity, each time more pointed, of winning the *campesino* masses. . . .

Within a month and a half, two small columns of eighty and of a hundred forty men, constantly surrounded and harassed by an army which mobilized thousands of soldiers, crossed the plains of Camagüey, arrived at Las Villas, and began the job of cutting the island in two.

It may seem strange, incomprehensible, and even incredible that two columns of such small size—without communications, without mobility, without the most elemental arms of modern warfare—could fight against well-trained, and above all, well-armed troops.

Basic is the characteristic of each group: the more uncomfortable the guerrilla fighter is, and the more he is initiated into the rigors of nature, the more he feels himself at home; his morale is higher, his sense of security greater. At the same time, he has learned to risk his life in every circumstance that might arise, to trust it to luck like a tossed coin; and in general, as a final result of this kind of combat, it matters little to the individual guerrilla whether or not he survives.

The enemy soldier in the Cuban example which presently concerns us, is the junior partner of the dictator; he is the man who gets the last crumbs left to him in a long line of profiteers that begins in Wall Street and ends with him. He is disposed to defend his privileges, but he is disposed to defend them only to the degree that they are important to him. His salary and his pension are worth some suffering and some dangers, but they are never worth his life: if the price of maintaining them will cost it, he is better off giving them up; that is to say, withdrawing from the face of guerrilla danger. From these two concepts and these two morals springs the difference which would cause the crisis of December 31, 1958. . . .*

By a simple law of gravity, the small island of 114,000 square kilometers and 6,500,000 inhabitants is assuming the leadership of the anti-colonial struggle in America, for there are important conditions which permit it to take the glorious, heroic and dangerous lead. The nations of colonial America which are economically less weak, those which are developing their national capitalism by fits and starts in a continual struggle, at times violent and without quarter, against the foreign monopolies, are gradually relinquishing their place to this small new power for liberty, since their governments do not find themselves with sufficient strength to carry the struggle to the finish. This is because the struggle is no simple matter, nor is it free of dangers nor exempt from difficulties. It is essential to have the backing of an entire people, and an enormous amount of idealism and the spirit of sacrifice, to carry it out to the end under the almost isolated conditions in which we are doing it in America. Small countries have previously tried to maintain this position; Guatemala, the Guatemala of the quetzal bird which dies when it is imprisoned in a cage, the Guatemala of the Indian Tecum Uman who fell before the direct aggression of the colonialists; and Bolivia, the Bolivia of Morillo, the prototype of martyrs for American independence, who yielded before the terrible difficulties of the struggle, in spite of having initiated it and having given three examples which are fundamental to the Cuban revolution: suppression of the army, the Agrarian Reform, and the nationalization of mines—a maximum source of wealth as well as of tragedy.

Cuba knows the previous examples, it knows the failures and the difficulties, but it knows also that it stands at the dawn of a new era in the world; the colonial pillars have been swept away before the impulse of the national and popular struggle, in Asia as in Africa. Now the tendencies to unification of the peoples are no longer given by their religions, by their customs, by their appetites, by their racial affinities or lack of them; it is given by the economic similarities of their social conditions and by the similarity of their desire for progress and recovery. . . .

---

*The day Batista was overthrown.

. . . It was some time ago that the English lion removed his greedy paws from our America, and the nice young Yankee capitalists installed the "democratic" version of the English clubs and imposed their sovereign domination in every one of the twenty republics.

These nations are the colonial feudal-estate of North American monopoly, "right in its own backyard"; at the present moment this is their *raison d'être* and the only possibility they have. If all the Latin peoples were to raise the banner of dignity, as has Cuba, monopoly would tremble; it would have to accommodate itself to a new politico-economic situation and to substantial cuts in its profits. But monopoly does not like to cut its profits, and the Cuban example—this "bad example" of national and international dignity—is spreading among the American countries. Every time that an upstart people sets up a cry of liberation, Cuba is accused; somehow or other Cuba is guilty, guilty because it has shown a way, the way of armed popular struggle against the supposedly invincible armies, the way of struggle in difficult terrain in order to exhaust and destroy the enemy away from his bases; in short, the way of dignity.*

---

*Ernesto "Che" Guevara died in Bolivia in 1967, while this volume's initial phases got under way.

Part IV

LOGIC AND PHILOSOPHY OF VALUES

THE UNITY OF OPPOSITES: A DIALECTICAL PRINCIPLE*

V. J. McGill and William T. Parry

INTRODUCTION

ALTHOUGH the unity of opposites and other dialectical principles have suffered various "refutations," and certain interpretations and misapplications have quite properly been laid to rest, dialectic is very much alive today. The Platonic-Aristotelian tradition continues, and both the Hegelian and the Marxian dialectic have many followers. The unity of opposites, which Lenin described as the most important of the dialectical principles,[1] states that a thing is determined by its internal oppositions.

The principle was first put forward by the Milesian philosophers of the sixth century B.C., and by their cotemporary, Heraclitus of Ephesus. It held its own through centuries of philosophic thought, though it took different forms which were seldom clearly distinguished. The purpose of the present paper is to separate various forms of the unity of opposites principle, to show that they are of unequal importance and that their consequences are very different.

The principle is not a complete method or philosophy. If one forgot all about the complementary principle that a thing is determined by its field or milieu, the result would be a one-sided distortion. It is well to emphasize at the beginning, therefore, that no attempt is to be made to describe all phases of method in one article, however desirable this might be, but to cover one phase intensively. Lack of space also precludes an investigation of the historical origin and con-

---

[1] V. I. Lenin, *Collected Works*, XIII (New York, 1927), p. 321.

*Reprinted by permission from *Science and Society*, Vol. XII No. 4, Fall, 1948, pp. 418-444.

text of the various forms of the unity of opposites. Some are still important today. We shall confine ourselves to two brief examples.

From the time of Heraclitus it has been pretty well agreed that change involves a unity of opposites, of being and non-being. It is not true to say that the world is (being) or that it is not (non-being), said Heraclitus, but that it is becoming. "You cannot step twice into the same river, for new waters are ever flowing in upon you." The supposed contradiction involved led the Eleatics to deny the reality of change, and has been employed to disparage change, ever since. The Hegelian dialectic, on the other hand, accepted the contradiction as a real aspect of the world, which is continually overcome and continually renews itself in the process of change.

Another famous historical example of the unity of opposites is the One-Many problem. The One, Plato has Parmenides say, must be many because it has parts, and the Many must be one, i.e., one Many. This paradox became the foundation of the system of Plotinus[2] and was also essential to the Christian doctrine of the trinity. The same problem reappears in contemporary discussions of the foundations of mathematics.

Thus Bertrand Russell, in his earlier treatment of classes in *The Principles of Mathematics*, finds it necessary to distinguish the class as one from the class as many. "In the class as many," he says, "the component terms, though they have some kind of unity, have less than in required for a whole, they have in fact just so much unity as is required to make them many, and not enough to prevent them from remaining many."[3] Later on he concludes that it is more correct "to infer an ultimate distinction between a class as many and a class as one, to hold that the many are only many, and are not also one."[4] But this raises the question what we are talking about when we refer to the class as many. It seems to be *one* in some sense. Although Russell ventures an answer, he nevertheless confesses that there are "puzzles in this subject which I do not yet know how to solve."[5] This and other difficulties were avoided in *Principia Mathematica* (1910) by a solution which involves the denial of the existence of classes, and by the development of the theory of logical atomism. Russell's new position

---

[2]*Ennead* VI, 9.
[3]B. Russell, *Principles of Mathematics* (New York, 1903; 2nd ed., 1938), p. 69.
[4]*Ibid.*, p. 76.
[5]*Ibid.*, p. 77.

permitted statements about classes, even the null-class, though classes were interpreted as fictions. Apparently the one-many problem was resolved only by translating statements about classes into statements about individuals similar to a given individual.

THE MEANING OF OPPOSITES

The meaning of the unity of opposites[6] will naturally depend on our understanding of "opposites." We shall distinguish the strict or formal sense of the term from the more concrete meanings which occur in dialectical writings and also in ordinary discourse.

(1) In this paper A and -A always stand for strict opposites, i.e., properties which cannot both be true of the same event E (except when E lies in a borderline or transitional range). Thus A and -A can stand for contradictories which cannot both be true, nor false of the same E, or for contraries which cannot both be true of the same E, but may be both false (providing that E in no case lies in a borderline or transitional range). Black and non-black, and infant and non-infant, are examples of contradictories; black and white, and infant and adult, are examples of contraries. This usage conforms to ordinary formal logic except for the parenthetical phrase: "providing that E does not lie in a borderline or transitional range." This phrase, however, is crucial, since it appears to constitute a principal difference between dialectic and formal logic. Let us take the contraries boy and man. Most boys are plainly not men, and most men are plainly not boys, though they may have some boyish features, but there are also many borderline or transitional cases in which any decision would be arbitrary and untenable. We have to say "yes and no" or "neither nor." It is to these stretches that our parenthetical phrase refers.

Our definition of "strict opposites" entails a revision of two principal laws of formal logic, viz.: the law of excluded middle and the law of non-contradiction and all other laws of formal logic which involve negation. The laws are restricted to cases which do not fall in borderline or transitional stretches. In these cases it is not true that everything is either A or -A, and it is not false that anything is both A and -A. Yet our assertion that these laws do not hold for these stretches

---

[6]It should be noted that the dialectician recognizes the conflict as well as the unity of opposites, as was especially emphasized by Lenin, *Selected Works*, XI (New York, n.d.), p. 82.

involves no contradiction, since we have defined A and -A as mutually exclusive except in transitional ranges.*

(2) The term "opposites" is also used with other meanings that differ from the strict sense defined above. What we describe below as "identical polar opposites," "opposite determinations," and "oppositely directed forces" are not strict opposites, though they are not, on that account, as we shall see, any less important.

FORMS OF THE PRINCIPLE

The principle of the unity of opposites has been interpreted in the following ways:

1. (a) *The conception (or perception) of anything involves the conception (or perception) of its opposite.*

To understand anything is to distinguish it from its opposite. This is recognized by non-dialectical logicians.** To perceive anything is to distinguish it from its background, which is necessarily different (contrary) in color or other sense-quality.

1. (b) *The existence of a thing involves the existence of an opposite.*

The existence of a thing depends upon the existence of certain other things, bound to it by a necessary relation: Thus no employer without employee. This principle does not hold universally for contraries or contradictories. Thus the existence of fallible men does not imply the existence of infallible men, though the existence of men does (biologically) imply the existence of non-men, e.g., plants or animals.

---

*In Hegelian and Marxist literature the term "contradiction" is used in a very broad sense, to include conflicts and opposing forces (see, for example, Henri Lefebvre, *A la Lumière du Materialisme Dialectique*, I, *Logique formelle, Logique dialectique* (Paris, 1948), p. 174 and *passim*), but also in the sense of formal or logical contradiction, which is much narrower. In the first sense, the state of the world or a segment of it is always contradictory, though the contradiction is also being overcome. Contradiction thus represents a stage of truth and reality, often of a very high order. In the second sense, on the other hand, contradiction is an unfortunate impasse of thought arising from mistake or ignorance. Anyone who falls into contradiction must give up his position. He has not got the truth at all, though the contradiction may help him to find it. To avoid this double use of "contradiction," the present authors have used the term only in the latter sense (though modified to take account of the "fringe").

**J. N. Keynes, *Studies and Exercises in Formal Logic*, 4th ed. (London, 1928), p. 58. "The thinking of anything as A involves its being distinguished from that which is not A."

2. *Polar opposites are identical.*

3. *A concrete thing or process is a unity of opposite determinations.*

4. *A concrete system or process is simultaneously determined by oppositely directed forces, movements, tendencies, i.e., directed toward A and -A.*

5. *In any concrete continuum, whether temporal or non-temporal, there is a middle ground between two contiguous opposite properties A and -A, i.e., a stretch of the continuum where it is not true that everything is either A or -A.*

6. *In any concrete continuum, there is a stretch where something is both A and -A.*

Of these six senses of the unity of opposites, the first four do not run counter to traditional formal logic. Forms 5 and 6, on the other hand, clearly involve a revision of formal logic. Sense 4 does not assert that something in both A and -A, but only that it contains oppositely directed forces. Forms 2 and 3 appear to involve logical contradiction, but they really do not, as we shall see below.

THE IDENTITY OF OPPOSITES

The unity of opposites is sometimes equated with the identity or coincidence of opposites. But there may be unity, even interpenetration, without complete coincidence or identity. Thus One and Many may be conceived as forming an inseparable unity of some sort, which would in fact specifically exclude identity. In general, *unity* of opposites seems to imply diversity, and to exclude identity in the strict sense.

There are, however, two cases at least in which it is possible to speak of the identity of opposites, though even here "identity" can not be taken in a strict sense. The first is the "fringe" phenomenon, to be discussed later. The other is the so-called identity of polar opposites. In any ordinary sense, polar opposites, or contraries, such as black and white, hot and cold, cannot be identical. But when you abstract sufficiently from circumstances, contraries such as "positive" and "negative" are interchangeable and indistinguishable. Of course, if you specify that the positive is, for example, positive electricity, and the negative, negative electricity, a distinction can be made. In arithmetic and logic there are also systems in which each of a set of symbols may be interchanged for another of the set (or itself) according to a certain rule, without affecting the truth of any proposition.*

---

*There is, for instance, the well-known duality of Boolean algebra.

This identity of opposites occurs only on levels of high abstraction, and the terms are not really opposites, but *forms* of opposition, related to opposites as propositional forms are related to propositions.* (The *unity* of polar opposites, on the other hand, is commonplace. For example, pure white and pure black are hypothetical end-terms of a continuum of intensities, and can be understood only in terms of it.)

Hegel made a great contribution, in spite of his exaggerations, by exhibiting the identity of opposites on certain levels of abstraction. Modern theory of axiom-sets confronts the same problem in a different form. It becomes the problem of interpretation. The abstract system may be "meaningless," but if it can be interpreted as a meaningful system, its usefulness is demonstrated.

OPPOSITE DETERMINATIONS

A concrete thing or process is a unity of opposite determinations (Form 3). Thus everything, it is said, is both abstract and concrete, both universal and particular. A man, for example, is always a concrete particular which can occupy only one space-time track. Yet all of his characteristics seem to be abstract, capable of occurring in many places simultaneously. We say that a man is an electrician, a broker, that he is silent, wise or foolish. Since such adjectives describe a man's nature, this nature must be regarded as abstract and universal. This contradiction is accepted, and embodied in the so-called theory of the concrete universal. A judgment such as "Jones is wise," it is said, is expressible in abstract terms as: "The individual is the universal."[7] But here a distinction must be made. "Jones is wise" does not mean that Jones is identical with wisdom, but that Jones *has* wisdom. The apparent contradiction is resolved by recognizing different meanings of "is."

Actuality and potentiality are also opposite determinations, for what is actual cannot be merely potential, nor vice versa, yet everything is both actual and potential. But the contradiction again is only apparent. The actual characteristics of a man, for example, are those which are manifest at a particular time, whereas the potential characteristics, or "dispositional" traits, are those which would be manifest if appropriate

---

[7]See Hegel, *The Logic of Hegel* (from the *Encyclopaedia*), tr. by Wallace, 2nd ed. (Oxford, 1892), Section 166, p. 297.

*A propositional form (or propositional function) is an expression such as "x is a philosopher" or "2 R 3," which becomes a proposition when an appropriate substitution is made.

stimuli were presented. It is clear, therefore, that (except for the borderline cases to be discussed later) nothing is both actual and potential in the same respect at the same time, and that there is accordingly no contradiction (except that involved in all transitions).

Another important example of opposite determinations is the unity of structure and function in tissues, organs and organisms. Structure and function are demonstrably interdependent, and neither could exist without the other. They are inseparable, but also distinguishable, like the convex and concave sides of a curve. Still another example, already mentioned, is the unity of one and many. Though what is one cannot be many, a class appears to be both. To dispel the contradiction, it is sufficient to specify what is one, and what is many, e.g., 12 disciples, and one class of 12 disciples. The difficulty arises only on levels of abstraction where logic, evidently, has resources to cope with it.

In Aristotle's philosophy, form and matter, and act and potency, were fundamental, and the tradition has continued with modifications to the present day. The unities of opposite determinations are forms of common experience, and furnish a conceptual framework presupposed by scientific inquiries. The precise interdependence of the determinations in concrete cases sets problems for the special sciences.

OPPOSITELY DIRECTED FORCES

Form four of the unity of opposites principal states: A concrete system or process is simultaneously determined by oppositely directed forces, movements, tendencies. Thus a planetary orbit is determined at every point by oppositely directed forces. Similarly, a society, or its development, may be determined (say) by conflict between productive forces and property relations (relations of production). In the psychobiological organism the phenomenon is always in evidence. The opposite forces acting upon the organism, however, are typically expressed by means of antagonistic skeletal muscles—flexors and extensors; or by smooth muscles—radial and circular fibers. In all examples, forces operate in different directions. The flexor pulls in, the extensor out. The employers' aim is reducing labor costs, the employees' aim is higher wages. Gravity in case of a planet induces movement toward the center of the sun, whereas inertia determines movement in a straight line.

The term "force" does not retain the same meaning when applied in different fields. The reduction of social forces to physical, or mechanical forces, is mechanism, whereas the reduction of physical forces to social or psychological forces is teleology (vitalism), and neither form of reductionism has proved successful. Psychological goals and motivations, social movements and tendencies, cannot be profitably treated as *mere* movements, differing only in direction and acceleration. On the other hand, psychological and social forces or movements do always *involve* directed and accelerated motion. This is the common denominator of "force" as employed in these different fields. In all examples of the unity of opposites, in form 4, there is a system acted upon by two forces in such a way that, if one of these forces grew weaker the whole system would veer in the direction of A, whereas, if the other force grew weaker, the whole system would veer in the contrary direction, -A. Thus if the gravitational pull of the sun decreased sufficiently, the earth's motion would approximate to a straight line; if the earth lost sufficient momentum, it would be deflected toward the sun. Similarly, when employer groups become much stronger, compared to the employee organizations, wages tend to fall, or prices to rise, and a whole series of changes commonly results; if conversely, the employee organizations become comparatively stronger, wages tend to rise, and a whole train of oppositely directed motions will ensue. Instead of silent submission, withdrawal and disunity, there is now vocal protest, demand of rights and labor solidarity. Instead of prudent retirement from shop windows, the employee goes on and purchases needed commodities. Instead of stopping at home, the family goes out for entertainment. On the psychobiological level, we may also find oppositely directed motions, although of course we also find a great deal more. In any rhythmic activity, such as walking, both flexors and extensors are pulling simultaneously, in opposite directions, though when one is contracted, the other is only partially contracted. The character of the activity is basically determined by the relative strength of the contractions of these antagonistic muscles. If in walking, the contraction of the extensors is extraordinarily greater than that of the flexors, acceleration and direction of movement is shifted upward.

If the law of the unity of opposites is to be applied to the subject matter of physics, sociology and psychology, *in the same sense*, then the common denominator, so far as one can see, would have to be: *Oppositely directed forces or movements within a system determine the movement of that system.* But as our discussion has suggested, this interpretation of the law is somewhat artificial. It might direct the scientist, investigating the behavior of a system, to the opposition movements within it, but since the movements referred to are mechanical, they would have to be reinterpreted if the system were psychological or sociological. The oppositely directed forces could only be understood when sufficient facts about the organism or society were known. While if the system were physical, the competent physicist would have the relevant data anyhow, and the law, it might be argued, would be of little use to him.

It is obvious that the law of the unity of opposites is not a law of physics, or of any other science, but a philosophical generalization of findings in various sciences. Its identical meaning in various kinds of systems is: Oppositely directed forces or movements within a system determine the movement of that system. In its more important interpretation, however, the law is systematically ambiguous, i.e., "forces" and "movements" are reinterpreted for every new kind of system investigated.

The problem is how such a philosophical generaliztion can be usefully employed. There is little doubt that philosophical generalizations and perspectives do sometimes give guidance to scientific work. Long before the evidence for organic evolution had accumulated, there was a philosophy of evolution based upon a certain amount of scientific knowledge which is supposed to have given impetus to investigations that finally established the importance of evolution in many fields of science. And similarly, before Newtonian physics came the Cartesian philosophy of a world machine, which is supposed to have supplied problems, direction and inspiration.

The question is how the law of the unity of opposites, in the fourth form, *can* give useful guidance to scientific work. That it actually does so in particular cases would be a historical question which lies beyond the compass of this brief paper. The law could provide desirable correction wherever scientific method overemphasizes the effect of external forces acting upon systems, and neglects their internal dynamics. Sometimes the spontaneity of organisms is not sufficiently recognized. The internal stimuli arising from complicated needs acquired by adult human beings, for example, are not adequately considered, and efforts are even made to explain complicated learning by blind or random trial and error, or by field forces acting entirely from outside the organism. Early behaviorists seemed to have assumed that given sufficient repetitions learning one thing is as easy as another, that conditioned responses can always be established, the organism being completely plastic and neutral. In sociology, similarly, the attempt has been made to explain basic human behavior by climate, terrain, technology or institutions of one kind or another, with little attention given to the needs and reaction patterns of the individual. Societies are often compared with respect to more or less external traits, such as population, geographical extent, or duration in time, without much acknowledgment of the crucial differences of internal structures. In anthropology an example that comes to mind is the extreme theory that civilizations and cultures develop mainly by a process of "diffusion." All such tendencies, and many more, illustrate the danger of neglecting those contrary forces internal to systems. The principle of the unity of opposites may therefore be said to express methodological experience, and revised judgments, in several fields of science.

The complementary principle, meanwhile, is not forgotten in dialectical literature. If the motion of a system is determined by the contrary forces or movements internal to it, it is also determined by the motions of other systems external to it, and by the systems to which it belongs. But the latter principle falls outside the scope of the present article.

THE FRINGE

The fifth form of the unity of opposites is: *In any concrete continuum, whether temporal or non-temporal, there is a middle ground between any two contiguous, opposite qualities A and -A,* i.e., a certain stretch S of the continuum where it is not true that everything is either A or -A. Thus the law of excluded middle, which states that S is always either A or -A is restricted. This restriction of the law of excluded middle may not appear to be a case of the unity of opposites because there is separation of opposites here rather than unity. However, as we shall see, the denial of this law is normally equivalent to the denial of the law of non-contradiction, and hence to form 6 of the principle. This fifth form of the unity of opposites applies to all contradictory properties, e.g., child and non-child, but also to contiguous *contrary* qualities, such as infant and child. Although most cases are either infants or children, there is an intermediate fringe in which this cannot be said. Non-contiguous contrary qualities, however, such as infant and old man, would have a middle ground in any case.

The dichotomy between child and adult is crude and unsatisfactory. There is a long stretch of the continuum S which is neither A nor -A. By applying the law of excluded middle as a kind of ideal or norm of thought we can reduce the size of S. We can distinguish between the neonate (two days or less) and the infant (more than two days and less than two years) and the child (at least two years but not more than sixteen), etc. By introducing intermediate terms, by use of the microscope, telescope and other analytic methods, it is possible to diminish S but not to eliminate it. The dichotomies established in accordance with the law of excluded middle prove periodically unsatisfactory, and are replaced by new dichotomies. The law of excluded middle, as Dewey says, specifies a condition *to be* satisfied,[8] which however, in certain stretches of a continuum, never *is* satisfied.

The sixth form of the principle is: *In any concrete continuum there is a stretch where something is both A and -A.* When the assumptions common to almost all logical systems are made, the law of non-contradiction is equivalent to the law of excluded middle.* But then the denial that the law of excluded middle holds universally is equivalent to the denial that the law of non-contradiction holds universally. And this is equivalent to the assertion that there is something for which the law fails. We may therefore infer from form 5 above that in any concrete continuum there is a stretch S where something is both A and -A. (The continuum, of course, may be temporal, as in growth or developmental processes, or static, as in the color spectrum.)

The same conclusion may be reached with the aid of Dr. M. Black's analysis,[9] by a direct approach. Suppose we have a series of colors and that we divide them into ten segments which are then numbered successively from 1 to 10. Now suppose that the colors in segments 1 to 4 are red, whereas those in segments 5 to 6 are doubtful, and those in segments 7 to 10 are not-red. Red therefore is excluded only from the range 7 to 10, while not-red is excluded only from the range 1 to 4. There is a sense, therefore, in which the ranges of application of red and non-red overlap, and the law of non-contradiction does not hold. The argument, in Dr. Black's generalized form, is as follows: If Lx means L is true of x and $-Lx$ means L is false of x, we may say that Lx is only definitely false for the range 7 to 10, whereas $-Lx$ is only

---

[8]John Dewey, *Logic, The Theory of Inquiry* (New York, 1938), p. 346.

[9]Max Black, "Vagueness," *Philosophy of Science*, IV, no. 4 (Oct., 1937), p. 435 f.

*There is, to be sure, the system of intuitionist logic of A. Heyting (see his "Die formalen Regeln der intuitionischen Logik," *Sitzungsberichte der Preussischen Akademie der Wissenschaften*, Physikalisch-Mathematische Klasse, 1930, p. 47-58), which asserts the law of non-contradiction while omitting the law of excluded middle; but this result is obtained by eliminating the law of double negation: (not not A is equivalent to A), and thus altering the usual meaning of negation. Such a system involves a revision of traditional logic, different from that which we propose, and may be disregarded for the present.

definitely false for the range 1 to 4. The "inability to find a logical interpretation of *doubtful* and *perhaps* in terms of the two truth values, truth and falsehood, forces us to admit that the ranges of application of Lx, 1 to 6, and of $-Lx$, 5 to 10, overlap in the fringe, 5, 6" ("Vagueness," *Philosophy of Science*, IV, No. 4, Oct., 1937, p. 436). "Whether the number of terms in the field of reference is finite or infinite," Dr. Black goes on to argue, "denial of the existence of a unique boundary between the domains of Lx and $-Lx$ leads to contradiction" (*ibid.*, p. 437).

THE UNITY OF OPPOSITES AND FORMAL LOGIC

The program of denying the unrestricted validity of formal logic is difficult, since our thinking has been molded by formal logic and it is embedded in our language. We shall go on thinking in terms of it anyhow, but the dialectician will always be mindful that the dichotomies he sets up are only approximate and can be improved. That is, the stretch S can be made smaller and more definite.

Another reason why denial of the unrestricted application of the law of non-contradiction and the law of excluded middle is difficult, is that these laws are confirmed by experience in innumerable instances. Usually, when one says, this is a chair, a goat, or a human being, the contradictories are manifestly impossible. We see at once that what we have before us could not be a non-chair, a non-goat or a non-human being. Either-or is also obviously valid throughout vast ranges of human experience. It is only in borderline cases that there is doubt. It is only in these cases that there could be any justification in saying that a certain thing is neither a chair nor a non-chair, or that it is both. There is no question that these laws have strong inductive support though the exceptions are also richly confirmed.

The main tradition of logic in the past, overlooking the exceptions, held that logical laws are universal and necessary truths, and hence impossible to establish by induction. The view taken was that they are intuitive certainties or, with Kant, *a priori* principles of the Understanding. A certain difficulty always attached to such interpretations, however. A great deal of experience of the oppositions in the world seemed necessary to the intuition, or to the operation of the Understanding. Neither was really *a priori* or *de novo*. Instantaneous logical convictions, like other convictions, now appear to have a history. Since the formation of logical concepts has been studied in children and variations of logical habits have been noted in different societies, it has become evident that the learning of logical laws is a protracted, cumulative process, which had its beginning perhaps in those first discriminations where figure is distinguished from its opposing ground, and in the first denials and frustrations—the "you can't have that" experience. Indeed, striving, success and frustration would seem necessary to any comprehension of negation.

The mainstream of modern logic has veered away from intuitionism, and few logicians today would talk about intuitive or transcendental necessities. The primitive propositions, or axioms, from which contemporary logic deduces its theorems are not affirmed to be self-evident, but are described as assumptions. When this course is taken, however, the usefulness of logic when applied to the concrete world remains mysterious. Why one set of assumptions should yield a system having important interpretations, another not, receives no answer.

This difficulty, which is often cited, can be avoided by an inductive approach. Since in the obvious ranges of experience, the formulae of formal logic are always confirmed, we may say that they have a probability of 1 or certainty in these ranges. Thus there are countless areas (which, however, need have no sharp boundaries) where the formula "not both A and -A" always holds. But in the transitional ranges, as we have seen, the general formula breaks down. In passing along the continuum from blue to green, the probability that colors will not be both blue and not-blue, runs from 1 to 0. In this sense we may say that the probability of a logical formula (i.e., where the quantifier is omitted) is determined by the ratio of favorable to the total number of cases. Favorable cases abound in the learning process. We are always discovering that different discriminations, interpretations, needs and objectives, which we had supposed to be jointly possible, are really incompatible. We have to learn in innumerable cases that ends without certain means are impossible, and that certain means, which seemed to conduce to an objective, are really inconsistent with it. Either A or -A, but not both, is richly confirmed in experience, and learning is a process of discovering what concrete properties exemplify A and -A. Each such discovery is a favorable case.

The unfavorable cases are also encountered in every field, though not nearly as frequently as the favorable. Unfavorable cases are those in which there is, in fact, no way of coming to a definite decision as to the application of a certain dichotomy. Subjects confronted with the continuum of colors in the spectrum will be able to distinguish two contiguous colors, such as blue and green, within the obvious ranges, but there is an intermediate range in which discrimination is impossible. Not only will subjects disagree among themselves as to which color it is, but any subject at different times will disagree with himself and, in certain cases, will be unable to decide whether the color is blue or non-blue, or blue or green. The formal logician may say that the color is, after all, either blue or non-blue, whether or not the subject can say which. But this presupposes that the word "blue" has an absolutely definite meaning, regardless of the way it is used. Where there is inescapable indecision as to the application of the term "blue" to an object, we might as well say that it is neither blue nor non-blue, as that it is either.

The same is true of Engels' example of living and dying:[10] Dying is a process that takes place in time, and there is therefore a stretch of the continuum in which neither "dead" nor "living" are applicable. You may try to get around the facts by saying that when properly analyzed, "dead" and "living" do not apply to the whole organism, but to the individual cells, some of which are dead, others living, at any particular time during the dying of the organism. But this merely shifts the difficulty from the organism to the cell. The cell also takes time to die, and for a certain stretch neither "living" nor "dead" can be applied. Moreover, the death of the organism cannot be properly reduced to a mere sum of dying cells because the cells are inter-dependent in dying as in living. On the empirical approach we are taking, the failure of formal logic to apply in such cases has an objective basis.

IS VAGUENESS SUBJECTIVE?

Bertrand Russell, on the one occasion on which he discussed this matter in print, employed the same example. "Death," he wrote, "is also a process; even when it is what is called instantaneous, death must occupy a finite time. If you continue to apply the name to the corpse, there must gradually come a stage of decomposition when the name ceases to be attributable, but no one can say precisely when this stage has been reached."[11] "Man" is also an indefinite term since there are doubtful prehistoric cases. There is no lack of exam-

---

[10]F. Engels, *Herr Eugen Dühring's Revolution in Science* (New York, 1939), p. 132 f.

[11]"Vagueness," *Australasian Journal of Philosophy*, I (1923), p. 88.

ples, but Russell attributes them, in every case, to the vagueness of language. "The law of excluded middle is true," he says, "when precise symbols are employed but it is not true when the symbols are vague, as in fact, symbols always are." Although the article sets out to prove that the failure of the law of excluded middle results from the vagueness of language only, no real argument is offered for this subjective explanation. "There is a tendency," he says, "in those who have realized that words are vague to infer that things also are vague. . . . This seems to be precisely a case of the fallacy of verbalism—the fallacy that consists in mistaking the properties of words for the property of things."[12] And yet nowhere does he even state criteria of objectivity and subjectivity.

This defect of Russell's article was remedied by a discussion by Max Black which is, in effect, an answer to Russell's subjective resolution of the problem. Vagueness cannot be explained as the absence of scientific precision, Black points out, since "the indeterminacy which is characteristic of vagueness is present also in all scientific measurement."[13] Vagueness is not a defect of language. It is not to be identified with ambiguity, since even the most precise and unambiguous terms are vague, the difference being that the ambiguous term will have more than one "fringe," or indeterminate area. "A symbol's vagueness," he holds, consists "in the existence of objects concerning which it is intrinsically impossible to say either that the symbol in question does, or does not, apply. The set of all objects about which a decision as to the symbol's application is intrinsically impossible is defined as the 'fringe' of the symbol's field of application."[14]

Black's argument for the objectivity of vagueness is interesting: If the vagueness of a symbol is subjective, he suggests, its use implies something about the speaker (psychological facts), whereas if it is objective its use implies something about the environment (physical facts). Thus an ambiguous symbol, which is clearly a subjective phenomenon, implies psychological, but not physical, facts. We can appeal to less equivocal symbols and the ambiguity disappears. In the case of vague symbols this is not true. Even when discrimination and linguistic precision are at the maximum, the fringe, though perhaps reduced in extent, is still demonstrable. Confronted by the continuous

---

[12]*Ibid.*, p. 84.
[13]"Vagueness," *Philosophy of Science* (1937), p. 429.
[14]*Ibid*, p. 430.

gradations of colors in the spectrum, even the most sensitive observers, employing the utmost refinements of language, are unable to eliminate the fringe. It is therefore reasonable to conclude that the fringe is an objective feature of the series observed. The same test is usually applied to determine the objectivity of the "reports" of scientific instruments, such as the telescope, which are analogous to human discriminators, or reporters. If a telescope "reports" a certain phenomenon, its objectivity is determined by employing other telescopes, located at higher altitudes, or tilted at a different angle, for example, to allow for the rotational velocity of the earth. If the phenomenon disappears when the conditions of observation are altered, it is not regarded as an objective feature of the stars observed.

One point is not sufficiently stressed by Professor Black. The subjectivity of the "report" of a given telescope is not decided merely by its conflict with the "reports" of other instruments, for the first telescope may be a superior one in the sense that it gives more objective reports. Many facts and theories are employed to establish the superiority of scientific instruments; for example, theories and facts about lenses, and the distorting effects of the earth's atmosphere. In the case of scales, the superiority of some scales has been correlated with the type of mechanism and materials used so that the accuracy can be predicted in advance. But even the most sensitive scale which records the most minute differences of load, will demonstrate the fringe, giving slightly different recordings for the same load at different times. The fact that the fringe is not eliminated under any conditions would indicate that the phenomenon is not merely verbal, nor merely subjective, but also objective. Dr. Black's further analysis of the phenomenon distinguishes three factors: symbol, subjects (or observers), and objects. We agree with him in stressing the fundamentally objective character of the situation.

The non-verbal character of the phenomenon, it might be added, is also shown by discrimination experiments, using dogs and other animals as subjects. Pavlov, for example, associated food with an illuminated circle, but no food with an ellipse of the same area. When the ellipse was of the proportion 2 to 1, the dogs readily distinguished the two figures, salivating to the circle but not to the ellipse. When the ellipse was gradually made thicker, the dogs were still able to discriminate. When the ratio of 9 to 8 was reached, however, and the ellipse was almost a circle, discrimination became impossible, and in three weeks of effort no progress was made. Evidently the limit of canine discrimination had been reached. If human adults were substituted for dogs, the fringe would be narrowed, and still more, if scientific instruments were used, but it would not be eliminated. The existence of the fringe does not seem, therefore, to be a wholly canine, human or an instrumental fact, but also a physical one. *Even the best instrument would fail to discriminate a mathematical line dividing A from -A*, since mathematical lines cannot be discriminated, and by all accounts, do not exist in nature.

Though the fringe is evidently not a mere psychological fact, the *size* of the fringe does vary with different observers, or groups of observers. Thus the size of the fringe, or the degree of vagueness of the symbol, is always respective to a class of observers. The size or degree is always *for* a given class of subjects, though the class may be a large one. The size of the fringe is a difficult conception, however, since the fringe has no distinct boundaries. No one can say with certainty exactly where it begins and where it ends. Professor Black has devised an ingenious technique for dealing with the difficulty,* and Professor Hempel[15] has contributed some improvements. Professor Black explains the vagueness of a symbol in terms of variations in its use by a given group of users, applying it to a given series of objects. He defines *"the consistency of application of a term"* to the members of a series. Suppose the series to be a series of chairs, running from the most obvious examples, such as a Chippendale chair, to ever more doubtful cases, and ending with a shapeless piece of wood. Almost all observers will call the first members of the series "chairs," and the last members of the series, "non-chairs." In other words, the consistency of application of the term "chair" and "non-chair" will be highest at the beginning and end of the series respectively. Toward the middle of the series the cases become more doubtful, however, and consistency decreases. The term "fringe" is henceforth used by Dr. Black with a new meaning, viz: the range of objects which are called "non-chairs" about as frequently as they are called

---

[15]C. G. Hempel, "Vagueness and Logic," *Philosophy of Science*, April, 1939, p. 168.

*More exactly, Dr. Black's technique enables him to eliminate the idea of the fringe as a definite set of objects. This he regards as a crude untenable notion, since it leads to logical contradiction by the kind of argument presented above in the section on the fringe.

"chairs." The vagueness of a symbol is to be measured by the curve on which this varying consistency is plotted.*

Two minor objections may be expressed. Vagueness should be defined not only by the conflicting discriminations of different observers, or of the same observer at different times, but also by the inability, or failure, of discrimination. Such failure, hesitation or blocked response is frequently met with in psychological studies of sensory discrimination. Secondly, discriminations of different observers, as of different scientific instruments, are not of equal accuracy. Such deficiencies in the formula, however, could probably be remedied. We must add that we believe (contrary to Professor Black) that the term "fringe" can be used in the original sense consistently, provided the laws of logic are stated with appropriate restrictions; and this is the practice we shall follow.

POSSIBLE LOGICS FOR DIALECTIC

The discussion so far poses the question: What alterations of formal logic are entailed by the principle of the unity of opposites in forms 5 and 6? It has been pointed out that the restriction of the law of excluded middle would mean a radical revision of logic; yet this has often been contemplated, even by Aristotle apparently. It seems still more drastic to restrict the law of non-contradiction; in fact, it has generally been considered unthinkable. The dialectician is as intent as anyone else to avoid self-contradiction, and continues to think of formal logic as prescribing an ideal for exact thought. There are several possibilities to be considered.

(a) One alternative available to the dialectician is to retain the

---

*If we refer to a member of the series of objects as x, let L and $-L$ stand for a term and its contradictory (e.g., "chair" and "non-chair"), let m be the number of discriminations of x as L, and n the number of discriminations of x as $-L$, then Professor Black defines "*the consistency of application of L to x as the limit to which the ratio m/n tends when the number of [discriminations of x] and the number of observers increase indefinitely*" (*loc. cit.*, p. 442). The "consistency profile" is the curve on which the consistency of application of L to x is plotted for every x in the series, from those most frequently called L to the least frequently. This curve is steep in the middle range if L is a precise symbol, and flat if it is a vague symbol. Professor Black proposes to measure vagueness by the flatness of this curve.

Professor Hempel has raised a technical objection to this method of measurement (based on the non-metric character of the series), and proposed an alternative formula which avoids this difficulty ("Vagueness and Logic," *Philosophy of Science*, April, 1939, p. 166).

principles of formal logic, but to assert them universally (if they involve negation) only for cases which are not in the fringe. It is not assumed here that the fringe has sharp boundaries, nor that it is so well defined that we can always tell whether an object falls in it or not. But it is assumed that for certain things we can decide definitely that they are *not* in the fringe between a certain property and its opposite. If we write "Fringe -A" for the fringe between A and -A, the law of excluded middle would be expressed in this fashion: For all *x* not in Fringe -A, either *x* is A or *x* is -A.

This scheme, if it can be worked out consistently, has several advantages. It retains traditional logic for the obvious cases while acknowledging existence of doubtful cases in the fringe. It also has the merit of fitting in with the inductive approach to logic, and appears to be the system presupposed by the conceptions of opposites and the fringe adopted in this paper. In addition to the statements of logical principles restricted, as above, to the non-fringe, we could also have unrestricted statements, in which, however, it would be asserted that the logical formula applies with a certain probability—a probability determined roughly by the ratio of favorable cases to the total cases in human experience. But for further refinement it must be remembered that not all observations are of equal accuracy and weight.

(b) An alternative procedure is to adopt the quantitative technique of Professor Black. Roughly, what he says is as follows: If we replace L and -L by consistency curves, representing the consistency of observers in applying these terms to a series of items, then the law of excluded middle, L or -L, may be restated in a form that is valid.*

---

*He replaces the propositional function Lx by $L(x, C)$, which means: "the symbol L applies to x with consistency C." When the consistency of application of L to x is C, then, by Black's definition, the consistency of application of -L to x is the reciprocal, $\frac{1}{C}$. Instead of the law of excluded middle in the form: "Every x is either L or -L," he has an operation which permits the transformation of $L(x, C)$ into $-L\left(x, \frac{1}{C}\right)$ (*loc. cit.*, p. 451 f.)

With appropriate changes, the law could also be stated for contiguous, *contrary* qualities which together exhaust a series. If a series begins with squarish rectangles ("plates") and gradually descends to very narrow rectangles ("sticks"), and "plates" and "sticks" are the only terms to be applied, the consistency curve may be expected to be similar to that where the terms are "plate" and "non-plate." See Livingston Welch's "A Prelmiinary Study of the Interaction of Conflicting Concepts of Children Between the Ages of 3 and 5 Years," *The Psychological Record*, II, 20 (1938).

This procedure differs from that of alternative (a) in denying the existence of the fringe as originally defined, i.e., as a class of objects qualitatively distinguished from the non-fringe. Any object that is L may be, so to speak, a little bit -L, if some people judge it so. The term "fringe" may still be used, but redefined (as explained above); and it is not required for the definition of "vagueness." This alternative is similar to the first, however, in involving an inductive approach.

(c) For the dialectician who wants logic to recognize the fringe, or borderline cases, there is a third alternative. He may adopt provisionally a three-value logic. Instead of the two-values true and false, the many-valued logic of Lukasiewicz (or rather one of these logics) introduces three truth values: 1, ½ and 0, or "certainly true," "doubtful," and "certainty false," as Lewis and Langford interpret them.[16] The middle term between true and false in this system is ½ or doubtful, and its application to the problem of the fringe is clear. There is a middle range of blue on the color spectrum which nearly all observers would call blue, and there is a middle range of green which almost no observers would call blue, and finally there is between blue and green a fringe which many observers would call blue, and many, non-blue. These latter judgments could be interpreted as ½ or doubtful, whereas the former attributions would be true and false, or 1 and 0, respectively. This logic, therefore, seems to be consistent with both the fifth and sixth forms of the principle of the unity of opposites. It is significant that neither the law of excluded middle nor the law of non-contradiction appears in this logic.

(d) The Heyting logic, to which we have already referred, also seems to allow for a fringe between A and -A, because it fails to assert the law of excluded middle and the law of double negation, --A=A. On the other hand the law of non-contradiction is asserted, which would exclude the sixth form of the principle of the unity of opposites.

It is not our purpose here to pass on the merits of these new logical developments, but only to point out that the dialectician who insists upon the importance of the fringe has a choice among several possible systems of logic.

DOES LOGIC APPLY TO THE WORLD?

Dialectic differs from formal logic in at least one important respect. It reformulates logical principles so as to allow for the existence of

----

[16]C. I. Lewis and C. H. Langford, *Symbolic Logic* (New York, 1932), p. 214, Cf. 2nd ed. (Dover Publications, 1959), p. 234.

the fringe. Its empirical confirmation is therefore much stronger than that of formal logic. The latter is confirmed throughout the range of obvious cases, but fails for the fringe, whereas dialectic holds for both. The probability of dialectical principles is determined, in a manner already explained, by the ratio of favorable to the total number of cases. Is such empirical evidence the only type available? There has been a persistent conviction that logical principles are self-evident and intuitively necessary. We do not deny the occurrence of intuitive certainties, but only insist that they be tested against the facts, and their origin traced in the learning process. Too many self-evident truths have turned out false to warrant any other course.

The view that logical laws are self-evident and immutable is to be rejected. So also the current conventionalism. The latter states that formal logic does not *describe* general features of the objective world, but *prescribes* verbal conventions. It is simply a set of rules for regulating scientific communication, those rules being preferable which best accomplish certain human ideals, such as precision and inclusiveness. Professor Nagel, who defends this view, interprets the principle of non-contradiction as requiring "that in a given context a term must not be applied to a given thing and also denied to it; and the principle of excluded middle is formulated in a corresponding way."* But he acknowledges that everyday language, and even the specialized languages of the sciences, do not entirely conform to these requirements.

There is no objection to formulating the laws of logic as rules for using language. But the fact that the laws can be interpreted ethically, as linguistic prescriptions, does not imply that they have no reference to the objective world. The materialist will want to know why some rules are more successful than others in regulating communication, organizing our knowledge—in achieving human ideals. He cannot escape the conviction that the success of an instrument depends upon properties of the object to which it is applied, as well as of the instrument itself and its user. He will also be curious about the ideals themselves. Do they vary from one society to another? Under what condi-

---

*Ernest Nagel, "Logic without Ontology," *Naturalism and the Human Spirit*, edited by Y. H. Krikorian (New York, 1944), p. 225. Of course, if the principle were formulated in the *same* way, it would say that in a given context a term must either be applied to a given thing or denied to it; which would oblige us to be omniscient. If weakened to a command to apply the compound term "either A or non-A" to any given thing, it would have the unfortunate consequence of making silence impossible. Perhaps the principle is to be formulated as a prohibition against denying both the terms A and non-A to a given thing.

tions are they learned? Such questions are relevant to the objective import of logic, and cannot be dismissed merely because our knowledge is still insufficient to furnish definitive answers.

Professor Nagel admits that the ideal of precision

> is not arbitrary, because communication and inquiry are directed to the achievement of certain objectives. . . . The assertion that this is so requires support by empirical evidence—evidence which it is possible to produce. But the available evidence is drawn from the study of the behavior of men engaged in inquiry; it does not come from a consideration of structural invariants found in other domains.[17]

It will be observed that on this view logical laws are instruments for the attainment of certain human objectives, and empirical evidence is admittedly required to show that they do in fact serve these purposes. It is regrettable that Dr. Nagel does not produce some of this evidence. Had he done so, we could perhaps discover whether it is his intention to admit as evidence only the behavior of men conducting an inquiry, or whether he would also include the facts of the world with which their inquiry deals. Dr. Nagel's position implies, in any case, that since logical laws are relative to human ideals and objectives, they may change with a change in these objectives; and secondly, that since particular logical laws are justified by empirical evidence, the weight of evidence might conceivably shift with circumstances in favor of other laws.

Professor Nagel, nevertheless, will not allow that logical principles can ever be established by empirical induction. His main argument is that logical principles cannot be refuted by negative instances. If there appears to be a negative instance, in any particular case, we always re-examine the empirical data to bring them into harmony with the logical principle. We never reject the principles themselves; for if we did not regard them as necessarily true, we would run counter to the established usage of the expressions they involve, such as "and" and "if . . . then."[18] He concludes that there is no clear sense in which logic can be experimentally verified.

> "Logical principles [he contends] are compatible with any order which the flux of events may exhibit; they could not be in disagreement with anything which inquiry may disclose, and if

---

[17]"Logic without Ontology," *op. cit.*, p. 226.
[18]*Ibid.*, p. 219.

they should ever require revision, the grounds for such alterations must lie elsewhere than in the subject matter of the natural sciences."[19]

But this passage is contradicted by a later one, in which he calls
attention to a recent suggestion:

> "That in order to develop the theory of subatomic phenomena
> in a manner conforming both to *experimental evidence* and to
> certain ideals of economy and elegance, a "logic" different from
> those normally employed may have to be instituted. The sug-
> gestion . . . calls attention to the fact in a striking way that under
> the pressure of *factual observation* and norms of convenience
> familiar language habits may come to be revised; and it indicates
> that the acceptance of logical principles as canonical need be
> neither on arbitrary grounds nor on grounds of their allegedly
> inherent authority, but on the ground that they effectively
> achieve certain postulated ends."[20]

It appears, then, that Dr. Nagel's denial of the relevance of empirical evidence to logic, which he makes a great deal of in his paper,
is difficult to carry out consistently .

It is true that when a logical principle appears to be violated, we
usually re-examine and revise the other data. The same thing is true
of the principles of physics. In every field we attempt to save the
general principles—whenever, that is, they are better established than
the data to which they are applied. But sometimes it is the principle
which is revised. Such revisions have occurred more than once in the
history of logic. For example, Kant corrected Aristotle's formulation
of the law of contradiction, omitting the reference to time, and the
superfluous expression of certainty.*

Many other examples could be given to show that logical principles,
like other scientific principles, are not sacrosanct prescriptions, but
modifiable to suit the purposes of logic, mathematics and other sciences. Thus Brouwer and other mathematical logicians have revised
logical formulations to fit the needs of mathematics.

---

[19]*Ibid.*, p. 220.

[20]*Ibid.*, p. 232; italics ours. The reference is to a paper by Birkhoff and von
Neumann.

*Cf. P. Popov, "The Logic of Aristotle and Formal Logic," *Philosophy and Phe-
nomenological Research*, VIII, p. 8 f. In the same way, modern logicians have
been obliged to deny the existential import of universal propositions.

It is true that logical principles seem to be intuitively true and self-evident. This is because (apart from the fringe) there appear to be no exceptions in our experience, and in the overwhelming majority of cases one is unable to *imagine* any. But fringe phenomena, as we have seen, have to be accepted. They oblige us to admit ranges of exceptions to formal logic, in every continuum. These exceptions, which dialectic incorporates into the statements of logical principles, are objective and important. As Dr. Black says, ". . . deviations from logical or mathematical standards of precision are all pervasive in symbolism; . . . to label them as subjective aberrations sets an impassable gulf between formal laws and experience and leaves the *usefulness* of the formal sciences an insoluble mystery."[21]

In general, the main objection to the view that logic has no objective import, but is merely a system of rules for organizing our knowledge, is that it fails to explain the enormous utility of this science. The conventionalism we have discussed admits the utility but makes a mystery of it.

CONCLUSION

We have not attempted in this paper to give new and interesting examples of the unity of opposites, but rather to distinguish six different forms this principle has taken in dialectical literature. It was found that some of these forms are subjective, having to do with conception and abstraction, others concrete and objective, that the last two forms required a revision of customary logic while the others did not. Naturally, an illustration of one form of the principle need not be an illustration of the others.

The same state of affairs, however, might illustrate various forms of the principle in different ways. A developing strike situation, for example, is determined by oppositely directed movements or tendencies (form 4). There is a tendency to strike but also an impulse to cautious withdrawal, and the outcome is determined by the composition of these tendencies and by the preponderance of one of them. Fringe phenomena (5, 6) could also have some significance. In the periphery there are employees who are neither clearly in (with) the union, nor outside (against) it. The outcome may depend, in part, upon the extent of this indeterminate or hybrid fringe. Another factor plays a part in such a situation. The language of the strike organizers may be too abstract, consisting of general slogans and appeals which

---

[21]Max Black in *Philosophy of Science, loc. cit.*, p. 429.

take little account of the concrete realities, ignoring the circumstances and hazards of the employees or the specific dispositions of the employer. The organizers have failed, in the specific situation, to achieve an effective integration of abstract and concrete, potential and actual (3).

It is well to emphasize that dialectical principles never by themselves provide any solution to concrete problems, afford no predictions. They describe only the most general determinations of processes or systems and cannot, of course, specify the outcome of any particular case. What the principle of the unity of opposites (forms 3, 4, 5 and 6) states is that in any system there is a unity of opposites of some kind appropriate to it, and that the specific interaction of the opposites determines the momentary character of the system, but also future states. The test of the principles, in this general form, would be: Does a change in the interrelation of the opposites bring about a change in the system? To revert to a previous example: Would the introduction of more specific and factual material into the union organizers' language, in place of purely abstract appeals and slogans, be apt to change the developing strike situation? Would a preponderance of one of the opposing forces change the system? Or, finally, would the narrowing of the fringe of doubtful employees who are neither clearly in, nor out of the union, or neither clearly with nor against it, have any appreciable effect on the system? The principle of the unity of opposites would enable you to predict that some change would result, but not what change.

The principle is, therefore, a standing invitation to acquire sufficient concrete knowledge to apply it successfully, to replace the variables of the general formula with concrete values. Hegel's whole philosophy is an insistence on this point, but it was Engels who gave the deeper materialist emphasis. It is clear that dialectic should not be compared to science, for it is not intended as a substitute for it, but as a framework for scientific inquiry. Its possible advantages are to be seen, rather, in comparison with the framework for inquiry provided by other philosophical traditions. What does the usual tradition of formal logic say? We have seen that it makes no provision for the fringe, and is obliged to overlook, for example, the mesoforms or intermediate forms which occur in the continuity of evolutionary development. And this tradition has also overemphasized the importance of propositions of the form *all A is B* and *at least one A is B,* usually ignoring the intermediate range of quantifiers which are practically most important. There has also been a strong tendency to restrict belief to certainty and outright rejection, as if the intermediate degrees of belief were not obviously the more significant. Along with this has gone the adulation of the syllogism, and a corresponding depreciation of the value of induction and concrete studies. The sterility of this logical tradition has been greatly remedied, but there is still much room for improvement. Other philosophical traditions have also laid down general principles of method. One emphasizes intuition; another, perception as the only test of truth; while still another insists that practice, without any commitment as to the nature of the world outside the laboratory, is a sufficient guide to inquiry. It is the obligation of the dialectician to demonstrate that his inductively grounded principles provide a better framework for inquiry than those of other schools. To do so, he would need to go far beyond the boundaries of this brief exploratory article, and in various directions. In particular, it would be necessary to exhibit the interrelation of the unity of opposites with other dialectical principles such as the transition from quantity to quality and the negation of negation.[22]

---

[22]With the exception of one slight change recommended by Dr. Parry, this essay has not been changed, except to change footnotes, incorporating some within the text—D.D.G.

A NEED DEFINITION OF 'VALUE'*

Rollo Handy

MUCH OF the recent controversy in meta-ethics is concerned with whether or not ethical statements are cognitive, whether or not they are descriptive, and whether or not ethical terms designate unique and nonnatural characteristics. Naturalists hold, in opposition to intuitionists, that ethical terms designate natural characteristics; and in opposition to emotivists, that ethical statements are cognitive and descriptive (and hence capable of being true or false). The purpose of this paper is to offer a definition of "value" within the naturalistic framework just mentioned. The relation of ethics to the social sciences, as a consequence of this definition, will also be discussed, as well as some topics in social philosophy.

Many nonnaturalists have criticized naturalistic definitions of ethical terms on the grounds that such definitions are not in accord with what "we mean," or with "common usage," or with "our language." Ewing has expressed this strongly when he argues that one must be able to say about an acceptable analysis of "good": "Well, this is what I meant all along, although I did not put it so clearly."[1] To the naturalists, however, it has often seemed both acceptable and necessary to prescribe the way in which ethical terms are to be used, rather than merely describing how those terms are used by some individual or group of individuals.[2] Since there seems to be no guarantee that any

[1] A. C. Ewing, *The Definition of Good* (London: Routledge, 1947), p. 43. Voicing similar criticisms, among others, are A. J. Ayer, *Language, Truth and Logic* (London: Gollancz, 1936), pp. 104-105, and W. D. Ross, *The Right and the Good* (Oxford: Clarendon Press, 1930), p. 11.

[2] For example, R. B. Perry, *Realms of Value* (Cambridge: Harvard University, 1954), p. 2; P. Kurtz, "Naturalistic Ethics and the Open Question," *Journal of Philosophy*, LII, No. 5 (March 3, 1955); R. Handy, "Naturalistic Definitions in Ethics and 'Common Usage,'" *Philosophy and Phenomenological Research*, XVI, No. 4 (June, 1956).

*Reprinted by permission from *The Philosophical Quarterly*. Vol. X, #39, April, 1960, pp. 156-163.

accepted usage is a proper one, since there are many meanings which are held to be in accord with accepted usage, and since in many areas (notably the sciences) progress has been made by redefining terms, no attempt will be made in this paper to offer a definition of "value" which corresponds exactly to "common usage." It also may be noted that one's introspective search for the meaning of ethical terms is not very good evidence that others mean the same thing when they use those terms. A. Stroll has proposed the use of questionnaire and interview tests to determine how ethical terms are actually employed,[3] but even a consensus on that issue would not preclude redefining those terms. The aim of this paper, then, is to prescribe a meaning for "value" which will be justified on grounds other than it agrees with "common usage."

Before offering this definition, some mention may profitably be made of how social scientists use the term "value." Very often, they define "value" in terms of what individuals desire or want, or in terms of what satisfies them.[4] This approach is very similar to Perry's famous definition of generic value: "any object of any interest." This approach has obvious merits for the practical work of the behavioral sciences. But many philosophers have been critical of such a scientific usage, holding that it leads to a vicious relativism; and have been critical of Perry's theory, holding that we may desire objects which are not good. While Perry has often answered this criticism, there still seems some point to the question: "Ought Y to value what he does in fact value?"

Yet all too often the attempts to escape cultural relativism amount to little more than saying: "Three cheers for the values of our set." Evidently one of the more seductive temptations facing the moralist is to make sweeping generalizations from the value system of a small group of people. One possible way of avoiding this type of narrowness is to set up criteria for "normality" which are not merely statistical nor based only on one culture. To discuss meaningfully what is good or bad for humans in general presupposes a general nature of man, a standard of normality applicable to all men.

---

[3]A. Stroll, *The Emotive Theory of Ethics* (Berkeley: University of California, 1954), pp. 84-85.

[4]For a rather typical example, see R. E. Carter, Jr., "An Experiment in Value Measurement," *American Sociological Review*, 21, No. 2 (April, 1956), especially note 5 on p. 157. C. L. Golightly has an interesting discussion of some recent, relatively complex, scientific views of the meaning of "value" in his "Value as a Scientific Concept," *Journal of Philosophy*, LIII, No. 7 (March 29, 1956).

Some interesting tests for "normality," in this sense, have been discussed recently by psychologists.[5] While the present writer is in sympathy with such efforts, there seem to be two pitfalls: (i) giving culture-bound criteria for "normality," even though the intention is to give criteria which apply to all cultures,[6] or (ii) defining "normal" so abstractly that, although the definition does have cross-cultural applicability, it has little practical use. As Cole himself points out, very often what is regarded as definitive of the normal person turns out to be (a) the modal case in a given society, or (b) the individual who acts effectively "in at least *seeming* conformity with the mores, ideals and beliefs" of a given society, or (c) the individual who deviates from the statistical norm of a society, but who gives "serious expression to that to which others are content to give mere lip service."[7] In any of these three cases, the definition of "normal" does not have cross-cultural applicability. A naturalistic theory of ethics (and metaethics) perhaps can be of some aid in the solution of the problems just mentioned. We may note, in this context, that even for some social scientists there is a strong value connotation to "normal." As Cole says, "*normal* is something good, sound, healthy, *right*."[8]

Somewhat similar issues arise in connection with making comparative value judgments about whole cultures. Can we describe "the sane society"? Can we meaningfully say that certain cultures are sick? Some anthropologists and sociologists assert that such judgments are meaningless: one culture cannot be judged in terms of the value system of another culture. In view of such considerations, a definition of "value" which would have some cross-cultural applicability and yet allow for differences in the value systems of different cultures would be useful.

---

[5]L. E. Cole, "The Normal Personality," ch. 24 of *Human Behavior: Psychology as a Bio-Social Science* (New York: World Book Co., 1953); C. S. Hall, "The Stabilized Personality," ch. 5 of *A Primer of Freudian Psychology* (New York: World Publishing Co., 1954); P. M. Symonds, "Normality," ch. 24 of *The Dynamics of Human Adjustment* (New York: Appleton-Century-Crofts, 1946); and E. Fromm, *Man for Himself* (New York: Rinehart, 1947). Fromm has also discussed what might be called the "normal" society: *The Sane Society* (New York: Rinehart, 1955).

[6]A very interesting discussion of this point is given by K. Horney, *The Neurotic Personality of Our Time* (New York: W. W. Norton, 1937), pp. 13-29. She argues that "there is no such thing as a normal psychology, which holds for all mankind" (p. 19).

[7]Cole, *op. cit.*, p. 820.

[8]*Ibid.*, p. 821.

II

The view which will be defended in this section of the paper is one which defines "value" in terms of human needs. In general, for generic value, *x is a value = x satisfies a human need.* This is intended to be parallel to Perry's position: "*x* is valuable = interest is taken in *x*."[9]

As applied to objects, institutions, etc., "satisfies a human need" refers to any need of any human. Should a doctor correctly find that Y needs a dose of morphine, then morphine is good for Y in that situation. Now at any given time, it is possible that a need exists for some person, or for everyone, which is not recognized. But on the proposed definition, an object which satisfies that need would be a value. In addition, an object which is not recognized as being able to satisfy a need, but which actually is capable of so doing, would also be a value. In regard to objects, then, a more adequate way of expressing the above equation is: *x is good for Y in situation z = x satisfies Y's need in situation z.* As applied to actions, the proposed definition of "value" is to be understood as follows: an action which results in the satisfaction of a human need is valuable. A contemplated but unperformed deed could be called valuable if it would satisfy a need when performed. In other words "satisfies" should be given a tenseless interpretation; either actual or potential satisfaction can be constitutive of value.

In addition, it is not intended that temporary states of satiety for x should result in x ceasing to be valuable. We can properly say that an individual has a need for x, even if, at a certain time, he is satisfied by the quantity of x he has. We are concerned mainly with the needs of humans in general, not with the momentary states of any particular individual. Thus food would still be a value, even if a given person were not at all hungry at a given moment.

For this theory, how "need" is defined is obviously important. Presumably we may depend upon the sciences for our definition of "need," and if more and more refined definitions are given as the sciences progress, so much the better. For the present, we may equate "need" with "an event or condition which aids the human to function adequately." The events or conditions may be located in the environment, in the organism, or may be bio-social. Warren's dictionary stresses the role of the environment by defining "need" in terms of "any factor or condition in the environment of an organism which assists to a marked extent in preserving its life and health or in furthering its

---

[9] R. B. Perry, *General Theory of Value* (Cambridge: Harvard University, 1926), p. 116.

usual modes of behaviour."[10] Patrick Mullahy says: "Needs are fundamentally outcomes of organism-environment instabilities and relations,
not of instabilities or pressures or tensions in an organism as an isolated entity."[11] It is likely that here, as in many areas, the most adequate approach is that of emphasizing both the biological and social
aspects of the person.

The view of "need" just presented leaves much to be desired in the
way of precision, but it is adequate for our present purposes. Considerable scientific work has been done as to what is necessary for
human functioning, especially on the biological level. On the cultural
level, much work remains to be done: what one culture regards as
general good functioning may be very different from what another
culture sees as good human behavior. The suggestion of this paper is
to leave both the determination of what needs humans have, and the
definition of "need," to the sciences. This poses important methodological questions, especially in respect to non-physiological needs.
A generic human nature is presupposed, and it is notorious that one's
conception of the nature of man is only too likely to be influenced by
cultural, ideological, and philosophic biases. In principle, however, the
question seems to be an empirical one. If humans have a need for X,
the consequences of depriving them of X and supplying them with X
(in various degrees) should be such as can be studied scientifically.
A. H. Maslow, for example, has recently developed a list of basic
human needs suggested by empirical research, and he also mentions
much of the work being done in the area.[12] Presumably suggested
lists of needs can be tested by the usual methods of science, although
conclusive results may not be available for some time to come.

It should also be emphasized here that there is no intention to
restrict human needs to biological ones, nor to reduce all human
needs to biological functioning. Our social and cultural needs obviously play an extremely important role in our lives. The child who is
sent to bed without his supper, to take a commonplace example,
suffers much more from the deprivation of affection and acceptance
than he does from the deprivation of food. Mullahy mentions "the
need for 'good feeling,' for euphoria, for security."[13] Humans have a
great variety of needs on many levels. (Recently, some have made

---

[10]H. C. Warren, ed., *Dictionary of Psychology* (Boston: Houghton Mifflin, 1934),
p. 176.
[11]P. Mullahy, "A Philosophy of Personality," reprinted in H. Brand, ed., *The
Study of Personality* (New York: John Wiley, 1954), p. 51.
[12]A. H. Maslow, *Motivation and Personality* (New York: Harper, 1954), ch. 5.
[13]Mullahy, *op. cit.*, p. 52.

an attempt to dispense with the view that humans have many needs, and have argued that what are taken as separate needs are really aspects of *one* basic need. Carl Rogers describes the one fundamental need as the striving to actualize, maintain, and enhance the organism; Kurt Goldstein refers to it as "self-actualization."[14] It may well be that this approach is the more fruitful one for the sciences. If so, the above formulation could be modified so that instead of referring to the satisfaction of diverse needs, one would refer to the satisfaction of the various aspects of the one fundamental human need. For the purposes of the value theory under discussion, whether it is more adequate to view humans as having many needs, or as having one basic need which takes many forms, does not seem to be of crucial importance.)

If the need-theory of value is accepted, it is clear that value statements are cognitive, descriptive, and naturalistic. In principle they are either true or false. If x satisfies a human need, then "x is a value" is a descriptive statement like many other descriptive statements in science. This theory makes value statements objective in an important sense of that term. For whether or not x is a value does not depend upon what any individual thinks, or upon an individual's attitude toward x. Possibly a whole class or a whole culture could go wrong, either about what human needs are, or about what will satisfy those needs.

Although value statements are objective, then, according to this view, they are not absolute. Different cultures will generate different needs: an individual living under modern capitalism has markedly different needs compared to an individual living in a simple food-gathering economy. Although some needs would be identical or remarkably similar for all cultures, others would differ very much. There also may be a kind of evolution of some cultural needs. Men of the Palæolithic period had needs which were not identical with those of the later men of Neolithic times, and these men of the new stone age had fewer needs than contemporary men. Technological advance produces new needs.[15] Values, then, are not absolute; they are relative to needs. As needs change, values change.

---

[14]C. R. Rogers, *Client-Centered Therapy* (Boston: Houghton Mifflin, 1951), pp. 487-491. K. Goldstein, *The Organism* (New York: American Book Co., 1939), pp. 194-207.

[15]See V. G. Childe, *Man Makes Himself* (New York: Mentor Book ed., 1951), especially pp. 20-37.

III

At this point, it is appropriate to consider the relation of the theory under discussion to Perry's interest theory of value. Many of the criticisms of Perry emphasize that there are things which are objects of interests, but yet which are bad. A sadist has a strong interest in inflicting pain; yet we want to call that interest bad. Perry has repeatedly replied to this criticism; he distinguishes between generic value and the morally good. Inflicting pain may have generic value and still be morally bad, since moral goodness depends upon an organization of interests; the ultimate standard for Perry is harmonious happiness.[16] While Perry has answered the critics well on this point, it will be argued here that the need-theory has some advantages in regard to this matter. Needs are presumably more stable than interests. Interests can be perverse, distorted, and unhealthy. Needs also may be, but they are likely to be so to a lesser extent. On the view of "need" given earlier, it may be said that a sadist has a need, as well as an interest, in inflicting pain. But it seems more direct and meaningful to speak of this need conflicting with other of his needs than it does to speak of a like interest conflicting with other interests. If "value" is defined in terms of human needs, rather than in terms of interests, it would be simpler in many cases to decide between opposing claims. An individual might well have an interest in exploiting other individuals economically, but not have a need to exploit them.

The need-theory also lends itself to a more straightforward distinction between what is objectively valuable for an individual and what he subjectively thinks is valuable. It could be rather difficult, at times, to distinguish between what a person thinks is an interest of his, and what his interest really is. It would be less difficult to distinguish between what an individual thinks his need is, and what it actually is. The difference is one of degree, not of kind. Needs and interests overlap a good deal, of course, but it seems that some, at least, of the things that Perry wants to accomplish can be accomplished more economically through the use of the need-definition of "value."

It might be argued, however, that even though there would be gains in substituting "need" for "interest," the result would be an overly great narrowing of the meaning of "value." Are there not many things which we want to call valuable which do not satisfy needs? In reply, it may be pointed out that the view of "need" given here is

---

[16]Perry, *Realms of Value,* pp. 11-13, pp. 90-92; and *General Theory of Value,* pp. 134-137.

rather broad, although it is not equivalent to "interest." Since the aim
has been to prescribe a meaning for "value," the objection need not
be a crucial one. Perhaps some things which one would like to call
valuable could not be called valuable under the proposed definition.
If other advantages exist for the theory, however, this change in usage
could be tolerated. In the present context, the issue could be put this
way: is it more useful to emphasize the "being for" or "being against"
aspects of value judgments, as Perry does,[17] or the kind of objectivity
resulting from the need-theory? How one answers this question depends upon many things, and ultimately metaphysical questions may
be involved. The thesis defended here is that the need-theory is the
more useful, since (in theory) the sciences can objectively determine
what the needs of humans are, and considering all cultures, there is
likely to be a greater uniformity of needs than there is of interests.

According to the view presented here, what happens if needs conflict? It is clear that not only will different individuals have needs
which conflict, but also that one person may have needs which are
not in harmony with other of his needs. A "sick" society, for example,
may produce such a conflict of needs that its members become neurotic, judged by the standards of that culture. What is needed, then,
for a general value theory, is a postulate stating that the greatest
possible number of need-satisfactions is to be chosen over any lesser
number of satisfactions. Now in some sense, this is an arbitrary postulate, but it is no more arbitrary than, as Edel has remarked in a somewhat different context, "the choice of health over sickness, realistic
appraisal over neurotic anxiety, life over death."[18] Many problems
could be raised as to how needs are to be added together, how the
sums of needs are to be compared, etc. This is not the place to discuss
them, since the view is being sketched only in broad outline.

IV

Certain consequences of this view may be pointed out, however.
Since the theory calls for the greatest possible satisfaction of the needs
of all men, the existence of any elite group which depends for the
high degree of satisfaction of its needs upon the low degree of satisfaction of the majority, would be condemned. The economic and cultural exploitation of colonial, minority, or depressed economic groups

---

[17]Perry, *Realms of Value*, p. 7.

[18]A. Edel, "Some Trends in American Naturalistic Ethics," in M. Farber, ed.,
Philosophic Thought in France and the United States (Albany: State University
of New York Press, 1968), p. 610.

so that a few could enjoy the good things of life in abundance, would be wrong. Such a view, then, would have important consequences for social practice: ethics, social philosophy, and the sciences would all be closely related.

Attention may now be turned to the problem of making cross-cultural value statements. As Edel has pointed out, there is an interesting correlation between social, political, and economic events, on the one hand, and the attitude of naturalistic writers on ethics, on the other hand. For some time we had a great emphasis on cultural relativity, and in the very recent past some attempts to construct an "all-human" ethics.[19] To repeat, although philosophers have often been anxious to construct a theoretical framework which will allow cross-cultural judgments, practising anthropologists, whose opinions should be taken very seriously, often feel that this is not possible.

On the need-theory, the following could be said:

(i) If (and it certainly seems to be so) different cultures produce different human needs, then one type of cultural relativism is inescapable. Looking at the matter either historically or taking a cross-cultural view of contemporary societies, it is a fact that different groups of humans have valued very different things. On an *a priori* basis, one can always say that all those who differ from one's own view are wrong, but this will be satisfying only to those who accept the same values. Like it or not, some form of cultural relativism is necessary if a general value system is to have any relation to empirical facts.

(ii) Some degree of cross-cultural value judgments can be meaningfully made, however. Other things being equal, a culture which does not offer many means of satisfying some of the basic human needs (assuming that there are some which are universal) is inferior to a culture which offers more means of satisfying those needs. For example, other things being equal, a culture in which the socio-economic organization allows many people to starve is inferior to one whose organization gives everyone adequate food.

The problem becomes more complicated when needs which vary from culture to culture are considered. If culture A produces a greater need for affection in its citizens than culture B does, it scarcely seems possible, on the basis of current knowledge, to say that one of the cultures is superior to the other in this respect. However, we can say that a culture which produces certain strong needs, but not the means of satisfying them, is inferior to a culture which does offer the means

---

[19]*Ibid.*, pp. 589-590.

of satisfying the needs of that culture. Hence some cross-cultural judgments in this area are possible.

(iii) As more and more knowledge is gained by the social sciences, we can more accurately make the kind of value judgments just described. Perhaps some day psychologists will be able to give a rather precise description of how much, and what type, affection a person needs. It may turn out that people living in different societies will need different amounts of affection, but still we may know more about how much affection is necessary under given conditions.

V

Earlier it was said that the definition of "value" given in this paper was not an attempt to describe how people do use the term, but rather an attempt to prescribe a meaning. What are some of the advantages accruing from a need-definition which would make this theory preferable to other theories which also prescribe a meaning for "value"?

In the first place, this theory obviously brings ethics and the sciences into a close relation. Many writers on ethics today would not view this as an advantage. However, in the light of the successes the sciences have had in the past, it seems as though ethics could certainly profit by a close association with the sciences. Secondly, this theory gives to the sciences the task of determining precisely what human needs are. If this question is to be answered at all, it will be answered by the sciences. Thirdly, the proposed definition of "value" does not seem hopelessly out of accord with some of the ways in which ethical terms are used. It is doubtful that people in general use ethical terms either exclusively or mainly in any of the ways proposed in recent meta-ethical analyses. Perhaps most people use ethical terms in several ways; some of these may well be inconsistent. The need-definition of "value" seems no more peculiar than many other analyses.

Some writers on ethics have stressed the intimate relations of "value" and "need," without adopting the approach advocated in this paper.[20]

---

[20]For example, S. Hook, "The Desirable and Emotive in Dewey's Ethics," in S. Hook, ed., *John Dewey: Philosopher of Science and Freedom* (New York: Dial, 1950), p. 213; A. Edel, *op. cit.*, p. 610; M. Farber, "Professor Reulet on 'Being, Value, and Existence,'" *Philosophy and Phenomenological Research*, X, No. 1 (September, 1949), p. 88; M. Farber, "False Abstractionism and the Problem of Objective Knowledge," *Proceedings of the XIth International Congress of Philosophy*, Vol. X (Amsterdam: North-Holland Publishing Co., 1953), p. 201. Dewey closely relates "value" to something approximating the view of "need" given in this paper in his *Theory of Valuation* (Chicago: University of Chicago, 1939), p. 57. Fromm discusses an ethical view similar to that of this paper in his *The Sane Society*, Ch. 2.

The view sketched here is intended only as a tentative one; perhaps a more useful formulation of the relation of "value" and "need" is possible. The theory under discussion does avoid the subjective aspects of some naturalistic theories, since whether or not something is a need depends upon objective, scientific, evidence. At the same time, it avoids the absolutistic nature of some of the nonnaturalistic theories. Finally, it allows some cognitively significant cross-cultural value judgments to be made. To many, these may seem qute inconclusive reasons for adopting a theory of ethics. Others, hospitable to the general philosophic orientation of this paper, may find the theory worthy of consideration.

ALIENATION AND SOCIAL ACTION[*]

Adam Schaff

THE WORD "alienation" is today one of those fashionable and hence suspect words.[**] It is very often used and therefore misused; it is an ambiguous and thereby obscure word; moreover, it gives rise to the defensive reactions of those who believe that what it represents is dangerous in practice and who are interested in maintaining a situation which, according to them, is worthwhile defending. These reactions stem from different ways of reasoning and practical attitudes; starting with those who consider that it is necessary to fight against all obscure and ambiguous words and ending with those who oppose the pessimism of the "philosophy of despair." There are, therefore, among the opposers, all those who believe in the traditions of neo-positivism and in the standpoint of the semantic analysis of terms.

In point of fact the theoretical concept of alienation has come to us in two ways, which although linked one to another are nonetheless different. The first one was Hegelianism, which exerted a constant influence, particularly on German humanism; the second was Marxism. At this point it is necessary to say that, genetically, Marxism was organically linked to Hegelianism; nevertheless, its conception of alienation is clearly different, and it was this conception which provoked in the 20th century, not only the renaissance, but also, more recently, the impetuous blossoming forth of this theory.

Fashion, in the intellectual sphere, may include some more or less marked elements of snobbishness, but almost never, or at least rarely, can it be reduced to snobbishness alone. It generally stems from the

[*]Reprinted by permission from *Diogenes*, #57, Spring (1967), pp. 64-82. Translated by Alessandro Ferace and Neldo Cantarella (with emendations by David H. DeGrood).

[**]This sketch was part of the book published to commemorate the 80th anniversary of Professor Tadeusz Kotarbinski.

social need to interpret some actual facts, and hence also from a new theoretical interest in certain ideas, an interest which, as Ludwik Krzywicki justly said, determines the "transfer of ideas."

Even if this were the only reason, the "fashion" of alienation would require a very accurate sociological and psychological analysis. On the other hand, the lack of clarity and the ambiguity of the term as it is currently used should not discourage research which aims at defining it precisely with the help of the methods of semantic analysis. It is the only way, if one wants to discover from whence comes the "fashion" of a given term or concept and on the other hand—and this is most important—if one wants to determine the perspective of their political value. This is the core of the problem: if the social need for the interpretation of certain phenomena manifests itself—and this determines the fashion of the given concept—it is generally because certain problems require an explanation so that social action can be perfected. Intellectual fashion is, therefore, only their spontaneous and unconscious expression. Reflection allows not only the achievement of consciousness of what lies beneath these spontaneous processes in the sphere of social ideas, but, moreover, renders explicit ideas hitherto not very clear and misleading because of their ambiguity. It can and must play an important role in the perfecting of social activities linked to this group of ideas.

It is this aspect of the problem which we will investigate first in this article and which explains the title.

1) I shall first try to define precisely the essential concepts. I will strive to do it in the spirit of the definition-project, which is to say I will convey the meaning of the words that I will use, as I understand them and as I intend to use them afterwards. Any other method is bound to fail because of the long history of the problem (which goes back at least to medieval philosophy) and of the consequent ambiguity of the term "alienation." Since I am not interested here in the history of the term, and it is possible to set it aside, I shall limit myself to pointing out that it will always be possible to find the fundaments or the impulses of anything that I may say of these questions in the course of history. Still this neither means that the definition that I adopt coincides with some other definition known in history nor that the whole structure of the concept and the consequent practical conclusions are identical to any one of the forms they took in the past. This is equally valid for the Marxist conception on which I rely and with which I identify myself as far as its guidelines are concerned.

Marx's conception was transformed in accordince with the transformations of his Weltanschauung and the ripening of his ideas on society; moreover, the development of social relations after Marx and above all the experiences of countries building socialism engender reflections which either did not appear in Marx or had not yet matured.

Let our point of departure be the difference between objectivation and alienation.

In the process of life, men enter into relationships through the intermediary of their various types of work, material and spiritual. To live, man transforms material reality, produces various goods in order to satisfy his physical human needs. But he also creates spiritual goods that must satisfy determined needs at different historic stages of the development of society. Man creates society itself, because he is involved in social relationships; and he creates the means which allow him to communicate with other men. In other words, man *acts* in order to live, but he also *lives* by acting; because man exists in regard to other men only *through the intermediary* of his works and he *is* for others the sum of what he has accomplished. But all human action, understood as acts, as well as all human work, understood as products, are the external projections of man, since man acts while thinking; and this is beyond doubt one of the characteristics which distinguish him from the rest of the animal world. What man thinks when he attempts to achieve an objective is transformed, when he acts, into an *objective* work, which is to say into something that exists beyond any human mind and independently from him. This is what I mean by *objectivation*. In short, *objectivation is the process of transformation, through action, of human thinking into material and spiritual products which have an objective existence, independent of human will and consciousness.* Needless to say, this process of objectivation is the basis and the condition of men's social life, since it satisfies their various needs and also permits them to communicate with one another and, therefore, to coexist.

Only when the meaning of objectivation has been explained—as the process and also the sum of acts and works of human activity—is it possible to understand the concept of "alienation."

The point of departure will be the observation of empirical facts in the sphere of man's social life. There are various products of human activity. They are the work of individuals, because only concrete and living individuals exist. But man, even if he exists as a concrete biological individual, is always a *social* individual, not only because he is the product of a certain society (physically and spiritually), but also because he can live and survive only in *society*, involved in its relations and the mechanism of its actions. Man's activities also are *social* in two ways, just as the *products* of man which also have a social function. The mechanism of this function may differ according to the social relations by which it is determined. The observation of social life proves that—even if man creates spiritual and material goods in order to satisfy certain needs of other men—in certain social conditions the products of human activity begin to function not only in an autonomous way, independently from the will and intentions of their makers, but even *contrarily* to their will and intentions, entangling their projects and even threatening in some way or other their makers. This is precisely what we call *alienation*. Therefore, *alienation is the process of functioning—given existing social relations —of men's products (material and spiritual) independently of the will and intentions of their authors, in a spontaneous way, disturbing men's plans and projects and threatening in some way their existence.* We call alienation a certain functioning of men's products in given social conditions, a functioning whose mechanism escapes the control of the individual and even of society, in such a way as to constitute a menace to their plans and even to their existence. The best illustration is the parable of the sorcerer's apprentice who after setting in motion certain forces is no longer able to dominate them.

We can, therefore, conclude our considerations about the mutual relations of objectivation and alienation.

Objectivation is a *necessary* phenomenon of the process of man's life. Without such an objectivation, men could neither exist (material and spiritual *production* is only a peculiar form of objectivation) nor coexist (were it only for the problem of communication).

Alienation, on the contrary, is not a *necessary* phenomenon of the process of man's life (not all the products of man are alienated, even if they always have an objective existence), but solely a *contingent* phenomenon. This depends on the social conditions according to which man's objectified products function. In certain social conditions, objectivation becomes alienation, in others it is not characterized by alienation (or it loses those characteristics when conditions are modified in a certain way). The general conclusion we can arrive at, and which is extremely important in order to continue with our considerations, is that the processes of alienation are a function of the entirety of social relations, and, depending on the structure of the *whole*, they may *appear* or *disappear*.

2) To better understand the meaning of the abstract concept of

"alienation," we must turn to some examples in which the term "alienation" most conveniently indicates the functioning of man's products.

Let us begin with the alienation of man's material products.

Let us examine the capitalist market, which was the particular object of Marx's attention. In the market there is merchandise; it has a definite price and value on the basis of which it is exchanged. Merchandise consists of material goods—products of man—which must satisfy certain material needs of man. But since in a capitalist society definite social relations prevail based on the relations of property, the product of human work changes character and becomes merchandise. Its function, which was to fulfill man's needs, no longer is conclusive, and it is its exchange function (creating capital) which gains the ascendancy. In the mechanism of the capitalist market, man's products start functioning not only in an autonomous way, independently of the will and plans of their maker (the scale of prices, the separation between goods intended to satisfy human needs and men anxious to satisfy these needs, of which the extreme example is the destruction of food products while people go hungry), but also against his objectives and plans, threatening his physical existence (shutdowns, crises of overproduction). This is a classical example of what is meant by the alienation of man's *material products*.

But alienation is not limited to the sphere of material products. The classic example of alienation in spiritual matters—considering what interested young Marx and his contemporaries—is religion.

If we refuse the mythological consciousness according to which God made man in his own image, we have to concede that the only rational thesis is Ludwig Feuerbach's, according to which *man* makes gods in his own image, a fact that can be demonstrated very easily on the basis of comparative studies in the field of the scientific study of religion. Man *creates* religion and in this respect the situation is analogous to his experience as producer of merchandise. In point of fact, the objectified products of his imagination in certain social conditions not only start to lead an independent existence, but also reach the point of threatening his existence: they engender persecution, inquisition, death on the pyre. There is no need to be particularly perspicacious in order to see the generalization of this problem when, in certain conditions, any ideology starts assuming the characteristics of a religion, with all the consequent dangers for man's freedom and happiness. According to Durkheim any ideology may function as a religion if it serves to render homogeneous a group on the basis of faith and not on the basis of scientifically verifiable convictions. And he was right. Marx and his contemporaries were also right when in their struggle for humanism they began attacking religious alienation. Because as long as one believes in the heteronomy of human destinies formed by extra- or super-human factors, and until one admits the thesis of the autonomous character of these destinies, according to which thesis they are formed *by* men and *for* men, it will not be possible to *realize*, in a consequent way, the view of humanism.

Let us take a striking current example: the discovery made by human genius of atomic disintegration and of automatization. It is incontestably an important province of the creation of the spirit which marks the beginning of a new epoch in the development of mankind, of an epoch that will surpass the social consequences of what has been called the industrial revolution. Here are, therefore, some discoveries which could make realizable the legendary paradise on earth, but functioning in certain social conditions they could threaten mankind with total destruction. This is a classic example of alienation: the threat is today known to everybody. *Nobody* wants to be annihilated. We have, therefore, the right to suppose reasonably that *everybody* would like to avoid this annihilation, nevertheless we are boldly moving towards the abyss. Never before has mankind found itself playing the role of the sorcerer's apprentice in such a clear and tragic way. This is precisely what I call a situation of alienation. The name is not important (if I use the traditional term it is because I could not find a better one), but what is in question are the *objective* social situations that are necessary to see and know in order to have the possibility to guarantee the efficacy of social actions destined to oppose them.

In this sense the term "alienation" admits a very large semantic function. "Alienation" designates in fact all the social processes in which man's products—material and spiritual—function in a social mechanism determined by definite social relations, not only independently of man but in opposition to the social objectives he has set for himself and even threatening his social existence.

If this conception of alienation is broad, it is, however, sufficiently exact to prevent identifying alienation with *every* objectivation and with what is called social evil.

If, for instance, traffic laws are in force independently of the will of the particular individuals who are obligated to cross the road in a disciplined way, nonetheless this is not alienation; just as the system of weights and measures socially accepted or the rules governing circulation on the roads, and so forth, are not alienation. Simply because in these instances there is no *opposition* to the social objectives of men (on the contrary, in all these cases it is a social convention which implements these objectives) nor is there any *danger* threatening their existence.

The same thing occurs if one tries to *identify* alienation with social evil. If it is true that alienation *is* a social evil, not all social evil is equivalent to alienation. We can cite epidemics for instance or suicides caused by an unhappy love affair. It is a question of the relation of the part to the whole and not of equivalence.

3) There is a particular problem related to matters of alienation which must be discussed separately. It is called *auto-alienation*. In certain literature of existentialist inspiration, alienation and auto-alienation are simply identified. It is a great mistake that calls for an explanation.

"Alienation" characterizes the process in which *man's products* become extraneous to him; they function independently and in spite of his will and plans. The *products* of man and not man himself are in a position of "alienation." Therefore, if we speak of the alienation of man, this term assumes a particular meaning. In this respect, chronologically, the oldest intuitions are linked to the analysis of religious alienation. The mechanism of this alienation consists in the fact that man projects some of his own characteristics in an absolute form on a superhuman being who is his own product. In this way, such qualities as goodness, knowledge, love, in an absolute sense, become the attributes of God, but at the same time man is deprived of these qualities when one compares him to the model of perfection he himself created. Here there is a double alienation. In the first place human characteristics are detached from man and they are "alienated," becoming an integral part of one of the products of man's mind functioning from that moment autonomously. In the second place man "grows poor" of the qualities which he has transposed outside of himself. This concept, belonging to Feuerbach, may be considered the first emergence of the idea of auto-alienation.

But there is also a much simpler interpretation. "Alienation" is the name given to the process during which man's products have an actual relation with their creator. This relation may also occur between the capabilities of man, his attitudes—in other words, between his personality considered as the ensemble of capabilities, attitudes, and the human individual who is the "bearer" of them. This occurs when, placed in the sphere of an economy based on trade, man and his personality become merchandise as well and are submitted to the laws and estimations of such an economy. This is the difference between work and free creation, between earning one's living and acting in order to satisfy human needs. In life and in literature this has different names: commercialization of culture, transformation into merchandise of feelings, cultural and scientific creation. The literature on the subject—including the *Communist Manifesto*—criticizes this situation in which everything that man has is on sale, and this causes him to adapt himself to the exigencies of buyers and to cease being himself. And in this sense he alienates himself. One of the aims of the Marxist ideal of the "total man" is to establish social conditions allowing man to act according to his needs and tastes, therefore, to create and not to work (this context explains why Marx considers work an alienation, an "inhuman" activity, while he thinks that creative activity is not only necessary to man, but characterizes him).

In the light of this reasoning, one also understands better the difference—typically Hegelian, but playing an important role for young Marx—between the "true man" and the real man. The real man, as he actually is, shows signs of alienation in regard to his "generic being," while the true man is free of them. But the "true man" is an ideal, a model.

Up to now we have approached the problem of auto-alienation from the point of view of the relationship "man—man's personality." This term has nevertheless another meaning which reappears generally in discussions on alienation. It is a question of the alienation of man as an individual in regard to society, to which is connected his non-engagement in society's dealings.

The literature of the "philosophy of despair"—works of philosophy as well as of belles-lettres—with its themes of solitude, of the individual lost in the crowd who does not find any meaning in life (seen as the objective one has in life), is rich and varied.

There is in it a lot of snobbishness and decadence, and it delights in the psychological analysis of sick individuals, and there is also a reactionary concept of the elite. But what this literature speaks of is a real problem that must not be forgotten because it is connected to new and negative social phenomena which the term "auto-alienation" suits very well.

Highly industrialized society brings with it, on one hand, the creation of huge urban agglomerations with all the positive and negative problems of what we call a mass-society. On the other hand, it also brings about the disintegration of traditional links among the different groups, starting with family ties, then professional ties, neighborhood ties, and confessional ties, that is to say the connections which, naturally and traditionally, determined the *participation* of the individual in society. The great city and, therefore, the culture of mass-society destroys the traditional links; but it also creates some new ones, more powerful in many aspects: trade unions, sports clubs, cultural associations, political parties, the links created by mass-culture conveyed by the press, by radio and television, etc. The individual man placed in this huge mechanism is connected to society by many more links than in the past, connections more powerful because it is a question of what conditions and forms his personality, as it is a question of his organic incorporation in the ensemble of the social structure, of the impossibility of living isolated outside of that structure and independently from it. There is, therefore, a clear integration and structuralization of society which determines a stricter integration of the individual in the society, at least in some aspects. This is not at all in contradiction with the disintegration which intervenes simultaneously within the social structure and which conditions the auto-alienation of the individual, in the sense of this term which interests us here.

Literature, good literature of course, goes further than dozens of scientific dissertations. To make myself clear, I will refer to Steinbeck's novel, *Grapes of Wrath*. The author describes in an extremely suggestive way, how, in their peregrinations to the West, a common destiny pushed men together in informal groups in which everybody could reciprocally count upon the other's help.

This factor has naturally been weakened by mass-society: man is a part of this society without which he cannot live, he depends on it in many respects, but he is an atom with which society can very well do without. This makes all the difference. This link, very powerful and organic on the one hand, on the other is very weak. This is why it is impossible to count on the help and solidarity of others (with the exception of particular alliances such as revolutionary groups, but this is not a characteristic of society as a whole). That is why it is easy to have relationships, but it is difficult to have friends (this is very clear in American society). Since this is the effect of deeply set rules governing a highly industrialized society, at least in the capitalist system, one is not only the object but also the subject of this disintegration. In other words, man loses the desire to involve himself in social problems; he confines himself more and more to the circle of his own narrow interests. This is, however, the principal *tendency*. Of course, this does not mean that in highly industrialized societies every tendency to take part in social life disappears totally. It can be found in groups having specific objectives, religious or revolutionary, for instance; but then they are exceptions which do not modify the principal tendency. At the level of society, such participation appears generally when it is a matter of defending national causes. Nevertheless, even in these cases the tendency towards disintegration is not conquered, simply the contradictory tendencies are overcome within one and the same society. The problem of auto-alienation still remains.

This is the "rational core" of the philosophy of the individual lost in the crowd. It has two aspects. The first is the problem of a certain disintegration of society for which the individual is something extraneous, and, by the same token, for the individual, society as well is something extraneous not requiring from the individual any emotional involvement. The second is that an exacerbated individualism similar to anarchism is manifesting itself amongst disintegrated individuals and at the same time a uniformity of life, above all spiritual, of the individual entangled in the mechanism of mass-society and culture which threatens to annihilate personality and borders upon the ghastly visions evoked in the fantastic novels of Zamiatine, Huxley, Orwell, and others.

This sum of complicated problems, which should be studied meticulously rather than rejected because of a defensive reaction, is characteristic of auto-alienation.

Therefore, it is clear from what we have said that it is necessary not to identify the problems of alienation and those of auto-alienation, and that those who try to reduce the problem of alienation simply to the problem of man who feels estranged in regard to society do not understand the issues at all, at least such as it is in the context of the Marxist tradition.

Secondly, it is equally true that the problem of auto-alienation has at least two aspects and that its current and simplified interpretation is a mistake which further confuses the already complicated picture of a very important contemporary social problem.

4) When we speak of "alienation" are we thinking of the subjective conditions of individuals—who feel "lonely," "lost," "deprived of the meaning of life,"—or of certain objective processes which influence the social position and the social improvement of individuals?

In the light of our reasoning the question is rather rhetorical. Nevertheless, those who ask it are right because the problem is not absolutely clear if one sticks to the current literature on the subject.

"Alienation" is the name given to certain *objective* processes in which man's products have certain relations with their creator. From this angle the question is meaningless. On the contrary, in the case of auto-alienation, it has some value.

In this case, in our usage, "auto-alienation" is the name given to certain *objective* processes in which the individual finds himself in a certain situation if it is a question of his attiude in regard to other men and society. These objective processes are evidently mirrored back in the consciousness of men who feel lonely, lost, without purpose. But their feelings are only a secondary phenomenon in regard to the objective processes which originated them. In other words, man is not alienated (in the sense of auto-alienation) because he feels so, but on the contrary, he feels certain things because he is in the objective situation called "auto-alienation."

To define this situation, one can use, as proposed by some—for instance, Professor S. Zolkiewski—the language of the theory of structuralism, analyzing it according to the structure of social relations (which can, therefore, reproduce themselves) which determine the individual existence of men. But it can also be done in another way, using, for instance, the traditional language of the socio-historical theory of Marxism. Personally, I am convinced that this is the better solution because I fear that a too universal application of the theory and methods of structuralism—which till now has brought lasting results only in linguistics—is not founded and results more from a fashion than from the real needs of research. It is, however, a minor question which requires verification in practice, in the course of research. It does not change at all the essence of our problem, namely, that of the objective character of the processes of alienation.

5) We have now concluded at least a superficial explanation of the concepts which interest us and which we are going to use in the course of our reasoning. It is time to ask a question: do these reasonings have a practical application? Or, in other words, can the category of alienation which is so widely disputed today be of any use in social action? If so, in which way?

My answer is affirmative; I see four areas, at least, which lend themselves to the concretization of the general thesis on the practical range of the category of alienation.

a) Let us start with the values of classification and knowledge that alienation brings with it.

The fact that there is a general theory and category of alienation allows the classification of certain social situations having characteristics which correspond to those generally attributed to the situation of alienation. Knowledge and diagnostics are made easy, if it is a question of contingent social action.

b) In practice what matters is precisely the function which permits the establishing of diagnostics.

In conformity with the general theory of alienation, as we know, the product of objectivation assumes the characteristics peculiar to the processes of alienation only when social relationships lend themselves to it. The very simple conclusion that we deduced previously is that a certain change in social relations makes it possible to overcome alienation. When the characteristics of alienation disappear, man's products—material and spiritual—start to function in conformity with the will and plans of their maker. They no longer function spontaneously.

Here are some examples:

Merchandise, on the capitalist market, has all the characteristics of the alienated product of man, because it functions in social conditions provided by capitalism which is founded on the relations of property. Therefore, to overcome this alienation—that brings with it not only the lack of planned production and crises but also as a consequence, shutdowns, hunger, poverty and the danger of imperialist wars, which threaten directly man's existence—it is convenient to transform the social relations that condition this alienation, and, in the first place, the relations of property. This was one of the fundamental ideas of Marx, the practical consequences of which have determined the line of development of our epoch.

The same occurs in the State in so far as it is an organization of physical coercion—"the troops of armed men" as Lenin said, such institutions as the army, the police, tribunals and prisons. In the perspective of Marxism it is an alienation whose genesis and development depend on actual social relationships: on the division of society into antagonistic classes based on the system of private property. The conclusion is to conquer this alienation and to thus extend social democracy; it is necessary to transform the social relations which condition alienation, the division of society into antagonistic classes, and this presupposes the elimination of the system of private ownership of the means of production which determine these classes.

Another example which belongs to the classic repertory of Marxism is religious alienation. There is no need to characterize it, it is too evident. We can pass directly to the practical conclusions. To overcome it, a change is necessary in social relationships, especially in the fields of culture and education, if this form of alienation is to be overcome, at least as a mass phenomenon, because it is too complicated a psychological phenomenon to relate simply to social relations and to suppose that only with these transformations, religious beliefs will disappear entirely and definitively.

We can try to generalize the significance of these examples from the point of view which interests us. *Any alienation can be overcome* (of course, by a more or less lengthy process), *if one knows what conditions it socially and if one modifies suitably the human relations which determine its functioning.*

c) This statement throws into relief not only the practical value of the category of alienation, but at the same time its power of mobilization as far as social action is concerned, social action being one of those elements upon which the optimistic character of Marxist humanism is founded (its adversaries would call it utopian and millenarian). Because if one ascertains that alienation is a social evil, one verifies at the same time that man, while acting socially, is always able to overcome this evil. It is a statement capable of stirring us to action, and thence an optimistic one, optimistic when compared to the metaphysics of evil, at least as expressed in some varieties of existentialism (Sartre's, for instance, that declares the unavoidable victory of evil regardless of what men do).

d) The range of this power of mobilization is magnified as one realizes that alienation is a *constant* social problem in any system. Alienation is in fact linked to the objectivation which is a constant and necessary phenomenon of any vital process on a human level. It is sufficient that certain social relations exist for objectivation to start functioning as alienation.

Is there always a valid formula? Are the social relationships that promote the processes of alienation known? There is no general formula, and in these conditions there can be no general remedy for the phenomenon.

We can draw two practical conclusions at least:

In the first case, the struggle against alienation is an endless process whose objective is to conquer a particular alienation and not alienation *in general*, which would be a utopia. This action is not only precise but its social range is vast: it tends to enlarge our knowledge of the world, even if we know full well that it is an endless process, as a mathematical series tends to a limit. Nevertheless, any stage of this process is of considerable practical importance to mankind—even if we know that it is endless, in the same way as it is important to cure an illness, even if we can reasonably assume that in the future the human organism will be seized by other illnesses.

The second conclusion is extremely important when we examine the problem of alienation in a socialist system. If there is no general formula concerning the genesis of alienation, we cannot exclude, a priori, the possibility of witnessing the development of social situations and relationships unknown to this moment which can engender new forms of alienation. There is only one thing to do: to discover the most general relation existing between objectivation and alienation, the detrimental effect of the latter on society and to be conscious of its being a social phenomenon which can be overcome only if one knows the social relations which provoke it, and transform them suitably. It is not a panacea, but certainly a very precious directive for practical action. It enables one to speak not only of the practical power that confines alienation, but also to include it in the praxeologic dictionary if a sufficiently broad significance is attributed to the concept of "good work."

6) What we just said brings us to the problem of alienation in socialism.

If in given social relationships, objectivation can always degenerate into alienation, we must ask ourselves a question. Is socialism, as a social structure, subject to this law or not?

The question would be useless and petty, considering the evidence of the problem, if it were not for some of the suggestions to be found in the works of the young Marx. He thought, at that time, that the elimination of economic alienation would bring about automatically, in some way, the disappearance of all the other forms of alienation. We can interpret this phenomenon with indulgence and admit that Marx thought only of the alienation peculiar to the system of private property which would disappear with it, or admit that his judgment of alienation was general and then simply recognize that he was wrong. On the other hand, considering the works he wrote in his maturity, one can rightfully doubt that he afterwards stuck to some of the ideas of his early work on the subject which were utopian in character.

When we speak of alienation in socialism after Marx, it is convenient to make a differentiation between two stages: the earlier stage—socialism—and the later stage—communism. They are fundamentally different from the point of view of their genetic links with capitalism, and, therefore, with private property and the division of society into classes.

Following the Marxist train of thought, it is banal to say that socialism, by definition and in fact, never fully overcomes *any* known alienation, not even economic. Even without mentioning the fact that in the light of Marxism, State and bureaucracy are by definition alienations (and yet in a socialist system they exist and must exist), still more evident are the problems of the division into classes that remain, of the differences between manual and intellectual labor, between work in the country and work in the city, etc. But even if it is the question of the fundamental basis—of economic alienation— it is nonetheless the very problem of property which still has to be resolved, because, according to Marx, the elimination of private property is not only a negative postulate that governs nationalization, but also—and perhaps above all—a positive postulate, i.e., socialization which transforms the citizens into co-owners. Without this it is impossible to achieve communism as "free associations of producers" according to Marx's terminology.

It is, therefore, evident that the persistence of processes of alienation in the socialist phase is, in the light of Marxism, an absolutely clear question from the theoretical point of view. If this is the actual situation, it is, therefore, not possible to exclude that, in new conditions, some phenomena of alienation—for instance, bureaucracy or the autonomization of the function of physical constraint—may be aggravated momentarily, and it is even possible to be faced with new forms of alienation, unknown up to that moment. From the theoretical point of view, it is not possible to reject such a possibility. From the practical point of view, it is impossible.

What can be said in this respect as far as communism is concerned? From a certain point of view, nowadays, the problem has no practical importance. Contrary to the illusions nurtured during a certain period, it can be now verified, in full conscience, that in so-called "socialist" countries, we are still very far from achieving a society in which the construction of communism will be a reality. If only on the basis of experience, we are compelled to reject Stalin's thesis (since it is a groundless revision of Marxism), according to which it is possible to build a communist society in a State system that permits an apparatus of physical coercion and a bureaucracy. It is, therefore, necessary to return to Marx's thesis, according to which communism can be victorious only on a world-wide scale, because only on this condition—

theoretically at least—could the State and also armed conflict disappear, and a material basis created permitting the distribution of material goods "to everybody according to his needs," without which —in Marx's opinion—"the ancient filthiness" might again reappear in another form.

It is, therefore, possible to erect the foundations or the framework of a communist society, but the road leading to its accomplishment is still very long and since the forms of transition to this new system, especially in highly industrialized countries, will differ from those we have known up to now, the form of this future society will be certainly different, and it is impossible, as of now, to say something known to be correct on the subject.

Nevertheless, some questions linked to alienation may and should interest us even in this long-range perspective.

It is necessary to ascertain, in the first place, that, theoretically, it is impossible to exclude the appearance of processes of alienation in this type of society. Since alienation cannot exist without the objectivation of human activities, it is impossible to exclude the appearance of certain processes of alienation, even transitory ones. We can foresee for instance that "the free association of producers," as Marx called it, will meet with great difficulties in struggling against the danger of alienation of the apparatus of management, planification and production, which—because of its international character at that moment and because of its needs for highly trained specialists—will have a natural tendency towards stabilization, which brings with it the danger of alienation.

Therefore, there cerainly will be some difficulties and possibilities of degeneration in the sense of processes of alienation. But there will be, in return, almost certainly better means to help in the struggle, including the use of electronic machines programmed for this purpose.

Such a society will have another problem, that of the participation of its members in community life—in other words, the struggle against all the phenomena of auto-alienation. The problem becomes the formation of the personality of men in the new society which fluctuates between the Scylla of anarchic individualism and the Charybdis of the destruction of personal individuality, with which the impulse of biochemistry passes from the sphere of fiction into that of real possibility.

But anything we might say about these fascinating subjects still belonging to the future pertains to science fiction. It is much better not to dwell upon them and simply be conscious of the vitality of these problems.

What is certain and important in the context of our considerations is that the category of alienation will always have, even in such a future, a practical value. If one does not take into account these problems in relation to man's action in a communist society, it will be impossible to build communism and—after its construction—either maintain or develop it.

NATURALISM IN THE *TAO* OF CONFUCIUS AND LAO TZU

Dison Hsueh-Feng Poe

I. COMMON GROUND AND DIVERGENT OUTLOOK

TRADITIONALLY, Confucianism is characterized as humanism and Taoism as mysticism. When probed deeper, however, Confucian humanism reveals its hidden foundation; and when shorn of similes, analogies, and obscure language, Taoist mysticism melts away. It is the central theme of this paper that in the teachings of Confucius and Lao Tzu in general, and for their two apparently conflicting but substantially complementary systems of *tao* in particular, there is one common ground: namely, naturalism.

The common ground of naturalism is this basic view: that the entire universe is self-operating without the guidance or intervention of supernatural forces, that, therefore, human life is governed not by capricious divine volition but by fixed laws of nature, and that man, as a rational being, ought to learn and follow *tao*—either the Confucian *tao* or the Taoist *tao*, which is in the last analysis what is taken (by Confucius or Lao Tzu) to be that part of the whole of the laws of nature, which man should discern and practice. To facilitate the presentation of the central theme of this paper, two pertinent interrelated points need clarification at the outset: the implication of naturalism and the meaning of *tao*.

Naturalism may lead to scientism, that is, seeking only facts and relationships between facts. With a philosopher, however, naturalism is almost always associated with axiology, searching for values and the comparison between value-systems. Likewise, naturalism may land itself in naked materalism, but not necessarily. If teleology is found in the laws of nature, naturalism may well be allied with idealism. Naturalism in alliance with axiology and idealism is precisely the type of naturalism embodied in the Confucian as well as the Taoist *tao*.

237

In the recorded teachings of the two early Chinese sages, the one same term *tao* is used in three senses, depending on the context of the pertinent passages: as nature's-*tao*, as Heaven's-*tao*, and as man's-*tao*. As a matter of fact, the terms Heaven's-*tao* and man's-*tao* are employed in many passages; the point to be borne in mind is that the one word *tao* may have any one of the three meanings. Nature's-*tao* denotes the totality of the laws of nature. Thus it is vast, intricate, infinite, and as a whole indescribable. This is properly the realm of science. Heaven's-*tao* is that part of the whole—that preferred, idealized part of the impartial, complex whole of the laws of nature—which, according to Confucius and Lao Tzu, each in his own way, man should understand and observe. (For instance, the Mean with Confucius and the Reversal with Lao Tzu.) This is axiology and this is idealism. As to man's-*tao*, it is of two kinds. Man's-*tao* of the right kind is what is based on or deduced from Heaven's-*tao*, both intelligible and practicable.* Man's-*tao* of the wrong kind includes all mistaken, improper, and, in short, unethical ways of doing things.

Inasmuch as *tao*—Confucian or Taoist—is ultimately linked with the laws of nature, and in so far as "ought" implies "can," it may be aptly said that both Confucianism and Taoism have naturalism as their common ground, notwithstanding their divergence in outlook and in preference. In each there are some inner inconsistencies, and between both there are as many similarities as differences.

In developing the central theme of the present paper and making clear certain implications and consequences, reference has to be made to the two sages' respective views on the following: (1) theology, (2) cosmology, (3) metaphysics, (4) *tao*, (5) epistemology, (6) human nature, (7) ethics and (8) government and politics.

II. THE *TAO* OF CONFUCIUS

(1) As a transmitter and not an originator, China's supreme sage and foremost teacher is conservative in form and by terminology, but rather radical in substance and by implication. The naturalism of Confucius is best revealed in his theology. Heaven (*T'ien*) is neither fate nor the Lord High above. Heaven to Confucius is nature plus teleology; namely, a moral order, self-operating and yet purposeful. Hence these two seemingly contradictory sayings: on the one hand, "My praying has been quite a long time"; and on the other, "Having

---

*Such as loyalty and filial piety with Confucius, and meekness and contentment with Lao Tzu.

offended Heaven, one has no place for praying."[1] Again, take ancestor-worship: on the one hand, "Make sacrificial rites to the spirits as if the spirits were present"; and on the other, "While unable yet to serve the living, how are we able to serve the dead? . . . While we do not understand life how do we understand death?"[2] Actually, Confucian humanism is grounded in naturalism: "To treat the dead as dead is lack of human-heartedness; this should not be done. To treat the dead as living is lack of knowledge; this should not be done."[3] What should be done is to treat the dead *as if* they were still living. At any rate, no recorded teachings indicate that Confucius positively believes in God or God's directing the world in general and human affairs in particular.

(2) There is little of cosmology in Confucius' teachings. However, the conspicuous absence of any theory of divine creation attests his naturalism. What is more, there is ample suggestion that Heaven-and-Earth comes into being from the primal union of opposites (the unity-in-duality), the unitary-and-composite forces of *yin-yang*. As will be indicated in the concluding section, the very concept of *yin-yang* itself is an initial piece of naturalism.

(3) In metaphysics Confucius seems to identify ultimate reality with *tao*, with constancy (*ch'eng*), the overall qualities of all laws of nature: abstract, operative, ubiquitous, and eternal:

> The *tao* of Heaven-and-Earth may be completely summarized in one statement: it affects things with no double standard and so it produces things in an unfathomable manner. The *tao* of Heaven-and-Earth is all-inclusive and all-deep, high and shining, far-reaching and ever-enduring.[4]
>
> Constancy is the *tao* of Heaven. The achievement of constancy is the *tao* of man . . . by choosing what is good and holding it with steadfastness.[5]

What is abiding and unchanging is *tao*, which permeates the universe. All living creatures, all inorganic materials, and all human events vary and change in accordance with invariable and eternal laws of nature.

---

[1]*Lun Yü (Analects)*, Bk. VII, Ch. 35; Bk. III, Ch. 13. All translations in this paper are mine. I do acknowledge my indebtedness to many scholars, Western and Chinese, for their various English translations I have consulted over the years.

[2]*Ibid.*, Bk. XI, Ch. 11.

[3]*Li Chi (Book of Rites)*, T'an Kung, I, 69.

[4]*Chung Yung (the Doctrine of the Mean)*, Ch. XXVII, 7.

[5]*Ibid.*, Ch. XX, 18. I have chosen "constancy" for the original Chinese word "ch'eng," which is usually translated as "sincerity" or "realness."

(4) With Confucius *tao* is neither God-given nor man-made. *Tao* is nature-endowed and sage-discovered. Three passages are most instructive:

> "The endowment of Heaven is called nature [the nature of things]; operation of nature is called *tao;* and cultivation of *tao* is called education.[6]
>
> Wealth and Honor are what men desire. If they cannot be obtained in accordance with *tao* [namely in what is deemed by the sage to be the proper way] they should not be acquired. Poverty and lowliness are what men dislike. If they cannot be disposed of in accordance with *tao* they should not be avoided.[7]
>
> Man can enlarge *tao; tao* cannot enlarge man."[8]

It is self-evident that the preferred, idealized portion of the sum-total of the laws of nature has to be learned, chosen, and followed with exertion. "Operation of nature" is nature's-*tao*. "Cultivation of *tao*" is Heaven's-*tao*. And in acquiring Wealth and Honor by the proper way, it is man's-*tao* of the right kind.

Only when it is thus understood can there be a reconciliation between some otherwise glaring inconsistencies in the Confucian teachings of *tao*, which inconsistencies traditional Confucianists over the centuries either fail to see or wilfully ignore. Take, for instance, these two teachings:

> "What is called *tao* is that which may not be momentarily departed from. That which could be momentarily departed from is not *tao*.[9]
>
> I know how *tao* is not followed. The knowing ones go beyond it and the stupid ones do not reach it. I know how *tao* is not understood. The worthy ones go beyond it and the unworthy ones do not reach it."[10]

In the former statement it is Heaven's-*tao*, the ideal *tao* that should not be deviated from even for a single instant. In the latter statement it signifies that ordinary people are following man's-*tao* of the wrong kind.

---

[6]*Ibid.*, Ch. I, 1.
[7]*Lun Yü*, Bk. IV, Ch. 5.
[8]*Ibid.*, Bk. XV, Ch. 8.
[9]*Chung Yung*, Ch. I, 2.
[10]*Ibid.*, Ch. IV, 1-2.

Take another instance. "All things concurrently flourish without damaging one another. All principles of *tao* parallelly operate without colliding with one another."[11] This assumed harmony and perfection in nature as well as in *tao* is utter idealism. Naturally, it gives rise to difficulties. How about jungle life? How about wolves and sheep? The traditionalists' answer is that here it is a case of "birds and beasts." Even such an answer cannot explain away the inconsistency. And how about an authentic conflict between loyalty and filial piety? Here again the traditionalists have a ready-made answer: choose the greater virtue; enlarge one's filial love into loyalty to one's country. But despite these and other inconsistencies the Confucian *tao* does rest on the ground of naturalism, however much it may be entangled with idealism.

(5) In the achievement of *tao* there is a prerequisite, namely, knowledge of *tao*. "*Tao* is not remote from man. That which is taken to be *tao* and found remote from man may not be *tao*."[12] So, knowledge is important. In the process of learning, perseverance counts even though native capacities may differ. "Those who know by birth rank highest. Those who know through learning come next. Those who are handicapped and exert in learning come still next. Those who are handicapped and refuse to learn are of the lowest order."[13] What is more, the more one learns, the less adequate he finds himself. Above all, indeed, comes intellectual honesty. "Knowing it is knowing it; not knowing it is not knowing it: this is knowledge."[14] Suffice it to say, Confucian epistemology bears out the spirit of naturalism.

(6) The same spirit stands out in bold relief in his concept of human nature. "By nature, men are nearly alike; by habit, men are far apart."[15] Human nature is taken to be basically neutral, neither good nor bad. Goodness or badness lies in the way of doing things. Moreover, one's way of doing things is primarily a matter of habit-formation.

(7) The heart and core of the Confucian *tao* is its ethical theory. The center of the Confucian ethic is the supreme virtue of *jen* or human-heartedness. Why human-heartedness? Well, the fact that there is life (this is nature's-*tao*) postulates the intended and practiced care and love of life (this is Heaven's-*tao*), and this in turn demands

---

[11]*Ibid.*, Ch. XXX, 1.

[12]*Ibid.*, Ch. XIII, 1.

[13]*Lun Yü*, Bk. XVI, 9.

[14]*Ibid.*, Bk. II, 17.

[15]*Ibid.*, Bk. XVII, 2.

that all men should live and let-live (this is man's-*tao*; certainly of the right kind). This is why the five human relationships are so much stressed. This is why the *chün-tzu* (the ideal gentleman) is ready to sacrifice himself for the sake of humanity. "The determined scholar and the human-hearted person does not seek to live at the expense of human-heartedness but chooses to meet death in order to achieve human-heartedness."[16] Thus, the Confucian ethic as epitomized in the concept of human-heartedness may be labeled either as idealistic naturalism or naturalistic idealism.

Indeed, the highest Confucian ethical ideal is to achieve identity between man and Heaven:

> "It is only with utmost constancy that one can fully develop his own nature. Able to fully develop his own nature, one can fully develop other men's natures. Able to fully develop other men's natures, one can fully develop the natures of all creatures. Able to fully develop the natures of all creatures, one can assist the transforming and nourishing work of Heaven-and-Earth. Able to assist Heaven-and-Earth, man can achieve partnership with Heaven-and-Earth."[17]

Here nature's cosmic process and man's moral achievement meet in unison. It is idealism; yet it is grounded in naturalism.

(8) In the realm of government and politics, the naturalism of the Confucian *tao* is as elsewhere clear and abundant. To begin with, man is taken to be a political animal. Man has to live in a body politic just as fish in a pool of water. It is simply a fact, and no explanation, no rationalization is needed. Next, the state is regarded as the family writ large, with the ruler as the patriarch and the subjects as the children. Again, leadership always in the hands of the few is taken for granted, coinciding with what is known now as the "iron law of oligarchy." Moreover, the people's livelihood and economic well-being is stressed as the most basic governmental function. In addition, it may be pointed out that the Confucian utopia—the *ta-t'ung* society—resembles in structure and essence the contemporary ideal of democratic socialism. And above all, the strength and weakness of a government and the rise and fall of a regime are attributed not to the arbitrary will of Heaven nor to haphazard chance but to the operation of fixed principles. All these points vindicate the naturalism of the Confucian *tao* as regards government and politics.

---

[16]*Ibid.*, Bk. XV, 9.
[17]*Chung Yung*, Ch. XXII.

III. THE *TAO* OF LAO TZU

(1) If Confucius may be regarded as an agnostic, then more aptly may Lao Tzu be classified as an atheist. True, there are in the *Tao Te Ching* a few casual, perfunctory references to spirits. But there is in that Taoist classic nothing explicit or implicit suggesting God or Gods directing the universe and guiding human life. Neither retribution nor a life hereafter is taught. Such a truly negative theology testifies to Lao Tzu's thorough naturalism.

(2) One passage in the *Tao Te Ching* is definitively suggestive of a cosmology:

> "There is something nebulous and composite. Born before Heaven-and-Earth, silent and remote, self-existing and unchanging, turning round and unfailing, possibly it may be taken as the mother of the world. Knowing not its name, I term it as *tao*. Arbitrarily, I call it great. Great, it is receding. Receding, it is far-reaching. Far-reaching, it is returning. . . . Man models after Earth, Earth after Heaven, Heaven after *tao*, and *tao* after nature."[18]

It would be farfetched to read into these lines a sort of early theory of the expanding universe. Nevertheless, it is certain that such suggestive cosmology is naturalistic.

(3) In metaphysics, Lao Tzu takes *wu* or Non-being as the ultimate reality. "All things of the world stem from Being (*yu*), and Being stems from Non-being (*wu*)."[19] "The *tao* that can be described is not the eternal *tao*. The name that can be named is not the eternal name. Nameless, it is the beginning of Heaven-and-Earth. Nameable, it is the mother of all things."[20] Now what after all is this nameless Non-being? Nameless Non-being can only be *tao*, nature in the abstract, namely, the totality of the laws of nature, which is formless (beyond shape and figure), silent, intangible, and yet operative, ubiquitous, and eternal. That such a metaphysical theory is naturalistic *par excellence* can hardly be gainsaid.

(4) As to the central concept of *tao* itself, the following passage is most revealing:

---

[18]*Tao Te Ching (Book of Lao Tzu)*, Bk. I, Ch. 25. For the purpose of this paper it is immaterial whether Lao Tzu was a historical figure and in which century the *Tao Te Ching* was written.

[19]*Ibid.*, Bk. II, Ch. 40.

[20]Bk. I, Ch. 1.

"Looked at and not seen, that is called Invisible. Listened to and not heard, that is called Inaudible. Grabbed at and not touched, that is called Intangible. That which eludes these inquiries is taken to be a composite one. . . . It is called the formless Form and the imageless Image. It is called the Subtle and Elusive. Adherence to the *tao* of old still governs the Being of today. The ability to know the primal beginnings leads to the system of *tao*."[21]

The *tao* referred to here is the whole of the laws of nature (nature's-*tao*.)

What are some of the laws of nature that Lao Tzu prefers and idealizes and thus teaches man to understand and follow? Paradoxically, there are only two fundamental laws of nature that are emphasized and elaborated: Reversal and Meekness. Says Lao Tzu: "Reversal is the movement of *tao*. Meekness is the function of *tao*."[22] Both Reversal and Meekness are embodied in and represented by water. The ebb and flow of the tide signifies Reversal. Yielding, non-resistant, receptive, but at the same time integral, continuous, persistent, able to wear off the corners of, and sink holes into, solid rocks: such is the virtue and effect of the Meekness of water.

Because of the combination of naturalism and idealism, inconsistencies inevitably occur—just as in the case of Confucian *tao*. Take for instance these two passages from the *Tao Te Ching*: on the one hand, "The *tao* of Heaven benefits and harms not";[23] and on the other, "Heaven-and-Earth is unkind, treating all people as (sacrificial) straw-dogs. The sage is unkind, treating all people as (sacrificial) straw-dogs."[24] The pivotal point for us to observe here is that taking nature's *tao* as a whole everything is neutral. Hence, "Great *tao* is all-encompassing, indeed; it allows the turning to left as well as right."[25] Viewed from "great *tao*" (or nature's-*tao*), death is as natural as life, and chaos as order. Man prefers life and order. Naturally enough, there are many and varied ways of maintaining life and order. These various ways, preferred and idealized, give rise to diverse, conflicting systems of *tao;* and they too give rise to inconsistencies and difficulties within each system.

---

[21]Bk. I, Ch. 14.
[22]Bk. II, Ch. 40.
[23]Bk. II, Ch. 81.
[24]Bk. I, Ch. 5.
[25]Bk. I, Ch. 34.

(5) Is *tao* knowable and communicable? This is a problem of epistemology. "He who knows speaks not. He who speaks knows not."[26] Again, "He who knows is not extensively learned. He who is extensively learned does not know."[27] Still again, "When the superior scholar hears about *tao* he arduously endeavors to achieve it. When the average scholar hears about *tao* it appears to him as something and as nothing. When the inferior scholar hears about *tao* he laughs aloud; if not laughed at, it would not be *tao*."[28] It may readily be seen that *tao* is knowable and communicable. However, it requires insight and cultivation. What is more, knowledge and practice are not one and the same.

(6) In the observance or violation of *tao* (Heaven's-*tao*, according to Lao Tzu), human nature has its vital part to play. It is asserted repeatedly that man clings too much to life; and, because of this, man has unceasing desires—not just for the simple necessities of life but for the manifold luxuries of life, such as wealth, position, honor, power, and the like. The result of it all is that there is profound struggle and conflict and damage in society. "The reason why we have great trouble is because we have a body. When we no longer consider our body what trouble have we?"[29] Such an interpretation of human nature is decidedly naturalistic.

(7) The whole ethic of Lao Tzu is built on the premise of renunciation. Renunciation is rather the logical outcome of the two basic principles of Reversal and Meekness:

> "I have three treasures to possess and preserve. The first is compassion; the second, frugality; and the third, no venture to lead the world.[30]
>
> Man while alive is gentle and weak, and when dead stiff and strong. All creatures including trees and grasses are soft and fragile while alive, and dry and brittle when dead. Thus, the hard and rigid are followers of Death whereas the gentle and weak are followers of Life."[31]

The four cardinal virtues taught by Lao Tzu are meekness, humility, tolerance, and contentment. Man is to imitate water. However idealis-

---

[26]Bk. II, Ch. 56.
[27]Bk. II, Ch. 81.
[28]Bk. II, Ch. 41.
[29]Bk. I, Ch. 13.
[30]Bk. II, Ch. 67.
[31]Bk. II, Ch. 76.

tic the Taoist ethic may be, it is none the less founded on naturalism.

(8) The political philosophy of Lao Tzu is a thoroughgoing individualism, bordering on anarchism.

> "The more prohibitions exist in the world, the poorer the people become. The more sharp weapons men have, the more chaotic the state turns. The more technologies men develop, the more odd novelties are made. The more laws and decrees are issued, the more thieves and robbers there are."[32]

So Lao Tzu advocates *wu wei* or non-action. His famous paradox is: "While doing nothing, nothing is undone."[33] Various explanations have been attempted. One is that the ruler should do nothing, leaving everything to be done by ministers and bureaucrats. Another is that the government should do little, allowing the people to do things themselves. No explanation is satisfactory.

Actually there is an insoluble inconsistency involved. Lao Tzu suggests that the government should remedy the ills by tackling them at their roots:

> "Those of ancient times who excel in achieving *tao* do not seek to enlighten the people but to keep them in ignorance. The reason why the people are difficult to govern is that they abound in knowledge.[34]
>
> Therefore, in governing the people, the sage has their minds emptied, their bellies filled, their wills weakened, and their bones strengthened. The sage always keeps the people devoid of knowledge and devoid of desire."[35]

What an odd idea! Any attempt at keeping the people devoid of knowledge and desire—regardless of its rationale or possibility—would lead to law, coercion, and totalitarianism.

IV. DIFFERENCES AND SIMILARITIES

From the foregoing presentation it should be evident (it is hoped) that the Confucian *tao* and the Taoist *tao*, though divergent in outlook, are both grounded in naturalism. It is ironical, then, that the popular Taoist religion has claimed Lao Tzu as its founder. On the

---

[32]Bk. II, Ch. 57.
[33]Bk. II, Ch. 48.
[34]Bk. II, Ch. 65.
[35]Bk. I, Ch. 3.

other hand, it is instructive, indeed, that many attempts, including the last one after the founding of the Chinese Republic in 1912, at turning Confucianism into an organized, ritualistic religion have failed.

The dominant ingredient in the composition of the common ground of naturalism is the then already traditional concept of *yin-yang*. This concept, later developed into an elaborate, mystical philosophy, was initially a piece of naturalism, derived from the observation of natural phenomena characterized by the union of opposites, from the prevalence of dichotomies, such as day and night, ebb and flow, blossoming and withering. Confucius and Lao Tzu are profoundly influenced by the *yin-yang* concept. In Confucianism it is acknowledged that "one *yin* and one *yang* comprise what is called *tao*."[36] In Taoism it is believed that "all creatures, bearing *yin* and embracing *yang*, emerge from the blending of the two forces."[37]

Perhaps it is chiefly because of their common naturalism and common *yin-yang* ingredient that there are in the teachings of the two sages as many similarities as differences. Usually their differences are overemphasized and their similarities lost sight of. Let us enumerate some of the meaningful similarities:

First, Confucianism is too often taken to be idealistic and Taoism more materialistic. This is because Confucianism stresses virtues and believes in the achievement of identity between man and Heaven, whereas Taoism belittles virtues and exalts the preservation of life. This view is rather superficial. The economic foundation of morality and government is no less recognized by Confucius. And to stand for, as Lao Tzu does, the renunciation of worldly gains of all sorts is just as much idealistic.

Second, it is not infrequently asserted that the Taoist *tao* stands for the interest of the individual and the Confucian *tao* that of society. This is an oversimplification. If each person lives a simple, frugal, unambitious life and thus minds his own business, there would result a happy social harmony. Why is not renunciation and non-action championed also for the sake of society? On the other hand, Confucius, too, urges the importance of "humane administration," such as light

---

[36] *I Ching (Book of Changes)*, Hsi Tz'u, Part 1.

[37] *Tao Te Ching*, Bk. II, Ch. 42. Another passage brings out fully the *yin-yang* concept: "Thus Being and Non-being manifest each other; difficulty and ease complement each other; length and shortness compare with each other; height and depth incline toward each other; tone and sound harmonize with each other; front and back follow each other." *Ibid.*, Bk. I, Ch. 2.

taxation, minimal servitude, and the like, genuinely in the interest of the individual subject.

Third, the contrast between Confucian authoritarianism and Taoist *laissez faire* must be understood with some reservation. Recorded in the *Analects* is this saying of the Master: "In hearing law-suits, I might serve as well as anybody. But how better it must be to make law-suits no longer necessary."[38] According to this ideal good government may result in less government. Contrariwise, as has been pointed out in the preceding section, any sincere Taoist effort to "keep the people devoid of knowledge and devoid of desire" would end in totalitarianism, in which case Confucian authoritarianism would pale into insignificance.

Last, it is a common, deep-rooted belief, and very much warranted, that Taoism advocates renunciation and Confucianism actionism; yet a footnote should be added to this belief. True, it is renunciation not to seek, and when offered or acquired, to decline or give up, rank, wealth, and power. But in so doing how much is required of understanding, resoluteness and exertion, mental, psychological, and spiritual; in a word, an inward kind of actionism! Likewise with Confucian actionism. Yes, it is to serve the government and the people, ready to sacrifice one's own life and the lives of one's own family; yet such actionism is possible only when accompanied with the renunciation of one's ego and body. To sum up, there are between the two systems of *tao* perhaps more similarities than differences.

---

[38]*Lun Yü*, Bk. XII, Ch. 13.

AFTERWORD

IN AN ESSAY entitled "Concerning the Jews," Mark Twain offered a rather dour estimate of the human species. Discoursing on the subject of prejudice, Twain avowed he held no prejudices towards any race, color, caste or creed. "Indeed," said Twain, "I can stand any society. All that I care to know is that a man is a human being —that is enough for me; he can't be any worse." This bit of whimsy came to mind repeatedly as I read through the essays of this book. I think what prompted my thinking towards Twain's deliciously expressed misanthropy was in itself an example of the affinity of opposites. Here I was, reading small monographs from which emanated a formidable humanist *esprit*, acting as one taking a word association test by reaching mentally for a contrary view of humanity.

It was as if I were trying to furnish an illustration of one application of the principle of the unity of opposites, a subject ably examined by McGill and Parry in an essay bearing that title. In any event, whether or not my analysis of the psychodynamics directing my ruminations to Mark Twain is correct, I was impressed by what I saw as a marked quality of anthropocentrism characterizing the philosophical stance of so many of the authors.

A well-founded sense of modesty keeps me from undertaking a comparative analysis and evaluation of the sixteen essays herein contained. The reader finds compelling analyses and critiques of naturalism, idealism, pragmatism, formal logic, the conceit of an ahistorical, now-and-for-all-time scientific method, and a variety of barnacles that still cling to philosophic thought. Here too are excellent expositions of Marxist thought systems and their applicability. Also there is a penetrating analysis of the influence of liberalism on United States economic and foreign policy in the 20th Century. In brief, I compliment the editorial staff for having conceived such a book as this and for the generally high quality of their selections.

Having dealt so summarily with the substantive aspects of the

249

various writings, a limitation imposed by discretion (I am not formally trained in philosophy), I would like to return to the view of man and the attitude towards the human condition that came through to me from most of the essays and which I assume to be characteristic of dialectical materialism. Man can improve himself and his condition is implied where it is not stated. Moreover, there is the implication that a radical change in the arrangement of human life is imperative (the *status quo* finds no champions among these authors). Coming through loud and clear is the spirit of Marx's exhortation to first understand, then *change* the human condition. Lastly, I sensed a confident optimism as the dominant mood of the greater part of the selections. Were the several authors to amalgamate into a bookmaking operation, I have no doubt they would be giving handsome odds in favor of man's future (and they would be doing it while radiating a cheerful self-assurance that would likely dishearten potential takers).

To one who considers the aptest commentaries of the times to be those found in the book, *Catch 22*, the film, *Dr. Strangelove*, the cartoons of Jules Feiffer and the columns of Art Buchwald, I was exhilarated by this optimism. I am sure none of the authors would deny or minimize the reality of the assorted lunacies, moral imbecilities and perverse follies that characterize the current political scene and constitute the day-to-day doings of our "security managers," their academic mentors and much of society besides. The terminology, which provides satirists with so rich an abundance of material, amounts to an admission of insanity: MIRV, ABM, first- and second-strike capability, favorable kill ratio, overkill, and their indispensable creation of the "think tank" mentality—credibility. The world itself is a perpetual hostage to what goes by the name of deterrence, and the whole crazy business is justified as necessary to defend the principle of the sanctity and dignity of human life! How then can the authors escape concluding that man's prospects are dismal? How can they maintain their commitment to a philosophical framework that holds man on the loftiest of pedestals?

I believe the answer to these questions is to be found in the basic features of dialectical materialism. Obviously, the materialist does not accept the idea of a fixed human nature, nor the related idea of an inherent moral defect in the human character. Thus, despite abundant evidence from history that tends to support the idea of the presence of evil in man, the materialist sees man himself as an interacting process rather than a discrete entity, thus rejecting the concept of a non-material, enduring property called evil. The changed environment brings on modifications in man's ways of responding, a continuing process referred to as history. In short, there is at least as compelling evidence for man's capacity to make life-promoting adjustments as there is for his self-annihilative tendencies. Seeing wonderful possibilities in a generally plastic and yielding material world, the materialist contemplates an inviting tomorrow, remaining invulnerable to the pessimism expressed in Twain's remark.

In his admirably succinct Foreword, Professor Dunham takes up the dilemma of the observer-participant. Dunham points out the hazards of divorcement and overemphasis of either, then goes on to propose how and why a synthesis is to be brought about. In a few short sentences, Dunham at one stroke reveals a seminal mind and a major challenge of the materialist philosophy. It seems to me that the adroitness needed to manage the contraries of observation versus participation is precisely as Dunham describes it. Much of this book, it seems to me, speaks to that need.

STANLEY E. WEISBERGER

EPILOGUE
IMPERIALISM AND IRRATIONALISM

B ACK IN 1877, Engels in *Socialism: Utopian and Scientific*, offered this opinion: "Their political and intellectual bankruptcy is scarcely any longer a secret to the bourgeoisie themselves." Ninety years ago it required an Engels, perhaps, to see this; today the bankruptcy is announced by the defaulters themselves. Thus, in the summer of 1965, Richard Goodwin, then an Assistant to the President of the United States, said:

> "We are not sure where we are going. . . . We know there are new problems, but the intellectual resources of this nation—the historic reservoir of social progress—do not readily provide the answers."[1]

The very air is foul with more than smog and tear gas. These are only the more apparent effluvia emanating from the decay of a social order. Were Gibbon working now on the decline and fall of the United States empire, his notebooks would be overflowing.

Debasement is decay's product as well as its intention; I do not doubt that the debasement is not only systematic but also is deliberate. Not least among its virtues, surely, is the fact that it is profitable, too. At its heart is irrationalism; the eclipse of reason, the denial of science, the repudiation of causation. The normal result is cynicism; the abnormal is sadism. The finale is Fascism.

The levels vary. There is the overpriced rot usurping more and more of the shelf space in U.S. bookstores; here one finds no motivation, no real feeling, no difficulties, no doubt, no warmth, no love, no pity, no thought; no human beings. These are less pretentious, but otherwise not very different from such best-selling "books" as those by Spillane. The same is increasingly true for the movies—not

---

[1]Quoted by Richard Rovere, *The New Yorker*, August 14, 1965.

only at American Legion stag parties, and Times Square "art" houses, but more and more on the screens of those neighborhood moviehouses that manage to survive. Again, the central and common feature is mindlessness mixed with brutality.

Joseph Wood Krutch, an elder statesman of literary critics and still rather "old-fashioned" in some of his tastes, thinks the "emphasis on violence, perversion and nihilism" that characterizes much of current U.S. fiction and playwriting "seemed rooted in contempt for the world." He offered this view:

> "Seldom, if ever before, has any of the arts been so dominated by an all-inclusive hatred. Once the writer hated individual 'bad men.' Then he began to hate instead the society which was supposed to be responsible for the creation of bad men. Now his hatred is directed not at individuals or their societies but at the universe in which bad men and bad societies are merely expressions of the fundamental evil of the universe itself."[2]

Here is the way a new novel is advertised in the *New York Times* (May 3, 1967): ". . . a labyrinth of cruelty, pain, blood, welts, screams, moans, torture, bondage and—delight . . . whippings, cuffings, the ecstasy of contact. . . ."

Russell Baker, the "Observer" of the *New York Times*, noted (August 3, 1967) that it is a rare evening in watching television that one does not witness as part of the "entertainment," "a whole battalion of victims bludgeoned, machine-gunned, bayoneted, pistol-whipped, gunned down, mashed under tank treads, beaten senseless with fists and otherwise despatched." Here are the words of that same newspaper's movie critic, Bosley Crowther (July 4, 1967), describing a current film epic: ". . . violent explosions, bark of guns, the whine of bullets and the spinning bodies of men mortally hit provide the aural and visual stimulation for an excitement of morbid lust."

On Broadway—somewhat less so, off-Broadway and off-off-Broadway—as Walter Kerr wrote in a very recent *New York Times* (January 26, 1969):

> "Nowadays, it's not good form to ask what a play is about. Aboutness is out, content is irrelevant, conscious design is suspect.

---

[2] In *The Saturday Review*, May 6, 1967. For an earlier and incisive analysis of these trends, see Sidney Finkelstein, *Existentialism and Alienation in American Literature* (New York: International, 1965), especially pp. 285-98. The neglect of this book by the commercial press is a fine tribute to its author.

A play is simply a series of impressions that happen to happen in a certain unordained sequence. . . . We're supposed to sit quietly, keep our responses open, and never, never strain for coherence."

What we have referred to in the above paragraphs is a steeper decline than the literary reflections of alienations; these continue, but do not represent as full a repudiation of reason as must modern productions.[3]

Another significant and particular source—and expression—of irrationalism in the United States is racism. A useful examination of this connection was produced by Reese Cleghorn, an editor of the *Atlanta* (Ga.) *Journal*; it is a pamphlet badly entitled *Radicalism—Southern Style: A Commentary on Regional Extremism*.[4] I say badly entitled because this is a study not of radicalism but of reaction and especially of the George Wallace movement.

The point for present purposes, however, is that Mr. Cleghorn emphasizes that the Wallace movement reflects the irrationalism so characteristic of dominant Southern politics; he says this irrationalism reflects the racism that afflicts the South in particular—an ideology in open conflict with elementary democratic principles. The thinking, writes Mr. Cleghorn, is paranoid and stems from feelings "of guilt, obsessive defensiveness, close mindedness"; the feelings themselves, of course, stem from enslavement and oppression and super-exploitation of others, though Mr. Cleghorn is not quite so clear on the latter point. But he is clear as to the irrationalism fostered by racism—itself the quintessence of irrationalism; here is another and striking example of racism's cost to Americans of all colors.

Reason's eclipse takes many other and sometimes rather elusive or highly sophisticated forms. The entire tendency towards a technocratic, arithmetic, *counting* methodology especially in sociology is part of this; the tendency towards eliminating causation either explicitly or by denying the possibility of evaluating causes, or by affirming the infinitude of causation—where everything is cause to everything else and therefore no cause per se can be discovered—especially in historiography; the a-human writing of Herman Kahn and the

---

[3]In addition to the Finkelstein book cited earlier, see: S. Finkelstein, "The Artistic Expression of Alienation," and Howard D. Langford, "The Imagery of Alienation," in H. Aptheker, ed., *Marxism and Alienation* (New York: Humanities Press, 1965); Gaylord C. LeRoy, *Marxism and Modern Literature* (New York: AIMS, 1967); Arnold Kettle and V. G. Hanes, *Man and the Arts* (New York: AIMS, 1968).
[4]Jointly issued in 1969 by the Southern Regional Council in Atlanta and the American Jewish Committee in New York City.

efforts of Z. K. Brzezinski; the apocalyptic visions of Norman O. Brown, with his insistence that it is only the subjective and the so-called unconscious that matter rather than the objective and the conscious; A. H. Maslow's rejection of social renovation as central to making possible the better life and replacing this (basic to the concept of utopia as well as the concept of revolution) with efforts at the release of psychic impulses so that one would not have Utopia but rather "Eupsychia"; the most recent writings of Herbert Marcuse with their reflections of near despair and their emphasis again upon the subjective and psychological; and efforts to apply existentialism to social questions, as in the work of John Wild, which in fact effectively rule out of the social sciences the possibility of ascertaining objective reality; or in the religion of Timothy Leary whose discoverer insists that: "We must entertain nonverbal methods of communication if we are to free our nervous system from the tyranny of the stifling simplicity of words."[5]

In addition to the well-known attacks upon values and ethics—either as unknowable or as irrelevant to "science"—there are growing signs of a repudiation of the Enlightenment as a whole. There certainly is value in calling attention to areas of neglect in the entire Enlightenment tradition, including its highest, or Marxian, aspect; I mean, for example, such questions as the nature of power, of evil, of psychology as a whole. But this is something else than, for example, Ronald V. Sampson's essay, "The Bramble of Power," where one reads: "*Only* by appealing to the private individual can we give meaning to the legitimate ideals of Progress, Democracy and Socialism."[6] Mr. Sampson concludes—quite logically, given his "only":

> "Long-term action needs to be undertaken at the level of psycho-therapy, family mores, child nurture and an education, cooperative and not competitive, that is devoted to rearing the whole creative potential of man through the work of his hands and his brain in a life that is not divorced from nature."

It does not reflect any denial of the consequence of Mr. Sampson's essay to remark that such writing is not only pre-Marxian; it is pre-

---

[5]Full bibliographical reference would require excessive space; but see, in particular, N. O. Brown, *Love's Body* (N.Y., 1966); John Wild, *Existence and the World of Freedom* (Englewood Cliffs, N.J., 1963); and Timothy Leary and Richard Alpert, "The Politics of Consciousness Expansion," *The Harvard Review*, I (Summer, 1963)—quoted matter from p. 35.

[6]In *The Nation*, December 16, 1968; italics added.

Owenite, and we will not go forward by retreating. Clearly, a competitive society will have a competitive education; one struggles on all levels—including the educational—but one never forgets the *strategy*, namely, the transforming of society.

Perhaps the most dramatic, recent reflection of the flight from reason is the fantastic fad of McLuhan, or of McLuhancy. Significantly, it is the United States—including its academic community—which has most ardently embraced this shoddiness and made of it a veritable cult of the "in." The English scholar, D. W. Harding, in a penetrating analysis of this phenomenon, observed:

> "McLuhan's glaring incoherences of thought and disregard of everyday observation are not confined to peripheral 'probes'; they occur at nodal points of the system. And yet the cult sprang up. Something in our education abets the willing suspension of common sense which a belief in McLuhan requires."[7]

In an important—and therefore neglected!—book, the distinguished English writer, Pamela Hansford Johnson, suggested that all "must know the basic reason for the deluge of sado-masochistic, 'hard-core' pornography." Here was her "basic reason":

> "This is not published by good, altruistic persons who believe they are helping to make a sweeter and more educated society. These may exist: but I have referred earlier to another force in commercial society, which is an infinitely powerful one. People and publishing the stuff because there is money in it. The motive is, quite simply, profit, and this is the way they can make a quick, sure turnover."[8]

This is, I think, the immediate reason; but it is not the basic one. For consider: profit-making has existed for some time, but the reason Mrs. Johnson wrote her book in this period is that today there is, as she said, "the deluge." Such a deluge appears only in a society which is dying; it reflects disintegration and it intensifies that disintegration. At the same time, for those who rule that society, the motive is not only making profit in the selling of such commodities but also inculcating inhumanity.

---

[7] In *New York Review of Books*, January 2, 1969. Sidney Finkelstein presented a devastating critique of McLuhan—*Sense and Nonsense of McLuhan* (N.Y., 1968); but for every ten who read Finkelstein there are ten thousand who read McLuhan —itself sufficient commentary on the eclipse of reason in the United States!

[8] *On Iniquity* (N.Y., 1968), p. 113.

Recently, Walter Lippmann was asked: "Are these the worst times there've been in your lifetime? For the country?"

Mr. Lippmann—whose active life in the United States goes back to the 1910s—replied: "Yes, I think so. I'm more worried about the state of the country than ever before. . . . What I see is the disintegration of hope and belief and will—will power and morale . . . we have despair and deterioration."[9]

Henry Steele Commager, a contemporary of Mr. Lippmann and his peer in distinction, expressed himself at about the same time, in very much the same way: "We find ourselves not only confused but impotent, impotent intellectually and morally. . . . We [have] lost confidence in ourselves, dissipated our energies, dissolved our dreams, substituted anti-principles for principles, anti-policies for policies . . . we have lost confidence in man."[10]

I think United States history does not show another occasion when so prestigious a body as The National Committee for an Effective Congress concluded after examining the state of the nation, that: "America has experienced two great crises in her history: the Civil War and the Economic Depression of the 1930s. The country may now be on the brink of a third trauma, a depression of the national spirit."[11] This Committee found "malaise," "frustration," "alienation," as appropriate words to describe dominant moods; it states that, "At all levels of American life, people share similar fears, insecurities and gnawing doubts to such an intense degree that the country may in fact be suffering from a kind of nervous breakdown."

The disintegration is most acute because the United States is the main bastion of what remains of imperialism; a centerpiece in the British *New Statesman* (October 27, 1967) generalized the matter this way: "The West is a civilization without a philosophy and is rotting at the core because of this." As for analysis, the author, James Hemming, went further than one is likely to find in the commercial U. S. press: "Man treated as worker-consumer, however fat his wage packet or salary cheque, is man without dignity, manipulated, degraded man, frustrated man, alienated man. This is exactly where commercialized society has got us."

Marx was not mentioned, presumably because the borrowing—even to verbiage—was so heavy that acknowledgement was held to be unnecessary!

---

[9]*New Republic,* December 9, 1967.
[10]*New York Times Book Review,* January 28, 1968.
[11]*New York Times,* December 26, 1967.

Neither Lippmann nor Commager nor the National Committee for an Effective Congress offer explanations for the unprecedented despair and alienation they describe. Similarly, Hans J. Morgenthau in asking "What Ails America?" sees "the decomposition of those ties of trust and loyalty which link citizen to citizen and the citizens to the government,"[12] but its source is not clear to him, except as this lies in the unspeakable war being waged by the U. S. government against the people of Vietnam. The latter, however, while carrying with it enormous capacity for damage and vitiation of the quality of U. S. life, is reflective of deeper sources of such damage and vitiation. That is, that the U. S. government is capable of waging so atrocious a war is itself symptomatic of more basic rot at its very foundations. True certainty it is, as W. E. B. DuBois warned in his remarkably prophetic way, back in 1904: "I believe that the wicked conquest of weaker and darker nations by white and stronger but foreshadows the death of that strength." But the path of racist conquest itself reflects the logic of a structurally parasitic and exploitive social order and there one has, I think, the root of the paranoia now dominating official U. S. conduct and policy.

In biblical language one may speak of the reality of retribution; in psychiatric language, of paranoia; in Marxist language, of antagonistic contradictions and the inexorable trauma these produce.

The heart of the difficulties lies in the fact that the U. S. social order is characterized by the private ownership of the means of production and the private appropriation of profit. Such relations and motivations are obsolete and therefore regressive. The obsolescence—manifested in the spread of socialism and the decline of colonialism—means that aggressive foreign policies and repressive domestic ones are not only anti-human but also doomed—I mean doomed in a practical sense. They are not viable and so U. S. policy—with all its wealth and power—goes from one disaster to another.

Admitting this for those wedded to the corpse is psychologically impossible; hence, real paranoia appears. That is, since reality is insufferable it is denied and a world whose content fits the needs of an obsolescent social order is imaginatively constructed. This means the repudiation of reason.

* * *

The alienation that is everywhere apparent may also be viewed as a sign of health and I think that to view it that way is nearer the truth

---

[12]*New Republic,* October 28, 1967.

than to see it as simply a reflection of sickness. Symptoms of sickness, indeed, are themselves physiological forms of struggle against illness; manifestations of alienation on a broad scale reflect the essential soundness of the population which increasingly finds intolerable the anti-human and irrational policies of its doomed rulers.

Professor Morgenthau complained rightly that "deception [by the U. S. government] is being practiced not occasionally as a painful necessity dictated by the reason of state, but consistently as a kind of light-hearted sport through which the deceiver enjoys his power."

More, deception is now normal because it is needed; the policy is so awful and so doomed that it must be enveloped in falsification. But the masses of people have quite different needs and in time—despite a natural, patriotic bias—will become persuaded that they are being fed a diet of deceit and will demand a change of menu. Indeed, what all the talk about radicalization means is that the mass of the people are in the process of becoming persuaded of this and are raising this demand.

But to trace this out further is another essay, and that must await another opportunity. . . .

Herbert Aptheker

BIBLIOGRAPHY*

Joseph Agassi. "The Confusion between Physics and Metaphysics in Standard Histories of Science." *Proceedings of the Xth International Congress for the History of Science.* Ed. H. Guerlac. (Paris, 1965.)

_____. "Methodological Individualism." *British Journal of Sociology,* 11, 1960.

_____. "The Nature of Scientific Problems and Their Roots in Metaphysics." *The Critical Approach: Essays in Honour of Karl R. Popper.* Ed. Mario Bunge. (New York, 1964.)

_____. "Revolutions in Science, Occasional or Permanent?" *Organon,* 3, 1966.

Alan Ross Anderson. "The Formal Analysis of Normative Systems." *The Logic of Decision and Action.* Ed. Nicholas Rescher. (University of Pittsburgh, 1967.)

_____ (with Nuel D. Belnap, Jr.). "The Pure Calculus of Entailment." *The Journal of Symbolic Logic.* Vol. 27, No. 1, March, 1962.

_____. "What Do Symbols Symbolize?: Platonism." *Philosophy of Science: The Delaware Seminar.* Vol. I. Ed. Edward Baumrin. (Interscience Publisher, 1963.)

Bertram Bandman. "The Fundamental Question of Ethics." *Mind,* January, 1965.

_____. "The Good Reasons Approach in Educational Discourse." *Studies in Philosophy and Education,* Winter, 1968.

_____. *The Place of Reason in Education.* (Ohio State University Press, 1967.)

_____. "What Makes an Educational Question Right or Wrong?" *Proceedings of the Philosophy of Education Society,* 1967.

A. Cornelius Benjamin. *An Introduction to the Philosophy of Science.* (New York: Macmillan, 1937.)

_____. *The Logical Structure of Science.* London, 1936.

_____

*Prepared by David H. DeGrood. This list is made up of living philosophers, mostly American. It is hoped that it fills a gap that most bibliographies possess.

_____. *Operationism.* (Charles C Thomas, 1955.)

_____. *Science, Technology and Human Values.* (University of Missouri, 1965.)

Gustav Bergmann. *Logic and Reality.* (Wisconsin University Press, 1960.)

_____. *Meaning and Existence.* (Wisconsin University Press, 1960.)

_____. *The Metaphysics of Logical Positivism.* (Wisconsin University Press, 1968.)

_____. *Realism: A Critique of Brentano and Meinong.* (Wisconsin University Press, 1967.)

Arnold Berleant. "The Experience and Criticism of Art." *Sarah Lawrence Journal,* Winter, 1967.

_____. "The Experience and Judgment of Values." *The Journal of Value Inquiry,* I, 1 (Spring, 1967.)

_____. "The Sensuous and the Sensual in Aesthetics." *Journal of Aesthetics and Art Criticism,* XXIII, 2 (Winter, 1964.)

Max Black. *A Companion to Wittgenstein's Tractatus,* Cornell, 1964.

_____. *Models and Metaphors.* (Cornell, 1962.)

_____. *The Nature of Mathematics.* (London, 1933.)

_____. *Problems of Analysis.* (Cornell, 1954.)

Albert E. Blumberg (with Herbert Feigl). "Logical Positivism." *Journal of Philosophy,* Vol. 28, 1931.

_____. "The Nature of Philosophic Analysis." *Philosophy of Science,* Vol. 2, 1935.

_____. "Science and Dialectics." *Science and Society,* Vol. 22, Fall, 1958.

May Brodbeck. *Readings in the Philosophy of the Social Sciences.* (Macmillan, 1968.)

Justus Buchler. *The Concept of Method.* (Columbia University Press, 1961.)

Justus Buchler. *Metaphysics of Natural Complexes.* (Columbia University Press, 1966.)

_____. *Nature and Judgment.* (Columbia University Press, 1955.)

_____. *Toward a General Theory of Human Judgment.* (Columbia University Press, 1951.)

Mario Bunge. *Causality.* (New York: Meridian, 1963.)

_____. *Foundations of Physics.* (Springer, 1967.)

_____. *The Myth of Simplicity.* (Prentice-Hall, 1963.)

_____. *Scientific Research,* 2 vols. (Springer, 1967.)

Peter Caws. "Aspects of Hempel's Philosophy of Science." *Review of Metaphysics,* Vol. XX, #4 (June, 1967).

_____. "The Functions of Definition in Science." *Philosophy of Science,* Vol. 26, #3 (July, 1959).

_____. *The Philosophy of Science.* (Princeton: Van Nostrand, 1965.)

_____. "Three Logics, or the Possibility of the Improbable." *Philosophy and Phenomenological Research,* Vol. XXV, #4 (June, 1965).

Noam Chomsky. *Aspects of the Theory of Syntax.* (M.I.T. Press, 1965.)

_____. *Cartesian Linguistics.* (Harper & Row, 1966.)

_____. *Language and Mind.* (Harcourt, Brace & World, in preparation.)

_____. *Syntactic Structures.* (The Hague: Mounton, 1957.)

C. West Churchman. *Challenge to Reason.* (New York: McGraw-Hill, 1968.)

_____ (with R. L. Ackoff). *Methods of Inquiry.* (St. Louis: Educational Publishers, 1950.)

_____. *Prediction and Optimal Decision.* (Prentice-Hall, 1961.)

_____. *Theory of Experimental Inference.* (New York: Macmillan, 1948.)

Tad S. Clements. *Science and Man: The Philosophy of Scientific Humanism.* (Charles C Thomas, 1968.)

Irving M. Copi. "Analytical Philosophy and Analytical Propositions." *Philosophical Studies,* 1953, Vol. 4.

_____. "Essence and Accident." *Journal of Philosophy,* 1954, Vol. 51.

_____. "Language Analysis and Metaphysical Inquiry." *Philosophy of Science,* 1949, Vol. 16.

_____. "Philosophy and Language." *Review of Metaphysics,* 1951, Vol. 4.

Maurice Cornforth. *Dialectical Materialism,* 3 vols. (New York: International, 1954.)

_____. *Marxism and the Linguistic Philosophy.* (New York: International, 1965.)

_____. *The Open Philosophy and the Open Society.* (New York: International, 1968.)

_____. *Science versus Idealism.* (New York: International, 1946.)

Auguste Cornu. "Bergsonianism and Existentialism." Contained in Marvin Farber's *Philosophic Thought in France and the United States.* (Albany: State University of New York Press, 1968.)

_____. *Karl Marx et Friedrich Engels: Leur vie et leur oeuvre.* 3 vols. Paris: Presses Universitaires de France, 1955.

_____. *The Origins of Marxian Thought.* (Charles C Thomas, 1957.)

Edward D'Angelo. *The Problem of Freedom and Determinism.* (University of Missouri Press, 1968.)

David H. DeGrood. *Haeckel's Theory of the Unity of Nature.* (Boston: Christopher, 1965.)
_____. *Philosophies of Essence.* (Groningen: Wolters-Noordhoff, 1970.)
Paul Diesing. "National Self-Determination and U. S. Foreign Policy." *Ethics,* 1967.
_____. "Objectivism vs. Subjectivism in the Social Sciences." *Philosophy of Science,* 1966.
_____. *Reason in Society,* 1962.
W. H. Dray. " 'Explaining What' in History." In P. Gardiner, ed., *Theories of History.* (Free Press, 1959.)
_____. *Laws and Explanation in History.* (Oxford University Press, 1957.)
_____. *Philosophy of History.* (Prentice-Hall, 1964.)
_____. "Toynbee's Search for Historical Laws." *History and Theory,* Vol. 1, No. 1, 1960.
Barrows Dunham. *The Artist in Society.* (New York: Marzani & Munsell, 1960.)
_____. *Giant in Chains.* (New York: Hill and Wang, 1965.)
_____. *Heroes and Heretics.* (New York: Alfred A. Knopf, 1964.)
_____. *Man Against Myth.* (New York: Hill and Wang, 1962.)
Loyd D. Easton. "Empiricism and Ethics in Dietzgen." *Journal of the History of Ideas,* 19, January, 1958.
_____. *Ethics, Policy, and Social Ends.* (William C. Brown, 1955.)
_____. *Hegel's First American Followers.* (Ohio University Press, 1967).
_____ (with Kurt Guddat). *Writings of the Young Marx on Philosophy.* (New York: Doubleday, 1967.)
Abraham Edel. *Anthropology and Ethics* (with May Edel), 1959.
_____. *Ethical Judgment,* 1955.
_____. *Method in Ethical Theory,* 1963.
_____. *Science and the Structure of Ethics,* 1961.
Marvin Farber. *Basic Issues of Philosophy.* (New York: Harper & Row, 1968.)
_____. *The Foundation of Phenomenology.* (State University of New York Press, 1967.)
_____. *Naturalism and Subjectivism.* (State University of New York Press, 1968.)
_____. *Phenomenology and Existence.* (New York: Harper & Row, 1967.)
James K. Feibleman. "The Logical Structure of the Scientific Method." *Dialectica,* 13, 1959.

James K. Feibleman. "The Role of Hypotheses in the Scientific Method." *Perspectives in Biology and Medicine,* II, 1959.

——————. "Testing Hypotheses by Experiment." *Perspectives in Biology and Medicine,* IV, 1960.

——————. "Types of Empirical Discoveries." *Systematics,* V, 1967.

Herbert Feigl. "Aims of Education for Our Age of Science." *Fifty-fourth Yearbook of the National Society for the Study of Education.* (University of Chicago Press, 1955.)

——————. "Existential Hypotheses." *Philosophy of Science,* Vol. 17, 1950.

——————. *The 'Mental' and the 'Physical.'* (University of Minnesota Press, 1967.)

——————. "Philosophy of Science." In R. Schlotter, ed., *Humanistic Scholarship in America.* (Prentice-Hall, 1964.)

Roger Garaudy. *From Anathema to Dialogue: A Marxist Challenge to the Christian Churches.* (New York: Herder and Herder, 1966.)

George R. Geiger. *John Dewey in Perspective.* (McGraw-Hill, 1964.)

——————. *Philosophy and the Social Order.* (Houghton Mifflin, 1947.)

——————. "Values and Social Science." *Journal of Social Issues,* VI, 4.

Neal W. Gilbert. *Renaissance Concepts of Method.* (New York: Columbia University Press, 1960.)

Ray Ginger. *Age of Excess.* (New York: Macmillan, 1965.)

Harry Girvetz. *Democracy and Elitism.* (Scribner, 1967.)

——————. *The Evolution of Liberalism.* (Collier, 1963.)

—————— (with George Geiger, Harold Hantz, & Bertram Morris). *Science, Folklore, and Philosophy.* (Harper & Row, 1966.)

Daniel Goldstick. "In Defense of a Dogma." *The Marxist Quarterly,* No. 13, Spring, 1965.

Adolf Grünbaum. "Carnap's Views on the Foundations of Geometry." In P. A. Schilpp, ed., *The Philosophy of Rudolf Carnap.* (Open Court, 1963.)

Adolf Grünbaum. *Geometry and Chronometry in Philosophical Perspective.* (University of Minnesota Press, 1968.)

——————. *Modern Science and Zeno's Paradoxes.* (Wesleyan University Press, 1967.)

——————. *Philosophical Problems of Space and Time.* (New York: Knopf, 1963.)

Rollo Handy. *A Current Appraisal of the Behavioral Sciences* (with Paul Kurtz). (Behavioral Research Council, 1964.)

——————. *Methodology of the Behavioral Sciences.* (Charles C Thomas, 1964.)

——————. "Philosophy's Neglect of the Social Sciences." *Philosophy of Science,* Vol. 25, No. 2, April, 1958.

_____. *Value Theory and the Behavioral Sciences*. (Charles C Thomas, 1969.)

David Hawkins. "The Creativity of Science." *Science and the Creative Spirit* (with Harcourt Brown, *et al.*). (Toronto, 1957.)

_____. "Design for a Mind." *Daedalus*, Vol. 91, No. 3 (Summer, 1962).

_____. *The Language of Nature*. (San Francisco: W. H. Freeman, 1964.)

_____. "Taxonomy and Information." *Boston Colloqium in the Philosophy of Science*, ed. Robert S. Cohen, Vol. III, 1968.

Carl G. Hempel. *Aspects of Scientific Explanation*. (New York: Free Press, 1965.)

_____. *Fundamentals of Concept Formation in Empirical Science*. (University of Chicago Press, 1952).

_____. *Philosophy of Natural Science*. (Prentice-Hall, 1966.)

_____. "Rational Action." *Proceedings and Addresses of the American Philosophical Association*, Vol. XXXV, 1961-1962.

Donald C. Hodges. "The Dual Character of Marxian Social Science." *Philosophy of Science*, Vol. XXIX, No. 4 (October, 1962).

_____. "Genetic Inquiry and Ideological Thought." *Inquiry*, Vol. 5, No. 3, Fall, 1962.

Donald C. Hodges. "The Informal Task of Political Semantics." *The Personalist*, Vol. XLIV, No. 2 (Spring, 1963).

_____. "The 'Intermediate Classes' in Marxian Theory." *Social Research*, Vol. 28, No. 1 (April, 1961).

Irving Louis Horowitz. *The Idea of War and Peace in Contemporary Philosophy*. (New York: Paine-Whitman, 1957.)

_____. *Philosophy, Science, and the Sociology of Knowledge*. (Charles C Thomas, 1961.)

_____. *Professing Sociology: Studies in the Life Cycle of a Social Science*. (Chicago: Aldine, 1968.)

_____. *Radicalism and the Revolt Against Reason*. (Southern Illinois Press, 1968.)

Jørgen Jørgensen. *The Development of Logical Empiricism*. (Chicago, 1951.)

_____. *A Treatise of Formal Logic*, 3 Vols., New York, 1962.

Jack Kaminsky. "Can 'Essence' Be a Scientific Term?" *Philosophy of Science*, XXIV, 1957.

_____. "Corrigibility and Law." *Philosophy of Science*, XXI, 1954.

_____ (with Raymond J. Nelson). "Scientific Statements and Statements about Humanly Created Objects." *Journal of Philosophy*, July, 1958.

Gabriel Kolko. *The Triumph of Conservatism*. (New York: Free Press, 1963.)

Yervant H. Krikorian, ed. *Naturalism and the Human Spirit.* (Columbia University Press, 1944.)

Corliss Lamont. *Freedom of Choice Affirmed.* (New York: Horizon Press, 1967.)

_____. *The Illusion of Immortality.* (New York: Ungar, 1965.)

_____. *The Philosophy of Humanism.* (New York: Ungar, 1965.)

V. J. McGill. *August Strindberg.* (Brentano, 1930.)

_____. *Emotions and Reason.* (Charles C Thomas, 1954.)

V. J. McGill. *The Idea of Happiness.* (Praeger, 1967.)

_____. *A Philosopher Meets a Novelist.* (Ithaca: Dragon Press, 1932.)

A. L. Mackay. "An Outsider's View of Science in Japan." *Impact* (UNESCO), 12, No. 3, 1962.

_____. "Science in Asia." In Guy Wint, *Asia: A Handbook to the Continent.* (Penguin, 1968.)

_____ (edited with Maurice Goldsmith). *The Science of Science.* (Penguin, 1966.)

_____ (with J. D. Bernal). "Towards a Science of Science." *Organon*, 3, 1966.

Edward H. Madden. *Chauncey Wright and the Foundations of Pragmatism.* (Seattle: University of Washington Press, 1963.)

_____. *Philosophical Problems of Psychology.* (New York: Odyssey, 1962.)

_____. *The Structure of Scientific Thought.* (Boston: Houghton Mifflin, 1960.)

_____ (with Ralph M. Blake and Curt J. Ducasse). *Theories of Scientific Method.* (Seattle: University of Washington Press, 1960.)

Herbert Marcuse. *One Dimensional Man: Studies in the Ideology of Advanced Industrial Society.* (Boston: Beacon, 1967.)

Norman Melchert. "The Independence of the Object in Critical Realism." *The Monist*, Vol. 51, No. 2 (April, 1967).

_____. *Realism, Materialism, and the Mind: The Philosophy of Roy Wood Sellars.* (Charles C Thomas, 1968.)

Shia Moser. *Absolutism and Relativism in Ethics.* (Charles C Thomas, 1968.)

Thomas Munro. *The Arts and Their Interrelations.* (Case Western Reserve University Press, 1967.)

_____. *Evolution in the Arts.* (Cleveland Museum of Art, 1963.)

_____. *Form in the Arts.* (Cleveland Museum of Art, 1968.)

Thomas Munro. *Toward Science in Aesthetics.* (Bobbs-Merrill, 1956.)

Ernest Nagel. *Logic Without Metaphysics.* (Free Press, 1956.)

_____. *Principles of the Theory of Probability.* (University of Chicago Press, 1939.)

_____. *Sovereign Reason.* (Free Press, 1954.)

_____. *The Structure of Science.* (Harcourt, Brace & World, 1961.)

Marvin K. Opler. *Culture and Mental Health.* (New York: Macmillan, 1959.)

_____. *Culture and Social Psychiatry.* (New York: Atherton Press, 1967.)

Enzo Paci. *Funzione delle Scienze e Significato dell'Uomo.* (Milan, 1963.)

_____. *Relazioni e Significati.* Vol. III, "Critica e Dialettica," (Milan, 1966).

_____. *Tempo e Relazione.* (Milan, 1961.)

_____. *Tempo e Verita' nella Fenomenologia di Husserl.* (Bari, 1961.)

Howard L. Parsons. "Man East and West." In B. L. Atreya, ed., *S. Radhakrishnan Souvenir Volume.* (Moradabad, India, 1964.)

_____. "Philosophy and the Problem of Man's Mental Health." *XIII Congreso Internacional de Filosofía,* Vol. II. (Mexico, 1963.)

_____. "Reality, Value, and Growth." *Journal of Philosophy,* Vol. L, No. 17, August, 1953.

_____. "Value and Mental Health in the Thought of Marx." *Philosophy and Phenomenological Research,* Vol. 24, No. 3 (March, 1964.)

Paul Piccone. "Objectivity, Teleology, and Functionalism." *The Monist,* Vol. 52, No. 3 (July, 1968).

_____. "Towards a Socio-Historical Interpretation of the Scientific Revolution." *Telos,* Spring, 1968.

John Herman Randall, Jr. "The Art of Language and the Linguistic Situation." *Journal of Philosophy,* LX, 1962.

John Herman Randall, Jr. *How Philosophy Uses Its Past.* (New York, 1963.)

_____. *The Meaning of Religion for Man.* (New York, 1968.)

_____. *Nature and Historical Experience.* (New York, 1958.)

Oliver L. Reiser. *Cosmic Humanism.* (Schenkman, 1966.)

_____. *The Integration of Human Knowledge.* (Porter Sargent, 1958.)

_____. *Man's New Image of Man.* (Boxwood Press, 1961.)

_____. *A New Earth and a New Humanity.* (Creative Age, 1942.)

Dale Riepe. "The Ethics of H. S. Sullivan." *The International Journal of Social Psychiatry,* XII, 4 (Autumn, 1966).

_____. "Flexible Scientific Naturalism and Dialectical Fundamentalism." *Philosophy of Science,* October, 1958.

——————— (with Solomon Levy). "Is Ethical Non-Attachment Naturalistically or Logically Defensible?" *Darshana*, VI, No. 3, July, 1966.

———————. *The Naturalistic Tradition in Indian Thought.* (University of Washington Press, 1961.)

Patrick Romanell (with Chauncey D. Leake). "Can We Agree? A Scientist and a Philosopher Argue about Ethics." (University of Texas Press, 1950.)

———————. "Romanticism and Croce's Conception of Science." *Review of Metaphysics*, Vol. 9, 1956.

———————. *Toward a Critical Naturalism.* (New York: Macmillan, 1958.)

Lynn E. Rose. *Aristotle's Syllogistic.* (Charles C Thomas, 1968.)

Adam Schaff. *Introduction to Semantics.* (Oxford: Pergamon, 1962.)

———————. *Marxism and the Individual.* (New York: McGraw-Hill, 1967.)

———————. *The Philosophy of Man.* (New York: Monthly Review Press, 1963.)

Trent Schroyer. *Alienation and the Dialectical Paradigm*, Doctoral Diss., 1968.

Roy Wood Sellars. *Evolutionary Naturalism.* (Chicago: Open Court, 1926.)

———————. *Lending a Hand to Hylas.* (Ann Arbor: Edwards Brothers, 1968.)

———————. *The Next Step in Democracy.* (New York: Macmillan, 1916.)

———————. *The Philosophy of Physical Realism.* (New York: Macmillan, 1932.)

Wilfrid Sellars. *Philosophical Perspectives.* (Charles C Thomas, 1967.)

———————. *Science and Metaphysics.* (London: Routledge & Kegan Paul, 1968.)

———————. *Science, Perception and Reality.* (London: Routledge & Kegan Paul, 1963.)

Howard Selsam. *Ethics and Progress.* (New York: International, 1965.)

———————. *Philosophy in Revolution.* (New York: International, 1957.)

John Somerville. *The Communist Trials and the American Tradition.* (New York: Cameron, 1956.)

———————. *The Philosophy of Marxism.* (New York: Random House, 1967.)

———————. *The Philosophy of Peace.* (New York: Liberty, 1954.)

———————. *Soviet Philosophy.* (New York: Philosophical Library, 1946.)

Paul M. Sweezy (with Paul A. Baran). *Monopoly Capital.* (Monthly Review Press, 1967.)

_____. *The Present as History*, 1953.

_____. *Socialism*, 1948.

_____. *The Theory of Capitalist Development*, 1942.

Vernon Venable. *Human Nature: The Marxian View*. (Cleveland: Meridian, 1966.)

Gregory Vlastos. "Isonomia Politike." In *Studien zur Gleicheitsvorstellung im griechischen Denken*. (Berlin, 1964.)

_____. "A Metaphysical Paradox." Presidential Address to the Eastern Division of the American Philosophical Association, No. 39, 1966.

Gregory Vlastos. "Minimal Parts in Epicurean Atomism." *Isis*, 56, 1965.

_____. "Zeno." *Encyclopedia of Philosophy*. (Macmillan.)

W. Preston Warren. "The Mote in the Eye of the Critic of Critical Realism." *Philosophy and Phenomenological Research*, Vol. XXVI, No. 1, September, 1965.

_____. "Realism 1900-1930: An Emerging Epistemology." *The Monist*, Vol. 51, No. 2, April, 1967.

Marx W. Wartofsky. *Conceptual Foundations of Scientific Thought*. (New York: Macmillan, 1968.)

_____. "Diderot and the Development of Materialist Monism." *Diderot Studies II*, ed. N. Torrey and O. Fellows. (Syracuse University Press, 1953.)

_____. "Metaphysics as Heuristic for Science." *Boston Studies in Philosophy of Science*, Vol. III. (New York, 1967.)

_____. "Temporal Description and the Ontological Status of Judgment." *Review of Metaphysics*. Part I, XIV, i (September, 1960); Part II, XIV, 2 (December, 1960).

Harry K. Wells. *Pavlov and Freud*, 2 Vols. (New York: International, 1960-1963.)

Leslie A. White. "The Concept of Culture." *American Anthropologist*, Vol. 61, 1959.

_____. "Culturology." *Encyclopedia of the Social Sciences*. (Collier-Macmillan, 1968.)

_____. *The Evolution of Culture*. (New York: McGraw-Hill, 1959.)

_____. *The Science of Culture*. (Grove, 1958.)

William Appleman Williams. *The Contours of American History*. (Cleveland: World, 1961.)

_____. *The Great Evasion*. (Chicago: Quadrangle, 1964.)

_____. *The Tragedy of American Diplomacy*. (New York: Delta, 1962.)

THE CONTRIBUTORS

Herbert Aptheker has been an activist and scholar in the areas of civil rights, civil liberties, anti-imperialism and socialism since 1936. He has published over twenty books in these areas; among the best known are: *American Negro Slave Revolts* (1943); *A Documentary History of the Negro People in the United States* (2 vols., 1951); *The Nature of Democracy, Freedom and Revolution* (1967). During 1969-70, he has been Visiting Lecturer in History, Bryn Mawr College, and since 1964 he has been Director of the American Institute for Marxist Studies.

Robert B. Carson is a political economist who teaches at the State University College, Oneonta, New York. He is presently preparing a study of contemporary American economic issues, and he has written on New York State railroads in the twentieth century and on the American Black Power Movement.

Edward D'Angelo is Assistant Professor of Philosophy at the University of Bridgeport. His current research interests include the problem of free will and determinism, Eastern European philosophy, the philosophy of education, and the area of critical thinking.

David H. DeGrood is Assistant Professor of Philosophy at the University of Bridgeport. His fields of interest are social philosophy, philosophy of culture, and ontology.

Barrows Dunham is an eminent American philosopher who has carefully analyzed the major crises and ideas of our time. He received his doctorate from Princeton in 1933, and has taught at Franklin & Marshall College, Temple University, and Beaver College. Presently Dunham is preparing a major work on ethics.

Marvin Farber is Distinguished Professor of Philosophy at the State University of New York at Buffalo, and is the founder and editor of *Philosophy and Phenomenological Research*. Dr. Farber is a past President of the American Philosophical Association. His writings include critical analyses of provocative movements of our time in philosophy.

Ernesto "Che" Guevara was killed (1967) during the early collection of these materials. The contribution chosen for this volume was appropriately retitled to fit our collection. Guevara's life gave hope to millions of oppressed people, and his death, like the deaths of many American leaders during this explosive period of world history, has only brought greater determination to progressive men around the globe.

Rollo Handy is Provost of the Faculty of Educational Studies at the State University of New York at Buffalo. Dr. Handy's main interests are in value theory and in the philosophy of the behavioral sciences.

James E. Hansen is Lecturer in Philosophy at Brock University; his main interests lie in dialectical philosophy and philosophies of *praxis*.

V. J. McGill is Professor of Philosophy at San Francisco State College. He is a member of the editorial board of *Philosophy and Phenomenological Research*, and has been President of the American Philosophical Association, Pacific Division (1968). McGill has written widely in the philosophy of literature and of psychology.

Alan Mackay is a member of Professor J. D. Bernal's Department of Crystallography in Birkbeck College, University of London. Apart from crystallography, Mackay has been concerned with promoting the study of the phenomenon of science itself by scientific methods.

Mihailo Marković is Professor of Philosophy at the University of Belgrade. He is a Member-Correspondent of the Serbian Academy of Sciences, Head of the section for the Methodology of Science in the Institute for Social Sciences (Belgrade), and member of the Council for the Coordination of Scientific Research.

William T. Parry is Chairman of the Philosophy Department of the State University of New York at Buffalo. A distinguished logician, Dr. Parry has been Sheldon Traveling Fellow from Harvard University (1931-1932), studying at the universities of Vienna, Warsaw, and Cambridge.

Howard L. Parsons is Bernhard Professor of Philosophy and Chairman of the Philosophy Department of the University of Bridgeport. He was President of the Society for the Philosophical Study of Dialectical Materialism (1962-1963). Parsons was also a founding member and sponsor of the board of the American Institute for Marxist Studies.

Dison Hsueh-Feng Poe is Professor of Philosophy at the University of Bridgeport. He has taught at Tsing Hua University, Central University, and Chengchi University. He served also as Deputy Director-General of CNRRA and was Vice Minister of Education. In 1962, he came to the United States as a Whitney-Fulbright scholar.

Dale Riepe is Professor of Philosophy at the State University of New York at Buffalo. Dr. Riepe was twice Fulbright scholar and once a Fellow of the American Institute of Indian Studies, studying in Asia on three occasions. His wide interests revolve about his fascination with Oriental Philosophy, particularly the naturalistic trends.

Adam Schaff is Professor of Philosophy at Warsaw University. He has worked in the fields of epistemology, philosophy of language, the methodology of the social sciences, and in the philosophy of man. He has studied at the Ecole des Sciences Politiques et Economiques in Paris and in the Soviet Union. Presently he is a member of the Central Committee of the Polish United Workers' Party.

Roy Wood Sellars, Emeritus Professor of the University of Michigan, is one of America's widely known philosophers. In 1923 Sellars was President of the Western Philosophical Association. His scholarly work has dealt with many areas of philosophic thought.

John Somerville is Professor of Philosophy at California Western University, having retired from Hunter College where he taught from 1939 to 1967. Somerville has done research in the U.S.S.R. as a Cutting Fellow of Columbia University and in the United States as a Rockefeller grantee. He has been editor of the translation journal *Soviet Studies in Philosophy* since 1962, and he is currently President of the Society for the Philosophical Study of Dialectical Materialism.

Stanley E. Weisberger is a Doctor of Speech at the State University College, Oneonta, New York. He served in the U. S. Armed Forces in World War II, and has since the war organized critical opposition to America's Cold War policy. He had previously taught at Brooklyn College and Northern Illinois University. Professor Weisberger has also been active in Civil Rights and the War Moratorium.

INDEX*

A

ABM, 250
Adams, Henry, 119f.
Agassi, Joseph, 260
Alpert, Richard, 255n.
American radicalism, 135
Analytic philosophy, 30f.
Anderson, Alan Ross, 260
Anselm, 24
Anton, John, 51n.
Aptheker, Herbert, 270
Arcesilaus, 23
Archimedes, 68
Aristotle, 5, 30, 33, 59, 102n., 104, 109, 189, 200, 205
Augustine, 29
Austin, J. L., 13, 57
Ayer, A. J., 74, 209n.

B

BACON, FRANCIS, 18, 24f., 33, 110, 140, 154
Bandman, Bertram, 260
Baran, Paul, 137
Barber, Bernard, 39n.
Batista, Fulgencio, 176, 178n.
Becker, Oskar, 33
Bell, Daniel, 46
Benjamin, A. C., 260f.
Bentham, Jeremy, 28
Bergmann, Gustav, 261
Bergson, Henri, 7, 87
Berkeley, George, 55ff., 59, 61ff., 99
Berleant, Arnold, 23n., 261

Bernal, J. D., 48n., 71
Bertalanffy, Ludwig von, 110
Beveridge, Albert, 129, 132
Black, Max, 193f., 197ff., 206, 261
Blanshard, Brand, 64
Blumberg, Albert E., 261
Boas, George, 16f., 21f.
Bohr, Niels, 46, 48
Boredom, 16f.
Bosanquet, Bernard, vii
Bourne, Randolph, 8f., 134, 138
Bouwsma, O. K., 6
Boyle, Robert, 62
Bradley, F. H., vii, 19, 64, 82
Brouwer, L. E. J., 205
Brown, Norman O., 255n.
Brzezinski, Z. K., 255
Buchler, Justus, 261
Bunge, Mario, 261
Burnham, James, 135

C

CABANIS, PIERRE-JEAN, 141
Camus, Albert, 7
Capitalism, 91, 123, 214
Carneades, 23
Carr, E. H., 44n., 45n.
Carson, Robert B., 270
Caws, Peter, 261f.
Ceteris paribus clause, 43, 45
Childe, V. G., 214
Chomsky, Noam, 262
Churchman, C. West, 262
Class-less science, 46n.
Class struggle, 16, 19, 47, 114

---

*Index prepared by Elaine A. DeGrood.

273